The Path to Rome

Hilaire Belloc

'. .. AMORE ANTIQUI RITUS, ALTO SUB NUMINE ROMAE'

This book has been published by:

Contact: sales@nuvisionpublications.com

URL: http://www.nuvisionpublications.com

Publishing Date: 2007

ISBN# 1-59547-854-X

Please see our website for several books created for
education, research and entertainment.

Specializing in rare, out-of-print books still in demand.

To every honest reader that may purchase, hire, or receive this book, and to the reviewers also (to whom it is of triple profit), greeting--and whatever else can be had for nothing.

If you should ask how this book came to be written, it was in this way. One day as I was wandering over the world I came upon the valley where I was born, and stopping there a moment to speak with them all--when I had argued politics with the grocer, and played the great lord with the notary-public, and had all but made the carpenter a Christian by force of rhetoric--what should I note (after so many years) but the old tumble-down and gaping church, that I love more than mother-church herself, all scraped, white, rebuilt, noble, and new, as though it had been finished yesterday. Knowing very well that such a change had not come from the skinflint populace, but was the work of some just artist who knew how grand an ornament was this shrine (built there before our people stormed Jerusalem), I entered, and there saw that all within was as new, accurate, and excellent as the outer part; and this pleased me as much as though a fortune had been left to us all; for one's native place is the shell of one's soul, and one's church is the kernel of that nut.

Moreover, saying my prayers there, I noticed behind the high altar a statue of Our Lady, so extraordinary and so different from all I had ever seen before, so much the spirit of my valley, that I was quite taken out of myself and vowed a vow there to go to Rome on Pilgrimage and see all Europe which the Christian Faith has saved; and I said, 'I will start from the place where I served in arms for my sins; I will walk all the way and take advantage of no wheeled thing; I will sleep rough and cover thirty miles a day, and I will hear Mass every morning; and I will be present at high Mass in St Peter's on the Feast of St Peter and St Paul.'

Then I went out of the church still having that Statue in my mind, and I walked again farther into the world, away from my native valley, and so ended some months after in a place whence I could fulfil my vow; and I started as you shall hear. All my other vows I broke one by one. For a faggot must be broken every stick singly. But the strict vow I kept, for I entered Rome on foot that year in time, and I heard high Mass on the Feast of the Apostles, as many can testify--to wit: Monsignor this, and Chamberlain the other, and the Bishop of *so-and-so--o--polis in partibus infidelium*; for we were all there together.

And why (you will say) is all this put by itself in what Anglo-Saxons call a Foreword, but gentlemen a Preface? Why, it is because I have noticed that no book can appear without some such thing tied on before it; and as it is folly to neglect the fashion, be certain that I read some eight or nine thousand of them to be sure of how they were written and to be safe from generalizing on too frail a basis.

And having read them and discovered first, that it was the custom of my contemporaries to belaud themselves in this prolegomenaical ritual (some saying in a few words that they supplied a want, others boasting in a hundred that they were too grand to do any such thing, but most of them baritoning their apologies and chanting their excuses till one knew that their pride was toppling over)--since, I say, it seemed a necessity to extol one's work, I wrote simply on the lintel of my diary, *Praise of this Book*, so as to end the matter at a blow. But whether there will be praise or blame I really cannot tell, for I am riding my pen on the snaffle, and it has a mouth of iron.

Now there is another thing book writers do in their Prefaces, which is to introduce a mass of nincompoops of whom no one ever heard, and to say 'my thanks are due to such and such' all in a litany, as though any one cared a farthing for the rats! If I omit this believe me it is but on account of the multitude and splendour of those who have attended at the production of this volume. For the stories in it are copied straight from the best authors of the Renaissance, the music was written by the masters of the eighteenth century, the Latin is Erasmus' own; indeed, there is scarcely a word that is mine. I must also mention the Nine Muses, the Three Graces; Bacchus, the Maenads, the Panthers, the Fauns; and I owe very hearty thanks to Apollo.

Yet again, I see that writers are for ever anxious of their style, thinking (not saying)--

'True, I used "and which" on page 47, but Martha Brown the stylist gave me leave;' or:

'What if I do end a sentence with a preposition? I always follow the rules of Mr Twist in his "'Tis Thus 'Twas Spoke", Odd's Body an' I do not!'

Now this is a pusillanimity of theirs (the book writers) that they think style power, and yet never say as much in their Prefaces. Come, let me do so ... Where are you? Let me marshal you, my regiments of words!

Rabelais! Master of all happy men! Are you sleeping there pressed into desecrated earth under the doss-house of the Rue St Paul, or do you not rather drink cool wine in some elysian Chinon looking on the Vienne where it rises in Paradise? Are you sleeping or drinking that you will not lend us the staff of Friar John wherewith he slaughtered and bashed the invaders of the vineyards, who are but a parable for the mincing pedants and bloodless thin-faced rogues of the world?

Write as the wind blows and command all words like an army! See them how they stand in rank ready for assault, the jolly, swaggering fellows!

First come the Neologisms, that are afraid of no man; fresh, young, hearty, and for the most part very long-limbed, though some few short and strong. There also are the Misprints to confuse the enemy at his onrush. Then see upon the flank a company of picked Ambiguities covering what shall be a feint by the squadron of Anachronisms led by old Anachronos himself; a terrible chap with nigglers and a great murderer of fools.

But here see more deeply massed the ten thousand Egotisms shining in their armour and roaring for battle. They care for no one. They stormed Convention yesterday and looted the cellar of Good-Manners, who died of fear without a wound; so they drank his wine and are to-day as strong as lions and as careless (saving only their Captain, Monologue, who is lantern-jawed).

Here are the Aposiopaesian Auxiliaries, and Dithyramb that killed Punctuation in open fight; Parenthesis the giant and champion of the host, and Anacoluthon that never learned to read or write but is very handy with his sword; and Metathesis and Hendiadys, two Greeks. And last come the noble Gallicisms prancing about on their light horses: cavalry so sudden that the enemy sicken at the mere sight of them and are overcome without a blow. Come then my hearties, my lads, my indefatigable repetitions, seize you each his own trumpet that hangs at his side and blow the charge; we shall soon drive them all before us headlong, howling down together to the Picrocholian Sea.

So! That was an interlude. Forget the clamour.

But there is another matter; written as yet in no other Preface: peculiar to this book. For without rhyme or reason, pictures of an uncertain kind stand in the pages of the chronicle. Why?

Because it has become so cheap to photograph on zinc.

In old time a man that drew ill drew not at all. He did well. Then either there were no pictures in his book, or (if there were any) they were done by some other man that loved him not a groat and would not have walked half a mile to see him hanged. But now it is so easy for a man to scratch down what he sees and put it in his book that any fool may do it and be none the worse--many others shall follow. This is the first.

Before you blame too much, consider the alternative. Shall a man march through Europe dragging an artist on a cord? God forbid!

Shall an artist write a book? Why no, the remedy is worse than the disease.

Let us agree then, that, if he will, any pilgrim may for the future draw (if he likes) that most difficult subject, snow hills beyond a grove of trees; that he may draw whatever he comes across in order to enliven his mind (for who saw it if not he? And was it not his loneliness that enabled him to see it?), and that he may draw what he never saw, with as much freedom as you readers so very continually see what you never draw. He may draw the morning mist on the Grimsel, six months afterwards; when he has forgotten what it was like: and he may frame it for a masterpiece to make the good draughtsman rage.

The world has grown a boy again this long time past, and they are building hotels (I hear) in the place where Acedes discovered the Water of Youth in a hollow of the hill Epistemonoscoptes.

Then let us love one another and laugh. Time passes, and we shall soon laugh no longer--and meanwhile common living is a burden, and earnest men are at siege upon us all around. Let us suffer absurdities, for that is only to suffer one another.

Nor let us be too hard upon the just but anxious fellow that sat down dutifully to paint the soul of Switzerland upon a fan.

When that first Proverb-Maker who has imposed upon all peoples by his epigrams and his fallacious half-truths, his empiricism and his wanton appeals to popular ignorance, I say when this man (for I take it he was a man, and a wicked one) was passing through France he launched among the French one of his pestiferous phrases, 'Ce n'est que le premier pas qui coute' and this in a rolling-in-the-mouth self-satisfied kind of a manner has been repeated since his day at least seventeen million three hundred and sixty-two thousand five hundred and four times by a great mass of Ushers, Parents, Company Officers, Elder Brothers, Parish Priests, and authorities in general whose office it may be and whose pleasure it certainly is to jog up and disturb that native slumber and inertia of the mind which is the true breeding soil of Revelation.

For when boys or soldiers or poets, or any other blossoms and prides of nature, are for lying steady in the shade and letting the Mind commune with its Immortal Comrades, up comes Authority busking about and eager as though it were a duty to force the said Mind to burrow and sweat in the matter of this very perishable world, its temporary habitation.

'Up,' says Authority, 'and let me see that Mind of yours doing something practical. Let me see Him mixing painfully with circumstance, and botching up some Imperfection or other that shall at least be a Reality and not a silly Fantasy.'

Then the poor Mind comes back to Prison again, and the boy takes his horrible Homer in the real Greek (not Church's book, alas!); the Poet his rough hairy paper, his headache, and his cross-nibbed pen; the Soldier abandons his inner picture of swaggering about in ordinary clothes, and sees the dusty road and feels the hard places in his boot, and shakes down again to the steady pressure of his pack; and Authority is satisfied, knowing that he will get a smattering from the Boy, a rubbishy verse from the Poet, and from the Soldier a long and thirsty march. And Authority, when it does this commonly sets to work by one of these formulae: as, in England north of Trent, by the manifestly false and boastful phrase, 'A thing begun is half ended', and in the south by 'The Beginning is half the Battle'; but in France by the words I have attributed to the Proverb-Maker, 'Ce n'est que le premier pas qui coute'.

By this you may perceive that the Proverb-Maker, like every other Demagogue, Energumen, and Disturber, dealt largely in metaphor--but this I need hardly insist upon, for in his vast collection of published and unpublished works it is amply evident that he took the silly pride of the half-educated in a constant abuse of metaphor. There was a sturdy boy at my school who, when the master had carefully explained to us the nature of metaphor, said that so far as he could see a metaphor was nothing but a long Greek word for a lie. And certainly men who know that the mere truth would be distasteful or tedious commonly have recourse to metaphor, and so do those false men who desire to acquire a subtle and unjust influence over their fellows, and chief among them, the Proverb-Maker. For though his name is lost in the great space of time that has passed since he flourished, yet his character can be very clearly deduced from the many literary fragments he has left, and that is found to be the character of a pusillanimous and ill-bred usurer, wholly lacking in foresight, in generous enterprise, and chivalrous enthusiasm--in matters of the Faith a prig or a doubter, in matters of adventure a poltroon, in matters of Science an ignorant Parrot, and in Letters a wretchedly bad rhymester, with a vice for alliteration; a wilful liar (as, for instance, 'The longest way round is the shortest way home'), a startling miser (as, 'A penny saved is a penny earned'), one ignorant of largesse and human charity (as, 'Waste not, want not'), and a shocking boor in the point of honour (as, 'Hard words break no bones'-- he never fought, I see, but with a cudgel).

But he had just that touch of slinking humour which the peasants have, and there is in all he said that exasperating quality for which we have no name, which certainly is not accuracy, and which is quite the opposite of judgement, yet which catches the mind as brambles do our clothes, causing us continually to pause and swear. For he mixes up unanswerable things with false conclusions, he is perpetually letting the cat out of the bag and exposing our tricks, putting a colour to our actions, disturbing us with our own memory, indecently revealing corners of the soul. He is like those men who say one unpleasant and rude thing about a friend, and then take refuge from their disloyal and false action by pleading that this single accusation is true; and it is perhaps for this abominable logicality of his and for his malicious cunning that I chiefly hate him: and since he himself evidently hated the human race, he must not complain if he is hated in return.

Take, for instance, this phrase that set me writing, *'Ce nest que le premier pas qui coute'*. It is false. Much after a beginning is difficult, as everybody knows who has crossed the sea, and as for the first *step* a man never so much as remembers it; if there is difficulty it is in the whole launching of a thing, in the first ten pages of a book, or the first half-hour of listening to a sermon, or the first mile of a walk. The first step is undertaken lightly, pleasantly, and with your soul in the sky; it is the five-hundredth that counts. But I know, and you know, and he knew (worse luck) that he was saying a thorny and catching thing when he made up that phrase. It worries one of set purpose. It is as though one had a voice inside one saying:

'I know you, you will never begin anything. Look at what you might have done! Here you are, already twenty-one, and you have not yet written a dictionary. What will you do for fame? Eh? Nothing: you are intolerably lazy--and what is worse, it is your fate. Beginnings are insuperable barriers to you. What about that great work on The National Debt? What about that little lyric on Winchelsea that you thought of writing six years ago? Why are the few lines still in your head and not on paper? Because you can't begin. However, never mind, you can't help it, it's your one great flaw, and it's fatal. Look at Jones! Younger than you by half a year, and already on the *Evening Yankee* taking bribes from Company Promoters! And where are you?' &c., &c.--and so forth.

So this threat about the heavy task of Beginning breeds discouragement, anger, vexation, irritability, bad style, pomposity and infinitives split from helm to saddle, and metaphors as mixed as the Carlton. But it is just true enough to remain fast in the mind, caught, as it were, by one finger. For all things (you will notice) are very difficult in their origin, and why, no one can understand. *Omne Trinum*: they are difficult also in the shock of maturity and in their ending. Take, for instance, the Life of Man, which is the Difficulty of Birth, the Difficulty of Death, and the Difficulty of the Grand Climacteric.

LECTOR. What is the Grand Climacteric?

AUCTOR. I have no time to tell you, for it would lead us into a discussion on Astrology, and then perhaps to a question of physical science, and then you would find I was not orthodox, and perhaps denounce me to the authorities.

I will tell you this much; it is the moment (not the year or the month, mind you, nor even the hour, but the very second) when a man is grown up, when he sees things as they are (that is, backwards), and feels solidly himself. Do I make myself clear? No matter, it is the Shock of Maturity, and that must suffice for you.

But perhaps you have been reading little brown books on Evolution, and you don't believe in Catastrophes, or Climaxes, or Definitions? Eh? Tell me, do you believe in the peak of the Matterhorn, and have you doubts on the points of needles? Can the sun be said truly to rise or set, and is there any exact meaning in the phrase, 'Done to a turn' as applied to omelettes? You know there is; and so also you must believe in Categories, and you must admit differences of kind as well as of degree, and you must accept exact definition and believe in all that your fathers did, that were wiser men than you, as is easily proved if you will but imagine yourself for but one moment introduced into the presence of your ancestors, and ask yourself which would look the fool. Especially must you believe in moments and their importance, and avoid with the utmost care the Comparative Method and the argument of the Slowly Accumulating Heap. I hear that some scientists are already beginning to admit the reality of Birth and Death--let but some brave few make an act of Faith in the Grand Climacteric and all shall yet be well.

Well, as I was saying, this Difficulty of Beginning is but one of three, and is Inexplicable, and is in the Nature of Things, and it is very especially noticeable in the Art of Letters. There is in every book the Difficulty of Beginning, the Difficulty of the Turning-Point (which is the Grand Climacteric of a Book)--

LECTOR. What is that in a Book?

AUCTOR. Why, it is the point where the reader has caught on, enters into the Book and desires to continue reading it.

LECTOR. It comes earlier in some books than in others.

AUCTOR. As you say ... And finally there is the Difficulty of Ending.

LECTOR. I do not see how there can be any difficulty in ending a book.

AUCTOR. That shows very clearly that you have never written one, for there is nothing so hard in the writing of a book--no, not even the choice of the Dedication--as is the ending of it. On this account only the great Poets, who are above custom and can snap their divine fingers at forms, are not at the pains of devising careful endings. Thus, Homer ends with lines that might as well be in the middle of a passage; Hesiod, I know not how; and Mr Bailey, the New Voice from Eurasia, does not end at all, but is still going on.

Panurge told me that his great work on Conchology would never have been finished had it not been for the Bookseller that threatened law; and as it is, the last sentence has no verb in it. There is always something more to be said, and it is always so difficult to turn up the splice neatly at the edges. On this account there are regular models for ending a book or a Poem, as there are for beginning one; but, for my part, I think the best way of ending a book is to rummage about among one's manuscripts till one has found a bit of Fine Writing (no matter upon what subject), to lead up the last paragraphs by no matter what violent shocks to the thing it deals with, to introduce a row of asterisks, and then to paste on to the paper below these the piece of Fine Writing one has found.

I knew a man once who always wrote the end of a book first, when his mind was fresh, and so worked gradually back to the introductory chapter, which (he said) was ever a kind of summary, and could not be properly dealt with till a man knew all about his subject. He said this was a sovran way to write History.

But it seems to me that this is pure extravagance, for it would lead one at last to beginning at the bottom of the last page, like the Hebrew Bible, and (if it were fully carried out) to writing one's sentences backwards till one had a style like the London School of Poets: a very horrible conclusion.

However, I am not concerned here with the ending of a book, but with its beginning; and I say that the beginning of any literary thing is hard, and that this hardness is difficult to explain. And I say more than this--I say that an interminable discussion of the difficulty of beginning a book is the worst omen for going on with it, and a trashy subterfuge at the best. In the name of all decent, common, and homely things, why not begin and have done with it?

It was in the very beginning of June, at evening, but not yet sunset, that I set out from Toul by the Nancy gate; but instead of going straight on past the parade-ground, I turned to the right immediately along the ditch and rampart, and did not leave the fortifications till I came to the road that goes up alongside the Moselle. For it was by the valley of this river that I was to begin my pilgrimage, since, by a happy accident, the valley of the Upper Moselle runs straight towards Rome, though it takes you but a short part of the way. What a good opening it makes for a direct pilgrimage can be seen from this little map, where the dotted line points exactly to Rome. There are two bends which take one a little out of one's way, and these bends I attempted to avoid, but in general, the valley, about a hundred miles from Toul to the source, is an evident gate for any one walking from this part of Lorraine into Italy. And this map is also useful to show what route I followed for my first three days past Epinal and Remiremont up to the source of the river, and up over the great hill, the Ballon d'Alsace. I show the river valley like a trench, and the hills above it shaded, till the mountainous upper part, the

Vosges, is put in black. I chose the decline of the day for setting out, because of the great heat a little before noon and four hours after it. Remembering this, I planned to walk at night and in the mornings and evenings, but how this design turned out you shall hear in a moment.

I had not gone far, not a quarter of a mile, along my road leaving the town, when I thought I would stop and rest a little and make sure that I had started propitiously and that I was really on my way to Rome; so I halted by a wall and looked back at the city and the forts, and drew what I saw in my book. It was a sight that had taken a firm hold of my mind in boyhood, and that will remain in it as long as it can make pictures for itself out of the past. I think this must be true of all conscripts with regard to the garrison in which they have served, for the mind is so fresh at twenty-one and the life so new to every recruit as he joins it, he is so cut off from books and all the worries of life, that the surroundings of the place bite into him and take root, as one's school does or one's first home. And I had been especially fortunate since I had been with the gunners (notoriously the best kind of men) and not in a big place but in a little town, very old and silent, with more soldiers in its surrounding circle than there were men, women, and children within its useless ramparts. It is known to be very beautiful, and though I had not heard of this reputation, I saw it to be so at once when I was first marched in, on a November dawn, up to the height of the artillery barracks. I remembered seeing then the great hills surrounding it on every side, hiding their menace and protection of guns, and in the south and east the silent valley where the high forests dominate the Moselle, and the town below the road standing in an island or ring of tall trees. All this, I say, I had permanently remembered, and I had determined, whenever I could go on pilgrimage to Rome, to make this place my starting-point, and as I stopped here and looked back, a little way outside the gates, I took in again the scene that recalled so much laughter and heavy work and servitude and pride of arms.

I was looking straight at the great fort of St Michel, which is the strongest thing on the frontier, and which is the key to the circle of forts that make up this entrenched camp. One could see little or nothing of its batteries, only its hundreds of feet of steep brushwood above the vineyards, and at the summit a stunted wood purposely planted. Next to it on the left, of equal height, was the hog back of the Cote Barine, hiding a battery. Between the Cote Barine and my road and wall, I saw the rising ground and the familiar Barracks that are called (I know not why) the Barracks of Justice, but ought more properly to be called the Barracks of petty tyrannies and good fellowship, in order to show the philosophers that these two things are the life of armies; for of all the virtues practised in that old compulsory home of mine Justice came second at least if not third, while Discipline and Comradeship went first; and the more I think of it the more I am convinced that of all the suffering youth that was being there annealed and forged into soldiery none can have suffered like the lawyers. On the right the high trees that stand outside the ramparts of the town went dwindling in perspective like a palisade, and above them, here and there, was a roof showing the top of the towers of the Cathedral or of St Gengoult. All this I saw looking backwards, and, when I had noticed it and drawn it, I turned round again and took the road.

I had, in a small bag or pocket slung over my shoulder, a large piece of bread, half a pound of smoked ham, a sketch-book, two Nationalist papers, and a quart of the wine of Brule--which is the most famous wine in the neighbourhood of the garrison, yet very cheap. And Brule is a very good omen for men that are battered about and given to despairing, since it is only called Brule on account of its having been burnt so often by Romans, Frenchmen, Burgundians, Germans, Flemings, Huns perhaps, and generally all those who in the last few thousand years have taken a short cut at their enemies over the neck of the Cote Barine. So you would imagine it to be a tumble-down, weak, wretched, and disappearing place; but, so far from this, it is a rich and proud village, growing, as I have said, better wine than any in the garrison. Though Toul stands in a great cup or ring of hills, very high and with steep slopes, and guns on all of them, and all these hills grow wine, none is so good as Brule wine. And this reminds me of a thing that happened in the Manoeuvres of 1891, *quorum pars magna;* for there were two divisions employed in that glorious and fatiguing great game, and more than a gross of guns--to be accurate, a hundred and fifty-six-- and of these one (the sixth piece of the tenth battery of the eighth--I wonder where you all are now? I suppose I shall not see you again; but you were the best companions in the world, my friends) was driven by three drivers, of whom I was the middle one, and the worst, having on my Livret the note 'conducteur mediocre'. But that is neither here nor there; the story is as follows, and the moral is that the commercial mind is illogical.

When we had gone some way, clattering through the dust, and were well on on the Commercy road, there was a short halt, and during this halt there passed us the largest Tun or Barrel that ever went on wheels. You talk of the Great Tun of Heidelburg, or of those monstrous Vats that stand in cool sheds in the Napa Valley, or of the vast barrels in the Catacombs of Rheims; but all these are built *in situ* and meant to remain steady, and there is no limit to the size of a Barrel that has not to travel. The point about this enormous Receptacle of Bacchus and cavernous huge Prison of Laughter, was that it could move, though cumbrously, and it was drawn very slowly by stupid, patient oxen, who would not be hurried. On the top of it sat a strong peasant, with a face of determination, as though he were at war with his kind, and he kept on calling to his oxen, 'Han', and 'Hu', in the tones of a sullen challenge, as he went creaking past. Then the soldiers began calling out to him singly, 'Where are you off to, Father, with that battery?' and 'Why carry cold water to Commercy? They have only too much as it is;' and 'What have you got in the little barrelkin, the barrellet, the cantiniere's brandy-flask, the gourd, the firkin?' He stopped his oxen fiercely and turned round to us and said: 'I will tell you what I have here. I have so

14

many hectolitres of Brule wine which I made myself, and which I know to be the best wine there is, and I am taking it about to see if I cannot tame and break these proud fellows who are for ever beating down prices and mocking me. It is worth eight 'scutcheons the hectolitre, that is, eight sols the litre; what do I say? it is worth a Louis a cup: but I will sell it at the price I name, and not a penny less. But whenever I come to a village the innkeeper begins bargaining and chaffering and offering six sols and seven sols, and I answer, "Eight sols, take it or leave it", and when he seems for haggling again I get up and drive away. I know the worth of my wine, and I will not be beaten down though I have to go out of Lorraine into the Barrois to sell it.'

So when we caught him up again, as we did shortly after on the road, a sergeant cried as we passed, 'I will give you seven, seven and a quarter, seven and a half', and we went on laughing and forgot all about him.

For many days we marched from this place to that place, and fired and played a confused game in the hot sun till the train of sick horses was a mile long, and till the recruits were all as deaf as so many posts; and at last, one evening, we came to a place called Heiltz le Maurupt, which was like heaven after the hot plain and the dust, and whose inhabitants are as good and hospitable as Angels; it is just where the Champagne begins. When we had groomed and watered our horses, and the stable guard had been set, and we had all an hour or so's leisure to stroll about in the cool darkness before sleeping in the barns, we had a sudden lesson in the smallness of the world, for what should come up the village street but that monstrous Barrel, and we could see by its movements that it was still quite full.

We gathered round the peasant, and told him how grieved we were at his ill fortune, and agreed with him that all the people of the Barrois were thieves or madmen not to buy such wine for such a song. He took his oxen and his barrel to a very high shed that stood by, and there he told us all his pilgrimage and the many assaults his firmness suffered, and how he had resisted them all. There was much more anger than sorrow in his accent, and I could see that he was of the wood from which tyrants and martyrs are carved. Then suddenly he changed and became eloquent:

'Oh, the good wine! If only it were known and tasted! ... Here, give me a cup, and I will ask some of you to taste it, then at least I shall have it praised as it deserves. And this is the wine I have carried more than a hundred miles, and everywhere it has been refused!'

There was one guttering candle on a little stool. The roof of the shed was lost up in the great height of darkness; behind, in the darkness, the oxen champed away steadily in the manger. The light from the candle flame lit his face strongly from beneath and marked it with dark shadows. It flickered on the circle of our faces as we pressed round, and

15

it came slantwise and waned and disappeared in the immense length of the Barrel. He stood near the tap with his brows knit as upon some very important task, and all we, gunners and drivers of the battery, began unhooking our mugs and passing them to him.

There were nearly a hundred, and he filled them all; not in jollity, but like a man offering up a solemn sacrifice. We also, entering into his mood, passed our mugs continually, thanking him in a low tone and keeping in the main silent. A few linesmen lounged at the door; he asked for their cups and filled them. He bade them fetch as many of their comrades as cared to come; and very soon there was a circulating crowd of men all getting wine of Brule and murmuring their congratulations, and he was willing enough to go on giving, but we stopped when we saw fit and the scene ended. I cannot tell what prodigious measure of wine he gave away to us all that night, but when he struck the roof of the cask it already sounded hollow. And when we had made a collection which he had refused, he went to sleep by his oxen, and we to our straw in other barns. Next day we started before dawn, and I never saw him again.

This is the story of the wine of Brule, and it shows that what men love is never money itself but their own way, and that human beings love sympathy and pageant above all things. It also teaches us not to be hard on the rich.

I walked along the valley of the Moselle, and as I walked the long evening of summer began to fall. The sky was empty and its deeps infinite; the clearness of the air set me dreaming. I passed the turn where we used to halt when we were learning how to ride in front of the guns, past the little house where, on rare holidays, the boys could eat a matelote, which is fish boiled in wine, and so on to the place where the river is held by a weir and opens out into a kind of lake.

Here I waited for a moment by the wooden railing, and looked up into the hills. So far I had been at home, and I was now poring upon the last familiar thing before I ventured into the high woods and began my experience. I therefore took a leisurely farewell, and pondered instead of walking farther. Everything about me conduced to reminiscence and to ease. A flock of sheep passed me with their shepherd, who gave me a good-night. I found myself entering that pleasant mood in which all books are conceived (but none written); I was 'smoking the enchanted cigarettes' of Balzac, and if this kind of reverie is fatal to action, yet it is so much a factor of happiness that I wasted in the contemplation of that lovely and silent hollow many miles of marching. I suppose if a man were altogether his own master and controlled by no necessity, not even the necessity of expression, all his life would pass away in these sublime imaginings.

This was a place I remembered very well. The rising river of Lorraine is caught and barred, and it spreads in a great sheet of water that must be very shallow, but that in its reflections and serenity resembles rather a profound and silent mere. The steeps surrounding it are nearly mountainous, and are crowned with deep forests in which the province reposes, and upon which it depends for its local genius. A little village, which we used to call 'St Peter of the Quarries', lies up on the right between the steep and the water, and just where the hills end a flat that was once marshy and is now half fields, half ponds, but broken with luxuriant trees, marks the great age of its civilization. Along this flat runs, bordered with rare poplars, the road which one can follow on and on into the heart of the Vosges. I took from this silence and this vast plain of still water the repose that introduces night. It was all consonant with what the peasants were about: the return from labour, the bleating folds, and the lighting of lamps under the eaves. In such a spirit I passed along the upper valley to the spring of the hills.

In St Pierre it was just that passing of daylight when a man thinks he can still read; when the buildings and the bridges are great masses of purple that deceive one, recalling the details of daylight, but when the night birds, surer than men and less troubled by this illusion of memory, have discovered that their darkness has conquered.

The peasants sat outside their houses in the twilight accepting the cool air; every one spoke to me as I marched through, and I answered them all, nor was there in any of their salutations the omission of good fellowship or of the name of God. Saving with one man, who was a sergeant of artillery on leave, and who cried out to me in an accent that was very familiar and asked me to drink; but I told him I had to go up into the forest to take advantage of the night, since the days were so warm for walking. As I left the last house of the village I was not secure from loneliness, and when the road began to climb up the hill into the wild and the trees I was wondering how the night would pass.

With every step upward a greater mystery surrounded me. A few stars were out, and the brown night mist was creeping along the water below, but there was still light enough to see the road, and even to distinguish the bracken in the deserted hollows. The highway became little better than a lane; at the top of the hill it plunged under tall pines, and was vaulted over with darkness. The kingdoms that have no walls, and are built up of shadows, began to oppress me as the night hardened. Had I had companions, still we would only have spoken in a whisper, and in that dungeon of trees even my own self would not raise its voice within me.

It was full night when I had reached a vague clearing in the woods, right up on the height of that flat hill. This clearing was called 'The Fountain of Magdalen'. I was so far relieved by the broader sky of the open field that I could wait and rest a little, and there, at last, separate from men, I thought of a thousand things. The air was full of midsummer, and its mixture of exaltation and fear cut me off from ordinary living. I now understood why our religion has made sacred this season of the year; why we have, a little later, the night of St John, the fires in the villages, and the old perception of fairies dancing in the rings of the summer grass. A general communion of all things conspires at this crisis of summer against us reasoning men that should live in the daylight, and something fantastic possesses those who are foolish enough to watch upon such nights. So I, watching, was cut off. There were huge, vague summits, all wooded, peering above the field I sat in, but they merged into a confused horizon. I was on a high plateau, yet I felt myself to be alone with the immensity that properly belongs to plains alone. I saw the stars, and remembered how I had looked up at them on just such a night when I was close to the Pacific, bereft of friends and possessed with solitude. There was no noise; it was full darkness. The woods before and behind me made a square frame of silence, and I was enchased here in the clearing, thinking of all things.

Then a little wind passed over the vast forests of Lorraine. It seemed to wake an indefinite sly life proper to this seclusion, a life to which I was strange, and which thought me an invader. Yet I heard nothing. There were no adders in the long grass, nor any frogs in that dry square of land, nor crickets on the high part of the hill; but I knew that little creatures in league with every nocturnal influence, enemies of the sun, occupied the air and the land about me; nor will I deny that I felt a rebel, knowing well that men were made to work in happy dawns and to sleep in the night, and everything in that short and sacred darkness multiplied my attentiveness and my illusion. Perhaps the instincts of the sentry, the necessities of guard, come back to us out of the ages unawares during such experiments. At any rate the night oppressed and exalted me. Then I suddenly attributed such exaltation to the need of food.

'If we must try this bookish plan of sleeping by day and walking by night,' I thought, 'at least one must arrange night meals to suit it.'

I therefore, with my mind still full of the forest, sat down and lit a match and peered into my sack, taking out therefrom bread and ham and chocolate and Brule wine. For seat and table there was a heathery bank still full of the warmth and savour of the last daylight, for companions these great inimical influences of the night which I had met and dreaded, and for occasion or excuse there was hunger. Of the Many that debate what shall be done with travellers, it was the best and kindest Spirit that prompted me to this salutary act. For as I drank the wine and dealt with the ham and bread, I felt more and more that I had a right to the road; the stars became familiar and the woods a plaything. It is quite clear that the body must be recognized and the soul kept in its place, since a little refreshing food and drink can do so much to make a man.

On this repast I jumped up merrily, lit a pipe, and began singing, and heard, to my inexpressible joy, some way down the road, the sound of other voices. They were singing that old song of the French infantry which dates from Louis XIV, and is called 'Aupres de ma blonde'. I answered their chorus, so that, by the time we met under the wood, we were already acquainted. They told me they had had a forty-eight hours' leave into Nancy, the four of them, and had to be in by roll-call at a place called Villey the Dry. I remembered it after all those years.

It is a village perched on the brow of one of these high hills above the river, and it found itself one day surrounded by earthworks, and a great fort raised just above the church. Then, before they knew where they were, they learnt that (1) no one could go in or out between sunset and sunrise without leave of the officer in command; (2) that from being a village they had become the 'buildings situate within Fort No. 18'; (3) that they were to be deluged with soldiers; and (4) that they were liable to evacuate their tenements on mobilization. They had become a fort unwittingly as they slept, and all their streets were blocked with ramparts. A hard fate; but they should not have built their village just on the brow of a round hill. They did this in the old days, when men used stone instead of iron, because the top of a hill was a good place to hold against enemies; and so now, these 73,426 years after, they find the same advantage catching them again to their hurt. And so things go the round.

Anyway Villey the Dry is a fort, and there my four brothers were going. It was miles off, and they had to be in by sunrise, so I offered them a pull of my wine, which, to my great joy, they refused, and we parted courteously. Then I found the road beginning to fall, and knew that I had crossed the hills. As the forest ended and the sloping fields began, a dim moon came up late in the east in the bank of fog that masked the river. So by a sloping road, now free from the woods, and at the mouth of a fine untenanted valley under the moon, I came down again to the Moselle, having saved a great elbow by this excursion over the high land. As I swung round the bend of the hills downwards and looked up the sloping dell, I remembered that these heathery hollows were called 'vallons' by the people of Lorraine, and this set me singing the song of the hunters, 'Entends tu dans nos vallons, le Chasseur sonner du clairon,' which I sang loudly till I reached the river bank, and lost the exhilaration of the hills.

I had now come some twelve miles from my starting-place, and it was midnight. The plain, the level road (which often rose a little), and the dank air of the river began to oppress me with fatigue. I was not disturbed by this, for I had intended to break these nights of marching by occasional repose, and while I was in the comfort of cities--especially in the false hopes that one got by reading books--I had imagined that it was a light matter to sleep in the open. Indeed, I had often so slept when I had been compelled to it in Manoeuvres, but I had forgotten how essential was a rug of some kind, and what a difference a fire and comradeship could make. Thinking over it all, feeling my tiredness, and shivering a little in the chill under the moon and the clear sky, I was very ready to capitulate and to sleep in bed like a Christian at the next

19

opportunity. But there is some influence in vows or plans that escapes our power of rejudgement. All false calculations must be paid for, and I found, as you will see, that having said I would sleep in the open, I had to keep to it in spite of all my second thoughts.

I passed one village and then another in which everything was dark, and in which I could waken nothing but dogs, who thought me an enemy, till at last I saw a great belt of light in the fog above the Moselle. Here there was a kind of town or large settlement where there were ironworks, and where, as I thought, there would be houses open, even after midnight. I first found the old town, where just two men were awake at some cooking work or other. I found them by a chink of light streaming through their door; but they gave me no hope, only advising me to go across the river and try in the new town where the forges and the ironworks were. 'There,' they said, 'I should certainly find a bed.'

I crossed the bridge, being now much too weary to notice anything, even the shadowy hills, and the first thing I found was a lot of waggons that belonged to a caravan or fair. Here some men were awake, but when I suggested that they should let me sleep in their little houses on wheels, they told me it was never done; that it was all they could do to pack in themselves; that they had no straw; that they were guarded by dogs; and generally gave me to understand (though without violence or unpoliteness) that I looked as though I were the man to steal their lions and tigers. They told me, however, that without doubt I should find something open in the centre of the workmen's quarter, where the great electric lamps now made a glare over the factory.

I trudged on unwillingly, and at the very last house of this detestable industrial slavery, a high house with a gable, I saw a window wide open, and a blonde man smoking a cigarette at a balcony. I called to him at once, and asked him to let me a bed. He put to me all the questions he could think of. Why was I there? Where had I come from? Where (if I was honest) had I intended to sleep? How came I at such an hour on foot? and other examinations. I thought a little what excuse to give him, and then, determining that I was too tired to make up anything plausible, I told him the full truth; that I had meant to sleep rough, but had been overcome by fatigue, and that I had walked from Toul, starting at evening. I conjured him by our common Faith to let me in. He told me that it was impossible, as he had but one room in which he and his family slept, and assured me he had asked all these questions out of sympathy and charity alone. Then he wished me good-night, honestly and kindly, and went in.

By this time I was very much put out, and began to be angry. These straggling French towns give no opportunity for a shelter. I saw that I should have to get out beyond the market gardens, and that it might be a mile or two before I found any rest. A clock struck one. I looked up and saw it was from the belfry of one of those new chapels which the monks are building everywhere, nor did I forget to curse the monks in

20

my heart for building them. I cursed also those who started smelting works in the Moselle valley; those who gave false advice to travellers; those who kept lions and tigers in caravans, and for a small sum I would have cursed the whole human race, when I saw that my bile had hurried me out of the street well into the countryside, and that above me, on a bank, was a patch of orchard and a lane leading up to it. Into this I turned, and, finding a good deal of dry hay lying under the trees, I soon made myself an excellent bed, first building a little mattress, and then piling on hay as warm as a blanket.

I did not lie awake (as when I planned my pilgrimage I had promised myself I would do), looking at the sky through the branches of trees, but I slept at once without dreaming, and woke up to find it was broad daylight, and the sun ready to rise. Then, stiff and but little rested by two hours of exhaustion, I took up my staff and my sack and regained the road.

I should very much like to know what those who have an answer to everything can say about the food requisite to breakfast? Those great men Marlowe and Jonson, Shakespeare, and Spenser before him, drank beer at rising, and tamed it with a little bread. In the regiment we used to drink black coffee without sugar, and cut off a great hunk of stale crust, and eat nothing more till the halt: for the matter of that, the great victories of '93 were fought upon such unsubstantial meals; for the Republicans fought first and ate afterwards, being in this quite unlike the Ten Thousand. Sailors I know eat nothing for some hours--I mean those who turn out at four in the morning; I could give the name of the watch, but that I forget it and will not be plagued to look up technicalities. Dogs eat the first thing they come across, cats take a little milk, and gentlemen are accustomed to get up at nine and eat eggs, bacon, kidneys, ham, cold pheasant, toast, coffee, tea, scones, and honey, after which they will boast that their race is the hardiest in the world and ready to bear every fatigue in the pursuit of Empire. But what rule governs all this? Why is breakfast different from all other things, so that the Greeks called it the best thing in the world, and so that each of us in a vague way knows that he would eat at breakfast nothing but one special kind of food, and that he could not imagine breakfast at any other hour in the day?

The provocation to this inquiry (which I have here no time to pursue) lies in the extraordinary distaste that I conceived that morning for Brule wine. My ham and bread and chocolate I had consumed overnight. I thought, in my folly, that I could break my fast on a swig of what had seemed to me, only the night before, the best revivifier and sustenance possible. In the harsh dawn it turned out to be nothing but a bitter and intolerable vinegar. I make no attempt to explain this, nor to say why the very same wine that had seemed so good in the forest (and was to seem so good again later on by the canal) should now repel me. I can only tell you that this heavy disappointment convinced me of a great truth that a Politician once let slip in my hearing, and that I have never

21

since forgotten. *'Man,'* said the Director of the State, *'man is but the creature of circumstance.'*

As it was, I lit a pipe of tobacco and hobbled blindly along for miles under and towards the brightening east. Just before the sun rose I turned and looked backward from a high bridge that recrossed the river. The long effort of the night had taken me well on my way. I was out of the familiar region of the garrison. The great forest-hills that I had traversed stood up opposite the dawn, catching the new light; heavy, drifting, but white clouds, rare at such an hour, sailed above them. The valley of the Moselle, which I had never thought of save as a half mountainous region, had fallen, to become a kind of long garden, whose walls were regular, low, and cultivated slopes. The main waterway of the valley was now not the river but the canal that fed from it.

The tall grasses, the leaves, and poplars bordering the river and the canal seemed dark close to me, but the valley as a whole was vague, a mass of trees with one Lorraine church-tower showing, and the delicate slopes bounding it on either side.

Descending from this bridge I found a sign-post, that told me I had walked thirty-two kilometres--which is twenty miles--from Toul; that it was one kilometre to Flavigny, and heaven knows how much to a place called Charmes. The sun rose in the mist that lay up the long even trends of the vale, between the low and level hills, and I pushed on my thousand yards towards Flavigny. There, by a special providence, I found the entertainment and companionship whose lack had left me wrecked all these early hours.

As I came into Flavigny I saw at once that it was a place on which a book might easily be written, for it had a church built in the seventeenth century, when few churches were built outside great towns, a convent, and a general air of importance that made of it that grand and noble thing, that primary cell of the organism of Europe, that best of all Christian associations--a large village.

I say a book might be written upon it, and there is no doubt that a great many articles and pamphlets must have been written upon it, for the French are furiously given to local research and reviews, and to glorifying their native places: and when they cannot discover folklore they enrich their beloved homes by inventing it.

There was even a man (I forget his name) who wrote a delightful book called *Popular and Traditional Songs of my Province*, which book, after he was dead, was discovered to be entirely his own invention, and not a word of it familiar to the inhabitants of the soil. He was a large, laughing man that smoked enormously, had great masses of hair, and worked by night; also he delighted in the society of friends, and talked continuously. I wish he had a statue somewhere, and that they would pull down to make room for it any one of those useless bronzes that are

22

to be found even in the little villages, and that commemorate solemn, whiskered men, pillars of the state. For surely this is the habit of the true poet, and marks the vigour and recurrent origin of poetry, that a man should get his head full of rhythms and catches, and that they should jumble up somehow into short songs of his own. What could more suggest (for instance) a whole troop of dancing words and lovely thoughts than this refrain from the Tourdenoise--

... Son beau corps est en terre
Son ame en Paradis.
Tu ris?
Et ris, tu ris, ma Bergere,
Ris, ma Bergere, tu ris.

That was the way they set to work in England before the Puritans came, when men were not afraid to steal verses from one another, and when no one imagined that he could live by letters, but when every poet took a patron, or begged or robbed the churches. So much for the poets.

Flavigny then, I say (for I seem to be digressing), is a long street of houses all built together as animals build their communities. They are all very old, but the people have worked hard since the Revolution, and none of them are poor, nor are any of them very rich. I saw but one gentleman's house, and that, I am glad to say, was in disrepair. Most of the peasants' houses had, for a ground floor, cavernous great barns out of which came a delightful smell of morning--that is, of hay, litter, oxen, and stored grains and old wood; which is the true breath of morning, because it is the scent that all the human race worth calling human first meets when it rises, and is the association of sunrise in the minds of those who keep the world alive: but not in the wretched minds of townsmen, and least of all in the minds of journalists, who know nothing of morning save that it is a time of jaded emptiness when you have just done prophesying (for the hundredth time) the approaching end of the world, when the floors are beginning to tremble with machinery, and when, in a weary kind of way, one feels hungry and alone: a nasty life and usually a short one.

To return to Flavigny. This way of stretching a village all along one street is Roman, and is the mark of civilization. When I was at college I was compelled to read a work by the crabbed Tacitus on the Germans, where, in the midst of a deal that is vague and fantastic nonsense and much that is wilful lying, comes this excellent truth, that barbarians build their houses separate, but civilized men together. So whenever you see a lot of red roofs nestling, as the phrase goes, in the woods of a hillside in south England, remember that all that is savagery; but when you see a hundred white-washed houses in a row along a dead straight road, lift up your hearts, for you are in civilization again.

23

But I continue to wander from Flavigny. The first thing I saw as I came into the street and noted how the level sun stood in a haze beyond, and how it shadowed and brought out the slight irregularities of the road, was a cart drawn by a galloping donkey, which came at and passed me with a prodigious clatter as I dragged myself forward. In the cart were two nuns, each with a scythe; they were going out mowing, and were up the first in the village, as Religious always are. Cheered by this happy omen, but not yet heartened, I next met a very old man leading out a horse, and asked him if there was anywhere where I could find coffee and bread at that hour; but he shook his head mournfully and wished me good-morning in a strong accent, for he was deaf and probably thought I was begging. So I went on still more despondent till I came to a really merry man of about middle age who was going to the fields, singing, with a very large rake over his shoulder. When I had asked him the same question he stared at me a little and said of course coffee and bread could be had at the baker's, and when I asked him how I should know the baker's he was still more surprised at my ignorance, and said, 'By the smoke coming from the large chimney.' This I saw rising a short way off on my right, so I thanked him and went and found there a youth of about nineteen, who sat at a fine oak table and had coffee, rum, and a loaf before him. He was waiting for the bread in the oven to be ready; and meanwhile he was very courteous, poured out coffee and rum for me and offered me bread.

It is a matter often discussed why bakers are such excellent citizens and good men. For while it is admitted in every country I was ever in that cobblers are argumentative and atheists (I except the cobbler under Plinlimmon, concerning whom would to heaven I had the space to tell you all here, for he knows the legends of the mountain), while it is public that barbers are garrulous and servile, that millers are cheats (we say in Sussex that every honest miller has a large tuft of hair on the palm of his hand), yet--with every trade in the world having some bad quality attached to it--bakers alone are exempt, and every one takes it for granted that they are sterling: indeed, there are some societies in which, no matter how gloomy and churlish the conversation may have become, you have but to mention bakers for voices to brighten suddenly and for a good influence to pervade every one. I say this is known for a fact, but not usually explained; the explanation is, that bakers are always up early in the morning and can watch the dawn, and that in this occupation they live in lonely contemplation enjoying the early hours.

So it was with this baker of mine in Flavigny, who was a boy. When he heard that I had served at Toul he was delighted beyond measure; he told me of a brother of his that had been in the same regiment, and he assured me that he was himself going into the artillery by special enlistment, having got his father's leave. You know very little if you think I missed the opportunity of making the guns seem terrible and glorious in his eyes. I told him stories enough to waken a sentry of reserve, and if it had been possible (with my youth so obvious) I would have woven in a few anecdotes of active service, and described great

24

shells bursting under my horses and the teams shot down, and the gunners all the while impassive; but as I saw I should not be believed I did not speak of such things, but confined myself to what he would see and hear when he joined.

Meanwhile the good warm food and the rising morning had done two things; they had put much more vigour into me than I had had when I slunk in half-an-hour before, but at the same time (and this is a thing that often comes with food and with rest) they had made me feel the fatigue of so long a night. I rose up, therefore, determined to find some place where I could sleep. I asked this friend of mine how much there was to pay, and he said 'fourpence'. Then we exchanged ritual salutations, and I took the road. I did not leave the town or village without noticing one extraordinary thing at the far end of it, which was that, whereas most places in France are proud of their town-hall and make a great show of it, here in Flavigny they had taken a great house and written over it ECOLE COMMUNALE in great letters, and then they had written over a kind of lean-to or out-house of this big place the words 'Hotel de ville' in very small letters, so small that I had a doubt for a moment if the citizens here were good republicans--a treasonable thought on all this frontier.

Then, a mile onward, I saw the road cross the canal and run parallel to it. I saw the canal run another mile or so under a fine bank of deep woods. I saw an old bridge leading over it to that inviting shade, and as it was now nearly six and the sun was gathering strength, I went, with slumber overpowering me and my feet turning heavy beneath me, along the tow-path, over the bridge, and lay down on the moss under these delightful trees. Forgetful of the penalty that such an early repose would bring, and of the great heat that was to follow at midday, I quickly became part of the life of that forest and fell asleep.

When I awoke it was full eight o'clock, and the sun had gained great power. I saw him shining at me through the branches of my trees like a patient enemy outside a city that one watches through the loopholes of a tower, and I began to be afraid of taking the road. I looked below me down the steep bank between the trunks and saw the canal looking like black marble, and I heard the buzzing of the flies above it, and I noted that all the mist had gone. A very long way off, the noise of its ripples coming clearly along the floor of the water, was a lazy barge and a horse drawing it. From time to time the tow-rope slackened into the still surface, and I heard it dripping as it rose. The rest of the valley was silent except for that under-humming of insects which marks the strength of the sun.

Now I saw clearly how difficult it was to turn night into day, for I found myself condemned either to waste many hours that ought to be consumed on my pilgrimage, or else to march on under the extreme heat; and when I had drunk what was left of my Brule wine (which then seemed delicious), and had eaten a piece of bread, I stiffly jolted down the bank and regained the highway.

In the first village I came to I found that Mass was over, and this justly annoyed me; for what is a pilgrimage in which a man cannot hear Mass every morning? Of all the things I have read about St Louis which make me wish I had known him to speak to, nothing seems to me more delightful than his habit of getting Mass daily whenever he marched down south, but why this should be so delightful I cannot tell. Of course there is a grace and influence belonging to such a custom, but it is not of that I am speaking but of the pleasing sensation of order and accomplishment which attaches to a day one has opened by Mass; a purely temporal, and, for all I know, what the monks back at the ironworks would have called a carnal feeling, but a source of continual comfort to me. Let them go their way and let me go mine.

This comfort I ascribe to four causes (just above you will find it written that I could not tell why this should be so, but what of that?), and these causes are:

1. That for half-an-hour just at the opening of the day you are silent and recollected, and have to put off cares, interests, and passions in the repetition of a familiar action. This must certainly be a great benefit to the body and give it tone.

2. That the Mass is a careful and rapid ritual. Now it is the function of all ritual (as we see in games, social arrangements and so forth) to relieve the mind by so much of responsibility and initiative and to catch you up (as it were) into itself, leading your life for you during the time it lasts. In this way you experience a singular repose, after which fallowness I am sure one is fitter for action and judgement.

3. That the surroundings incline you to good and reasonable thoughts, and for the moment deaden the rasp and jar of that busy wickedness which both working in one's self and received from others is the true source of all human miseries. Thus the time spent at Mass is like a short repose in a deep and well-built library, into which no sounds come and where you feel yourself secure against the outer world.

4. And the most important cause of this feeling of satisfaction is that you are doing what the human race has done for thousands upon thousands upon thousands of years. This is a matter of such moment that I am astonished people hear of it so little. Whatever is buried right into our blood from immemorial habit that we must be certain to do if we are to be fairly happy (of course no grown man or woman can really be very happy for long--but I mean reasonably happy), and, what is more important, decent and secure of our souls. Thus one should from time to time hunt animals, or at the very least shoot at a mark; one should always drink some kind of fermented liquor with one's food--and especially deeply upon great feast-days; one should go on the water

from time to time; and one should dance on occasions; and one should sing in chorus. For all these things man has done since God put him into a garden and his eyes first became troubled with a soul. Similarly some teacher or ranter or other, whose name I forget, said lately one very wise thing at least, which was that every man should do a little work with his hands.

Oh! what good philosophy this is, and how much better it would be if rich people, instead of raining the influence of their rank and spending their money on leagues for this or that exceptional thing, were to spend it in converting the middle-class to ordinary living and to the tradition of the race. Indeed, if I had power for some thirty years I would see to it that people should be allowed to follow their inbred instincts in these matters, and should hunt, drink, sing, dance, sail, and dig; and those that would not should be compelled by force.

Now in the morning Mass you do all that the race needs to do and has done for all these ages where religion was concerned; there you have the sacred and separate Enclosure, the Altar, the Priest in his Vestments, the set ritual, the ancient and hierarchic tongue, and all that your nature cries out for in the matter of worship.

From these considerations it is easy to understand how put out I was to find Mass over on this first morning of my pilgrimage. And I went along the burning road in a very ill-humour till I saw upon my right, beyond a low wall and in a kind of park, a house that seemed built on some artificial raised ground surrounded by a wall, but this may have been an illusion, the house being really only very tall. At any rate I drew it, and in the village just beyond it I learnt something curious about the man that owned it.

For I had gone into a house to take a third meal of bread and wine and to replenish my bottle when the old woman of the house, who was a kindly person, told me she had just then no wine. 'But,' said she, 'Mr So and So that lives in the big house sells it to any one who cares to buy even in the smallest quantities, and you will see his shed standing by the side of the road.'

Everything happened just as she had said. I came to the big shed by the park wall, and there was a kind of counter made of boards, and several big tuns and two men: one in an apron serving, and the other in a little box or compartment writing. I was somewhat timid to ask for so little as a quart, but the apron man in the most businesslike way filled my bottle at a tap and asked for fourpence. He was willing to talk, and told me many things: of good years in wine, of the nature of their trade, of the influence of the moon on brewing, of the importance of spigots, and what not; but when I tried to get out of him whether the owner were an eccentric private gentleman or a merchant that had the sense to earn little pennies as well as large ones, I could not make him understand my meaning; for his idea of rank was utterly different from mine and took no account of idleness and luxury and daftness, but was based entirely upon money and clothes. Moreover we were both of us Republicans, so the matter was of no great moment. Courteously saluting ourselves we parted, he remaining to sell wine and I hobbling to Rome, now a little painfully and my sack the heavier by a quart of wine, which, as you probably know, weighs almost exactly two pounds and a half.

It was by this time close upon eleven, and I had long reached the stage when some kinds of men begin talking of Dogged Determination, Bull-dog pluck, the stubborn spirit of the Island race and so forth, but when those who can boast a little of the sacred French blood are in a mood of set despair (both kinds march on, and the mobility of either infantry is much the same), I say I had long got to this point of exhaustion when it occurred to me that I should need an excellent and thorough meal at midday. But on looking at my map I found that there was nothing nearer than this town of Charmes that was marked on the milestones, and that was the first place I should come to in the department of the Vosges.

It would take much too long to describe the dodges that weary men and stiff have recourse to when they are at the close of a difficult task: how they divide it up in lengths in their minds, how they count numbers, how they begin to solve problems in mental arithmetic: I tried them all. Then I thought of a new one, which is really excellent, and which I recommend to the whole world. It is to vary the road, suddenly taking now the fields, now the river, but only occasionally the turnpike. This last lap was very well suited for such a method. The valley had become more like a wide and shallow trench than ever. The hills on either side were low and exactly even. Up the middle of it went the river, the canal and the road, and these two last had only a field between them; now broad, now narrow.

First on the tow-path, then on the road, then on the grass, then back on the tow-path, I pieced out the last baking mile into Charmes, that lies at the foot of a rather higher hill, and at last was dragging myself up the street just as the bell was ringing the noon Angelus; nor, however tedious you may have found it to read this final effort of mine, can you have found it a quarter as wearisome as I did to walk it; and surely between writer and reader there should be give and take, now the one furnishing the entertainment and now the other.

The delightful thing in Charmes is its name. Of this name I had indeed been thinking as I went along the last miles of that dusty and deplorable road--that a town should be called 'Charms'.

Not but that towns, if they are left to themselves and not hurried, have a way of settling into right names suited to the hills about them and recalling their own fields. I remember Sussex, and as I remember it I must, if only for example, set down my roll-call of such names, as--

28

Fittleworth, where the Inn has painted panels; Amberley in the marshes; delicate Fernhurst, and Ditchling under its hill; Arundel, that is well known to every one; and Climping, that no one knows, set on a lonely beach and lost at the vague end of an impassable road; and Barlton, and Burton, and Duncton, and Coldwatham, that stand under in the shadow and look up at the great downs; and Petworth, where the spire leans sideways; and Timberley, that the floods make into an island; and No Man's Land, where first there breaks on you the distant sea. I never knew a Sussex man yet but, if you noted him such a list, would answer: 'There I was on such and such a day; this I came to after such and such a run; and that other is my home.' But it is not his recollection alone which moves him, it is sound of the names. He feels the accent of them, and all the men who live between Hind-head and the Channel know these names stand for Eden; the noise is enough to prove it. So it is also with the hidden valleys of the Ile de France; and when you say Jouy or Chevreuse to a man that was born in those shadows he grows dreamy--yet they are within a walk of Paris.

But the wonderful thing about a name like Charmes is that it hands down the dead. For some dead man gave it a keen name proceeding from his own immediate delight, and made general what had been a private pleasure, and, so to speak, bequeathed a poem to his town. They say the Arabs do this; calling one place 'the rest of the warriors', and another 'the end', and another 'the surprise of the horses': let those who know them speak for it. I at least know that in the west of the Cotentin (a sea-garden) old Danes married to Gaulish women discovered the just epithet, and that you have 'St Mary on the Hill' and 'High Town under the Wind' and 'The Borough over the Heath', which are to-day exactly what their name describes them. If you doubt that England has such descriptive names, consider the great Truth that at one junction on a railway where a mournful desolation of stagnant waters and treeless, stonewalled fields threatens you with experience and awe, a melancholy porter is told off to put his head into your carriage and to chant like Charon, 'Change here for Ashton under the Wood, Moreton on the Marsh, Bourton on the Water, and Stow in the Wold.'

Charmes does not fulfil its name nor preserve what its forgotten son found so wonderful in it. For at luncheon there a great commercial traveller told me fiercely that it was chiefly known for its breweries, and that he thought it of little account. Still even in Charmes I found one marvellous corner of a renaissance house, which I drew; but as I have lost the drawing, let it go.

When I came out from the inn of Charmes the heat was more terrible than ever, and the prospect of a march in it more intolerable. My head hung, I went very slowly, and I played with cowardly thoughts, which were really (had I known it) good angels. I began to look out anxiously for woods, but saw only long whitened wall glaring in the sun, or, if ever there were trees, they were surrounded by wooden palisades which the owners had put there. But in a little time (now I had definitely yielded to temptation) I found a thicket.

You must know that if you yield to entertaining a temptation, there is the opportunity presented to you like lightning. A theologian told me this, and it is partly true: but not of Mammon or Belphegor, or whatever Devil it is that overlooks the Currency (I can see his face from here): for how many have yielded to the Desire of Riches and professed themselves very willing to revel in them, yet did not get an opportunity worth a farthing till they died? Like those two beggars that Rabelais tells of, one of whom wished for all the gold that would pay for all the merchandise that had ever been sold in Paris since its first foundation, and the other for as much gold as would go into all the sacks that could be sewn by all the needles (and those of the smallest size) that could be crammed into Notre-Dame from the floor to the ceiling, filling the smallest crannies. Yet neither had a crust that night to rub his gums with.

Whatever Devil it is, however, that tempts men to repose--and for my part I believe him to be rather an Aeon than a Devil: that is, a good-natured fellow working on his own account neither good nor ill-- whatever being it is, it certainly suits one's mood, for I never yet knew a man determined to be lazy that had not ample opportunity afforded him, though he were poorer than the cure of Maigre, who formed a syndicate to sell at a scutcheon a gross such souls as were too insignificant to sell singly. A man can always find a chance for doing nothing as amply and with as ecstatic a satisfaction as the world allows, and so to me (whether it was there before I cannot tell, and if it came miraculously, so much the more amusing) appeared this thicket. It was to the left of the road; a stream ran through it in a little ravine; the undergrowth was thick beneath its birches, and just beyond, on the plain that bordered it, were reapers reaping in a field. I went into it contentedly and slept till evening my third sleep; then, refreshed by the cool wind that went before the twilight, I rose and took the road again, but I knew I could not go far.

I was now past my fortieth mile, and though the heat had gone, yet my dead slumber had raised a thousand evils. I had stiffened to lameness, and had fallen into the mood when a man desires companionship and the talk of travellers rather than the open plain. But (unless I went backward, which was out of the question) there was nowhere to rest in for a long time to come. The next considerable village was Thayon, which is called 'Thayon of the Vosges', because one is nearing the big hills, and thither therefore I crawled mile after mile.

But my heart sank. First my foot limped, and then my left knee oppressed me with a sudden pain. I attempted to relieve it by leaning on my right leg, and so discovered a singular new law in medicine which I will propose to the scientists. For when those excellent men have done investigating the twirligigs of the brain to find out where the soul is, let them consider this much more practical matter, that you cannot relieve the pain in one limb without driving it into some other; and so I exchanged twinges in the left knee for a horrible great pain in the right. I sat down on a bridge, and wondered; I saw before me hundreds upon hundreds of miles, painful and exhausted, and I asked heaven if this was necessary to a pilgrimage. (But, as you shall hear, a pilgrimage is not wholly subject to material laws, for when I came to Epinal next day I went into a shop which, whatever it was to the profane, appeared to me as a chemist's shop, where I bought a bottle of some stuff called 'balm', and rubbing myself with it was instantly cured.)

Then I looked down from the bridge across the plain, and saw, a long way off beyond the railway, the very ugly factory village of Thayon, and reached it at last, not without noticing that the people were standing branches of trees before their doors, and the little children noisily helping to tread the stems firmly into the earth. They told me it was for the coming of Corpus Christi, and so proved to me that religion, which is as old as these valleys, would last out their inhabiting men. Even here, in a place made by a great laundry, a modern industrial row of tenements, all the world was putting out green branches to welcome the Procession and the Sacrament and the Priest. Comforted by this evident refutation of the sad nonsense I had read in Cities from the pen of intellectuals--nonsense I had known to be nonsense, but that had none the less tarnished my mind--I happily entered the inn, ate and drank, praised God, and lay down to sleep in a great bed. I mingled with my prayers a firm intention of doing the ordinary things, and not attempting impossibilities, such as marching by night, nor following out any other vanities of this world. Then, having cast away all theories of how a pilgrimage should be conducted, and broken five or six vows, I slept steadily till the middle of the morning. I had covered fifty miles in twenty-five hours, and if you imagine this to be but two miles an hour, you must have a very mathematical mind, and know little of the realities of living. I woke and threw my shutters open to the bright morning and the masterful sun, took my coffee, and set out once more towards Epinal, the stronghold a few miles away--delighted to see that my shadow was so short and the road so hot to the feet and eyes. For I said, 'This at least proves that I am doing like all the world, and walking during the day.' It was but a couple of hours to the great garrison. In a little time I passed a battery. Then a captain went by on a horse, with his orderly behind him. Where the deep lock stands by the roadside-- the only suggestion of coolness--I first heard the bugles; then I came into the long street and determined to explore Epinal, and to cast aside all haste and folly.

There are many wonderful things in Epinal. As, for instance, that it was evidently once, like Paris and Melun and a dozen other strongholds of the Gauls, an island city. For the rivers of France are full of long, habitable islands, and these were once the rallying-places of clans. Then there are the forts which are placed on high hills round the town and make it even stronger than Toul; for Epinal stands just where the hills begin to be very high. Again, it is the capital of a mountain district, and this character always does something peculiar and impressive to a town. You may watch its effect in Grenoble, in little Aubusson, and, rather less, in Geneva.

For in such towns three quite different kinds of men meet. First there are the old plain-men, who despise the highlanders and think themselves much grander and more civilized; these are the burgesses. Then there are the peasants and wood-cutters, who come in from the hill-country to market, and who are suspicious of the plain-men and yet proud to depend upon a real town with a bishop and paved streets. Lastly, there are the travellers, who come there to enjoy the mountains and to make the city a base for their excursions, and these love the hill-men and think they understand them, and they despise the plain-men for being so middle-class as to lord it over the hill-men: but in truth this third class, being outsiders, are equally hated and despised by both the others, and there is a combination against them and they are exploited.

And there are many other things in which Epinal is wonderful, but in nothing is it more wonderful than in its great church.

I suppose that the high Dukes of Burgundy and Lorraine and the rich men from Flanders and the House of Luxemburg and the rest, going to Rome, the centre of the world, had often to pass up this valley of the Moselle, which (as I have said) is a road leading to Rome, and would halt at fipinal and would at times give money for its church; with this result, that the church belongs to every imaginable period and is built anyhow, in twenty styles, but stands as a whole a most enduring record of past forms and of what has pleased the changing mind when it has attempted to worship in stone.

Thus the transept is simply an old square barn of rough stone, older, I suppose, than Charlemagne and without any ornament. In its lower courses I thought I even saw the Roman brick. It had once two towers, northern and southern; the southern is ruined and has a wooden roof, the northern remains and is just a pinnacle or minaret too narrow for bells.

Then the apse is pure and beautiful Gothic of the fourteenth century, with very tall and fluted windows like single prayers. The ambulatory is perfectly modern, Gothic also, and in the manner that Viollet le Duc in France and Pugin in England have introduced to bring us back to our origins and to remind us of the place whence all we Europeans came. Again, this apse and ambulatory are not perpendicular to the transept, but set askew, a thing known in small churches and said to be a symbol, but surely very rare in large ones. The western door is purely Romanesque, and has Byzantine ornaments and a great deep round door. To match it there is a northern door still deeper, with rows and rows of inner arches full of saints, angels, devils, and flowers; and this again is not straight, but so built that the arches go aslant, as you sometimes see railway bridges when they cross roads at an angle. Finally, there is a central tower which is neither Gothic nor Romanesque but pure Italian, a loggia, with splendid round airy windows taking up all its walls, and with a flat roof and eaves. This some one straight from the south must have put on as a memory of his wanderings.

The barn-transept is crumbling old grey stone, the Romanesque porches are red, like Strasburg, the Gothic apse is old white as our cathedrals are, the modern ambulatory is of pure white stone just quarried, and thus colours as well as shapes are mingled up and different in this astonishing building.

I drew it from that point of view in the market-place to the north-east which shows most of these contrasts at once, and you must excuse the extreme shakiness of the sketch, for it was taken as best I could on an apple-cart with my book resting on the apples--there was no other desk. Nor did the apple-seller mind my doing it, but on the contrary gave me advice and praise saying such things as--

'Excellent; you have caught the angle of the apse ... Come now, darken the edge of that pillar ... I fear you have made the tower a little confused,' and so forth.

I offered to buy a few apples off him, but he gave me three instead, and these, as they incommoded me, I gave later to a little child.

Indeed the people of Epinal, not taking me for a traveller but simply for a wandering poor man, were very genial to me, and the best good they did me was curing my lameness. For, seeing an apothecary's shop as I was leaving the town, I went in and said to the apothecary--

'My knee has swelled and is very painful, and I have to walk far; perhaps you can tell me how to cure it, or give me something that will.'

'There is nothing easier,' he said; 'I have here a specific for the very thing you complain of.'

With this he pulled out a round bottle, on the label of which was printed in great letters, 'BALM'.

'You have but to rub your knee strongly and long with this ointment of mine,' he said, 'and you will be cured.' Nor did he mention any special form of words to be repeated as one did it.

Everything happened just as he had said. When I was some little way above the town I sat down on a low wall and rubbed my knee strongly and long with this balm, and the pain instantly disappeared. Then, with a heart renewed by this prodigy, I took the road again and began walking very rapidly and high, swinging on to Rome.

The Moselle above fipinal takes a bend outwards, and it seemed to me that a much shorter way to the next village (which is called Archettes, or 'the very little arches', because there are no arches there) would be right over the hill round which the river curved. This error came from following private judgement and not heeding tradition, here represented by the highroad which closely follows the river. For though a straight tunnel to Archettes would have saved distance, yet a climb over that high hill and through the pathless wood on its summit was folly.

I went at first over wide, sloping fields, and some hundred feet above the valley I crossed a little canal. It was made on a very good system, and I recommend it to the riparian owners of the Upper Wye, which needs it. They take the water from the Moselle (which is here broad and torrential and falls in steps, running over a stony bed with little swirls and rapids), and they lead it along at an even gradient, averaging, as it were, the uneven descent of the river. In this way they have a continuous stream running through fields that would otherwise be bare and dry, but that are thus nourished into excellent pastures.

Above these fields the forest went up steeply. I had not pushed two hundred yards into its gloom and confusion when I discovered that I had lost my way. It was necessary to take the only guide I had and to go straight upwards wherever the line of greatest inclination seemed to lie, for that at least would take me to a summit and probably to a view of the valley; whereas if I tried to make for the shoulder of the hill (which had been my first intention) I might have wandered about till nightfall.

It was an old man in a valley called the Curicante in Colorado that taught me this, if one lost one's way going *upwards* to make at once along the steepest line, but if one lost it going *downwards*, to listen for water and reach it and follow it. I wish I had space to tell all about this old man, who gave me hospitality out there. He was from New England and was lonely, and had brought out at great expense a musical box to cheer him. Of this he was very proud, and though it only played four silly hymn tunes, yet, as he and I listened to it, heavy tears came into his eyes and light tears into mine, because these tunes reminded him of his home. But I have no time to do more than mention him, and must return to my forest.

I climbed, then, over slippery pine needles and under the charged air of those trees, which was full of dim, slanting light from the afternoon sun, till, nearly at the summit, I came upon a clearing which I at once recognized as a military road, leading to what we used to call a 'false battery', that is, a dug-out with embrasures into which guns could be placed but in which no guns were. For ever since the French managed to produce a really mobile heavy gun they have constructed any amount of such auxiliary works between the permanent forts. These need no fixed guns to be emplaced, since the French can use now one such parapet, now another, as occasion serves, and the advantage is that your guns are never useless, but can always be brought round where they are needed, and that thus six guns will do more work than twenty used to do.

This false battery was on the brow of the hill, and when I reached it I looked down the slope, over the brushwood that hid the wire entanglements, and there was the whole valley of the Moselle at my feet.

As this was the first really great height, so this was the first really great view that I met with on my pilgrimage. I drew it carefully, piece by piece, sitting there a long time in the declining sun and noting all I saw. Archettes, just below; the flat valley with the river winding from side to side; the straight rows of poplar trees; the dark pines on the hills, and the rounded mountains rising farther and higher into the distance until the last I saw, far off to the south-east, must have been the Ballon d'Alsace at the sources of the Moselle--the hill that marked the first full stage in my journey and that overlooked Switzerland.

Indeed, this is the peculiar virtue of walking to a far place, and especially of walking there in a straight line, that one gets these visions of the world from hill-tops.

When I call up for myself this great march I see it all mapped out in landscapes, each of which I caught from some mountain, and each of which joins on to that before and to that after it, till I can piece together the whole road. The view here from the Hill of Archettes, the view from the Ballon d'Alsace, from Glovelier Hill, from the Weissenstein, from the Brienzer Grat, from the Grimsel, from above Bellinzona, from the Princi-pessa, from Tizzano, from the ridge of the Apennines, from the Wall of Siena, from San Quirico, from Radicofani, from San Lorenzo, from Monte-fiascone, from above Viterbo, from Roncigleone, and at last from that lift in the Via Cassia, whence one suddenly perceives the City. They unroll themselves all in their order till I can see Europe, and Rome shining at the end.

But you who go in railways are necessarily shut up in long valleys and even sometimes by the walls of the earth. Even those who bicycle or drive see these sights but rarely and with no consecution, since roads also avoid climbing save where they are forced to it, as over certain passes. It is only by following the straight line onwards that any one can pass from ridge to ridge and have this full picture of the way he has been.

So much for views. I clambered down the hill to Archettes and saw, almost the first house, a swinging board 'At the sign of the Trout of the Vosges', and as it was now evening I turned in there to dine.

Two things I noticed at once when I sat down to meat. First, that the people seated at that inn table were of the middle-class of society, and secondly, that I, though of their rank, was an impediment to their enjoyment. For to sleep in woods, to march some seventy miles, the latter part in a dazzling sun, and to end by sliding down an earthy steep into the road, stamps a man with all that this kind of people least desire to have thrust upon them. And those who blame the middle-class for their conventions in such matters, and who profess to be above the care for cleanliness and clothes and social ritual which marks the middle-class, are either anarchists by nature, or fools who take what is but an effect of their wealth for a natural virtue.

I say it roundly; if it were not for the punctiliousness of the middle-class in these matters all our civilization would go to pieces. They are the conservators and the maintainers of the standard, the moderators of Europe, the salt of society. For the kind of man who boasts that he does not mind dirty clothes or roughing it, is either a man who cares nothing for all that civilization has built up and who rather hates it, or else (and this is much more common) he is a rich man, or accustomed to live among the rich, and can afford to waste energy and stuff because he feels in a vague way that more clothes can always be bought, that at the end of his vagabondism he can get excellent dinners, and that London and Paris are full of luxurious baths and barber shops. Of all the corrupting effects of wealth there is none worse than this, that it makes the wealthy (and their parasites) think in some way divine, or at least a lovely character of the mind, what is in truth nothing but their power of luxurious living. Heaven keep us all from great riches--I mean from very great riches.

Now the middle-class cannot afford to buy new clothes whenever they feel inclined, neither can they end up a jaunt by a Turkish bath and a great feast with wine. So their care is always to preserve intact what they happen to have, to exceed in nothing, to study cleanliness, order, decency, sobriety, and a steady temper, and they fence all this round and preserve it in the only way it can be preserved, to wit, with conventions, and they are quite right.

I find it very hard to keep up to the demands of these my colleagues, but I recognize that they are on the just side in the quarrel; let none of them go about pretending that I have not defended them in this book.

So I thought of how I should put myself right with these people. I saw that an elaborate story (as, that I had been set upon by a tramp who forced me to change clothes: that I dressed thus for a bet: that I was an officer employed as a spy, and was about to cross the frontier into Germany in the guise of a labourer: that my doctor forbade me to shave--or any other such rhodo-montade): I saw, I say, that by venturing upon any such excuses I might unwittingly offend some other unknown canon of theirs deeper and more sacred than their rule on clothes; it had happened to me before now to do this in the course of explanations.

So I took another method, and said, as I sat down--

'Pray excuse this appearance of mine. I have had a most unfortunate adventure in the hills, losing my way and being compelled to sleep out all night, nor can I remain to get tidy, as it is essential that I should reach my luggage (which is at Remiremont) before midnight.'

I took great care to pay for my glass of white wine before dinner with a bank-note, and I showed my sketches to my neighbour to make an impression. I also talked of foreign politics, of the countries I had seen, of England especially, with such minute exactitude that their disgust was soon turned to admiration.

The hostess of this inn was delicate and courteous to a degree, and at every point attempting to overreach her guests, who, as regularly as she attacked, countered with astonishing dexterity.

Thus she would say: 'Perhaps the joint would taste better if it were carved on the table; or do the gentlemen prefer it carved aside?'

To which a banker opposite me said in a deep voice: 'We prefer, madam, to have it carved aside.'

Or she would put her head in and say: 'I can recommend our excellent beer. It is really preferable to this local wine.'

And my neighbour, a tourist, answered with decision: 'Madame, we find your wine excellent. It could not be bettered.'

Nor could she get round them on a single point, and I pitied her so much that I bought bread and wine off her to console her, and I let her overcharge me, and went out into the afterglow with her benediction, followed also by the farewells of the middle-class, who were now taking their coffee at little tables outside the house.

I went hard up the road to Remiremont. The night darkened. I reached Remiremont at midnight, and feeling very wakeful I pushed on up the valley under great woods of pines; and at last, diverging up a little path, I settled on a clump of trees sheltered and, as I thought, warm, and lay down there to sleep till morning; but, on the contrary, I lay awake a full hour in the fragrance and on the level carpet of the pine needles looking up through the dark branches at the waning moon, which had just risen, and thinking of how suitable were pine-trees for a man to sleep under.

'The beech,' I thought, 'is a good tree to sleep under, for nothing will grow there, and there is always dry beech-mast; the yew would be good if it did not grow so low, but, all in all, pine-trees are the best.' I also considered that the worst tree to sleep under would be the upas tree. These thoughts so nearly bordered on nothing that, though I was not sleepy, yet I fell asleep. Long before day, the moon being still lustrous against a sky that yet contained a few faint stars, I awoke shivering with cold.

In sleep there is something diminishes us. This every one has noticed; for who ever suffered a nightmare awake, or felt in full consciousness those awful impotencies which lie on the other side of slumber? When we lie down we give ourselves voluntarily, yet by the force of nature, to powers before which we melt and are nothing. And among the strange frailties of sleep I have noticed cold.

Here was a warm place under the pines where I could rest in great comfort on pine needles still full of the day; a covering for the beasts underground that love an even heat--the best of floors for a tired man. Even the slight wind that blew under the waning moon was warm, and the stars were languid and not brilliant, as though everything were full of summer, and I knew that the night would be short; a midsummer night; and I had lived half of it before attempting repose. Yet, I say, I woke shivering and also disconsolate, needing companionship. I pushed down through tall, rank grass, drenched with dew, and made my way across the road to the bank of the river. By the time I reached it the dawn began to occupy the east.

For a long time I stood in a favoured place, just above a bank of trees that lined the river, and watched the beginning of the day, because every slow increase of light promised me sustenance.

The faint, uncertain glimmer that seemed not so much to shine through the air as to be part of it, took all colour out of the woods and fields and the high slopes above me, leaving them planes of grey and deeper grey. The woods near me were a silhouette, black and motionless, emphasizing the east beyond. The river was white and dead, not even a steam rose from it, but out of the further pastures a gentle mist had lifted up and lay all even along the flanks of the hills, so that they rose out of it, indistinct at their bases, clear-cut above against the brightening sky; and the farther they were the more their mouldings showed in the early light, and the most distant edges of all caught the morning.

At this wonderful sight I gazed for quite half-an-hour without moving, and took in vigour from it as a man takes in food and wine. When I stirred and looked about me it had become easy to see the separate grasses; a bird or two had begun little interrupted chirrups in the bushes, a day-breeze broke from up the valley ruffling the silence, the moon was dead against the sky, and the stars had disappeared. In a solemn mood I regained the road and turned my face towards the neighbouring sources of the river.

I easily perceived with each laborious mile that I was approaching the end of my companionship with the Moselle, which had become part of my adventure for the last eighty miles. It was now a small stream,

38

mountainous and uncertain, though in parts still placid and slow. There appeared also that which I take to be an infallible accompaniment of secluded glens and of the head waters of rivers (however canalized or even overbuilt they are), I mean a certain roughness all about them and the stout protest of the hill-men: their stone cottages and their lonely paths off the road.

So it was here. The hills had grown much higher and come closer to the river-plain; up the gullies I would catch now and then an aged and uncouth bridge with a hut near it all built of enduring stone: part of the hills. Then again there were present here and there on the spurs lonely chapels, and these in Catholic countries are a mark of the mountains and of the end of the riches of a valley. Why this should be so I cannot tell. You find them also sometimes in forests, but especially in the lesser inlets of the sea-coast, and, as I have said, here in the upper parts of valleys in the great hills. In such shrines Mass is to be said but rarely, sometimes but once a year in a special commemoration. The rest of the time they stand empty, and some of the older or simpler, one might take for ruins. They mark everywhere some strong emotion of supplication, thanks, or reverence, and they anchor these wild places to their own past, making them up in memories what they lack in multitudinous life.

I broke my fast on bread and wine at a place where the road crosses the river, and then I determined I would have hot coffee as well, and seeing in front of me a village called Rupt, which means 'the cleft' (for there is here a great cleft in the hillside), I went up to it and had my coffee. Then I discovered a singular thing, that the people of the place are tired of making up names and give nothing its peculiar baptism. This I thought really very wonderful indeed, for I have noticed wherever I have been that in proportion as men are remote and have little to distract them, in that proportion they produce a great crop of peculiar local names for every stream, reach, tuft, hummock, glen, copse, and gully for miles around; and often when I have lost my way and asked it of a peasant in some lonely part I have grown impatient as he wandered on about 'leaving on your left the stone we call the Nuggin, and bearing round what some call Holy Dyke till you come to what they call Mary's Ferry'... and so forth. Long-shoremen and the riparian inhabitants of dreadful and lonely rivers near the sea have just such a habit, and I have in my mind's eye now a short stretch of tidal water in which there are but five shoals, yet they all have names, and are called 'The House, the Knowle, Goodman's Plot, Mall, and the Patch.'

But here in Rupt, to my extreme astonishment, there was no such universal and human instinct. For I said to the old man who poured me out my coffee under the trellis (it was full morning, the sun was well up, and the clouds were all dappled high above the tops of the mountains): 'Father, what do you call this hill?' And with that I pointed to a very remarkable hill and summit that lie sheer above the village.

'That,' he said, 'is called the hill over above Rupt.'

'Yes, of course,' I said, 'but what is its name?'

'That is its name,' he answered.

And he was quite right, for when I looked at my map, there it was printed, 'Hill above Rupt'. I thought how wearisome it would be if this became a common way of doing things, and if one should call the Thames 'the River of London', and Essex 'the North side', and Kent 'the South side'; but considering that this fantastic method was only indulged in by one wretched village, I released myself from fear, relegated such horrors to the colonies, and took the road again.

All this upper corner of the valley is a garden. It is bound in on every side from the winds, it is closed at the end by the great mass of the Ballon d'Alsace, its floor is smooth and level, its richness is used to feed grass and pasturage, and knots of trees grow about it as though they had been planted to please the eye.

Nothing can take from the sources of rivers their character of isolation and repose. Here what are afterwards to become the influences of the plains are nurtured and tended as though in an orchard, and the future life of a whole fruitful valley with its regal towns is determined. Something about these places prevents ingress or spoliation. They will endure no settlements save of peasants; the waters are too young to be harnessed; the hills forbid an easy commerce with neighbours. Throughout the world I have found the heads of rivers to be secure places of silence and content. And as they are themselves a kind of youth, the early home of all that rivers must at last become--I mean special ways of building and a separate state of living, a local air and a tradition of history, for rivers are always the makers of provinces--so they bring extreme youth back to one, and these upper glens of the world steep one in simplicity and childhood.

It was my delight to lie upon a bank of the road and to draw what I saw before me, which was the tender stream of the Moselle slipping through fields quite flat and even and undivided by fences; its banks had here a strange effect of Nature copying man's art: they seemed a park, and the river wound through it full of the positive innocence that attaches to virgins: it nourished and was guarded by trees.

There was about that scene something of creation and of a beginning, and as I drew it, it gave me like a gift the freshness of the first experiences of living and filled me with remembered springs. I mused upon the birth of rivers, and how they were persons and had a name-- were kings, and grew strong and ruled great countries, and how at last they reached the sea.

But while I was thinking of these things, and seeing in my mind a kind of picture of The River Valley, and of men clustering around their home stream, and of its ultimate vast plains on either side, and of the white line of the sea beyond all, a woman passed me. She was very ugly, and was dressed in black. Her dress was stiff and shining, and, as I imagined, valuable. She had in her hand a book known to the French as 'The Roman Parishioner', which is a prayer-book. Her hair was hidden in a stiff cap or bonnet; she walked rapidly, with her eyes on the ground. When I saw this sight it reminded me suddenly, and I cried out profanely, 'Devil take me! It is Corpus Christi, and my third day out. It would be a wicked pilgrimage if I did not get Mass at last.' For my first day (if you remember) I had slept in a wood beyond Mass-time, and my second (if you remember) I had slept in a bed. But this third day, a great Feast into the bargain, I was bound to hear Mass, and this woman hurrying along to the next village proved that I was not too late.

So I hurried in her wake and came to the village, and went into the church, which was very full, and came down out of it (the Mass was low and short--they are a Christian people) through an avenue of small trees and large branches set up in front of the houses to welcome the procession that was to be held near noon. At the foot of the street was an inn where I entered to eat, and finding there another man--I take him to have been a shopkeeper--I determined to talk politics, and began as follows:

'Have you any anti-Semitism in your town?'

'It is not my town,' he said, 'but there is anti-Semitism. It flourishes.'

'Why then?' I asked. 'How many Jews have you in your town?'

He said there were seven.

'But,' said I, 'seven families of Jews--'

'There are not seven families,' he interrupted; 'there are seven Jews all told. There are but two families, and I am reckoning in the children. The servants are Christians.'

'Why,' said I, 'that is only just and proper, that the Jewish families from beyond the frontier should have local Christian people to wait on them and do their bidding. But what I was going to say was that so very few Jews seem to me an insufficient fuel to fire the anti-Semites. How does their opinion flourish?'

'In this way,' he answered. 'The Jews, you see, ridicule our young men for holding such superstitions as the Catholic. Our young men, thus brought to book and made to feel irrational, admit the justice of the ridicule, but nourish a hatred secretly for those who have exposed their folly. Therefore they feel a standing grudge against the Jews.'

41

When he had given me this singular analysis of that part of the politics of the mountains, he added, after a short silence, the following remarkable phrase--

'For my part I am a liberal, and would have each go his own way: the Catholic to his Mass, the Jew to his Sacrifice.'

I then rose from my meal, saluted him, and went musing up the valley road, pondering upon what it could be that the Jews sacrificed in this remote borough, but I could not for the life of me imagine what it was, though I have had a great many Jews among my friends.

I was now arrived at the head of this lovely vale, at the sources of the river Moselle and the base of the great mountain the Ballon d'Alsace, which closes it in like a wall at the end of a lane. For some miles past the hills had grown higher and higher upon either side, the valley floor narrower, the torrent less abundant; there now stood up before me the marshy slopes and the enormous forests of pine that forbid a passage south. Up through these the main road has been pierced, tortuous and at an even gradient mile after mile to the very top of the hill; for the Ballon d'Alsace is so shaped that it is impossible for the Moselle valley to communicate with the Gap of Belfort save by some track right over its summit. For it is a mountain with spurs like a star, and where mountains of this kind block the end of main valleys it becomes necessary for the road leading up and out of the valley to go over their highest point, since any other road over the passes or shoulders would involve a second climb to reach the country beyond. The reason of this, my little map here, where the dark stands for the valley and the light for the high places, will show better than a long description. Not that this map is of the Ballon d'Alsace in particular, but only of the type of hill I mean.

Since, in crossing a range, it is usually possible to find a low point suitable for surmounting it, such summit roads are rare, but when one does get them they are the finest travel in the world, for they furnish at one point (that is, at the summit) what ordinary roads going through passes can never give you: a moment of domination. From their climax you look over the whole world, and you feel your journey to be adventurous and your advance to have taken some great definite step from one province and people to another.

I would not be bound by the exaggerated zig-zags of the road, which had been built for artillery, and rose at an easy slope. I went along the bed of the dell before me and took the forest by a little path that led straight upward, and when the path failed, my way was marked by the wire of the telegraph that crosses to Belfort. As I rose I saw the forest before me grow grander. The pine branches came down from the trunks with a greater burden and majesty in their sway, the trees took on an appearance of solemnity, and the whole rank that faced me--for here the woods come to an even line and stand like an army arrested upon a downward march--seemed something unusual and gigantic. Nothing more helped this impression of awe than the extreme darkness beneath those aged growths, and the change in the sky that introduced my entry into the silence and perfume of so vast a temple. Great clouds, so charged with rain that you would have thought them lower than the hills (and yet just missing their tops), came covering me like a tumbled roof and gathered all around; the heat of the day waned suddenly in their shade: it seemed suddenly as though summer was over or as though the mountains demanded an uncertain summer of their own, and shot the sunshine with the chill of their heights. A little wind ran along the grass and died again. As I gained the darkness of the first trees, rain was falling.

The silence of the interior wood was enhanced by a bare drip of water from the boughs that stood out straight and tangled I know not how far above me. Its gloom was rendered more tremendous by the half-light and lowering of the sky which the ceiling of branches concealed. Height, stillness, and a sort of expectancy controlled the memories of the place, and I passed silently and lightly between the high columns of the trees from night (as it seemed) through a kind of twilight forward to a near night beyond. On every side the perspective of these bare innumerable shafts, each standing apart in order, purple and fragrant, merged into recesses of distance where all light disappeared, yet as I advanced the slight gloaming still surrounded me, as did the stillness framed in the drip of water, and beneath my feet was the level carpet of the pine needles deadening and making distant every tiny noise. Had not the trees been so much greater and more enduring than my own presence, and had not they overwhelmed me by their regard, I should have felt afraid. As it was I pushed upward through their immovable host in some such catching of the breath as men have when they walk at night straining for a sound, and I felt myself to be continually in a hidden companionship.

When I came to the edge of this haunted forest it ceased as suddenly as it had begun. I left behind me such a rank of trees aligned as I had entered thousands of feet below, and I saw before me, stretching shapely up to the sky, the round dome-like summit of the mountain--a great field of grass. It was already evening; and, as though the tall trees had withdrawn their virtue from me, my fatigue suddenly came upon me. My feet would hardly bear me as I clambered up the last hundred feet and looked down under the rolling clouds, lit from beneath by the level light of evening, to the three countries that met at my feet.

For the Ballon d'Alsace is the knot of Europe, and from that gathering up and ending of the Vosges you look down upon three divisions of men. To the right of you are the Gauls. I do not mean that mixed breed of Lorraine, silent, among the best of people, but I mean the tree Gauls, who are hot, ready, and born in the plains and in the vineyards. They stand in their old entrenchments on either side of the Saone and are vivacious in battle; from time to time a spirit urges them, and they go out conquering eastward in the Germanics, or in Asia, or down the peninsulas of the Mediterranean, and then they suck back like a tide homewards, having accomplished nothing but an epic.

Then on the left you have all the Germanics, a great sea of confused and dreaming people, lost in philosophies and creating music, frozen for the moment under a foreign rigidity, but some day to thaw again and to give a word to us others. They cannot long remain apart from visions.

Then in front of you southward and eastward, if you are marching to Rome, come the Highlanders. I had never been among them, and I was to see them in a day; the people of the high hills, the race whom we all feel to be enemies, and who run straight across the world from the Atlantic to the Pacific, understanding each other, not understood by us. I saw their first rampart, the mountains called the Jura, on the horizon, and above my great field of view the clouds still tumbled, lit from beneath with evening.

I tired of these immensities, and, feeling now my feet more broken than ever, I very slowly and in sharp shoots of pain dragged down the slope towards the main road: I saw just below me the frontier stones of the Prussians, and immediately within them a hut. To this I addressed myself.

It was an inn. The door opened of itself, and I found there a pleasant woman of middle age, but frowning. She had three daughters, all of great strength, and she was upbraiding them loudly in the German of Alsace and making them scour and scrub. On the wall above her head was a great placard which I read very tactfully, and in a distant manner, until she had restored the discipline of her family. This great placard was framed in the three colours which once brought a little hope to the oppressed, and at the head of it in broad black letters were the three words, 'Freedom, Brotherhood, and an Equal Law'. Underneath these was the emblematic figure of a cock, which I took to be the Gallic bird, and underneath him again was printed in enormous italics--

Quand ce coq chantera
Ici credit l'on fera.

Which means--

When you hear him crowing
Then's the time for owing.
Till that day--Pay.

While I was still wondering at this epitome of the French people, and was attempting to combine the French military tradition with the French temper in the affairs of economics; while I was also delighting in the memory of the solid coin that I carried in a little leathern bag in my

44

pocket, the hard-working, God-fearing, and honest woman that governs the little house and the three great daughters, within a yard of the frontier, and on the top of this huge hill, had brought back all her troops into line and had the time to attend to me. This she did with the utmost politeness, though cold by race, and through her politeness ran a sense of what Teutons called Duty, which would once have repelled me; but I have wandered over a great part of the world, and I know it now to be a distorted kind of virtue.

She was of a very different sort from that good tribe of the Moselle valley beyond the hill; yet she also was Catholic--(she had a little tree set up before her door for the Corpus Christi: see what religion is, that makes people of utterly different races understand each other; for when I saw that tree I knew precisely where I stood. So once all we Europeans understood each other, but now we are divided by the worst malignancies of nations and classes, and a man does not so much love his own nation as hate his neighbours, and even the twilight of chivalry is mixed up with a detestable patronage of the poor. But as I was saying--) she also was a Catholic, and I knew myself to be with friends. She was moreover not exactly of--what shall I say? the words Celtic and Latin mean nothing--not of those who delight in a delicate manner; and her good heart prompted her to say, very loudly--

'What do you want?'

'I want a bed,' I said, and I pulled out a silver coin. 'I must lie down at once.'

Then I added, 'Can you make omelettes?'

Now it is a curious thing, and one I will not dwell on--

LECTOR. You do nothing but dwell.

AUCTOR. It is the essence of lonely travel; and if you have come to this book for literature you have come to the wrong booth and counter. As I was saying: it is a curious thing that some people (or races) jump from one subject to another naturally, as some animals (I mean the noble deer) go by bounds. While there are other races (or individuals-- heaven forgive me, I am no ethnologist) who think you a criminal or a lunatic unless you carefully plod along from step to step like a hippopotamus out of water. When, therefore, I asked this family- drilling, house-managing, mountain-living woman whether she could make omelettes, she shook her head at me slowly, keeping her eyes fixed on mine, and said in what was the corpse of French with a German ghost in it, 'The bed is a franc.'

'Motherkin,' I answered, 'what I mean is that I would sleep until I wake, for I have come a prodigious distance and have last slept in the woods. But when I wake I shall need food, for which,' I added, pulling

45

out yet another coin, 'I will pay whatever your charge may be; for a more delightful house I have rarely met with. I know most people do not sleep before sunset, but I am particularly tired and broken.'

She showed me my bed then much more kindly, and when I woke, which was long after dusk, she gave me in the living room of the hut eggs beaten up with ham, and I ate brown bread and said grace.

Then (my wine was not yet finished, but it is an abominable thing to drink your own wine in another person's house) I asked whether I could have something to drink.

'What you like,' she said.

'What have you?' said I.

'Beer,' said she.

'Anything else?' said I.

'No,' said she.

'Why, then, give me some of that excellent beer.'

I drank this with delight, paid all my bill (which was that of a labourer), and said good-night to them.

In good-nights they had a ceremony; for they all rose together and curtsied. Upon my soul I believe such people to be the salt of the earth. I bowed with real contrition, for at several moments I had believed myself better than they. Then I went to my bed and they to theirs. The wind howled outside; my boots were stiff like wood and I could hardly take them off; my feet were so martyrized that I doubted if I could walk at all on the morrow. Nevertheless I was so wrapped round with the repose of this family's virtues that I fell asleep at once. Next day the sun was rising in angry glory over the very distant hills of Germany, his new light running between the pinnacles of the clouds as the commands of a conqueror might come trumpeted down the defiles of mountains, when I fearlessly forced my boots on to my feet and left their doors.

The morning outside came living and sharp after the gale--almost chilly. Under a scattered but clearing sky I first limped, then, as my blood warmed, strode down the path that led between the trees of the farther vale and was soon following a stream that leaped from one fall to another till it should lead me to the main road, to Belfort, to the Jura, to the Swiss whom I had never known, and at last to Italy.

But before I call up the recollection of that hidden valley, I must describe with a map the curious features of the road that lay before me into Switzerland. I was standing on the summit of that knot of hills

46

which rise up from every side to form the Ballon d'Alsace, and make an abrupt ending to the Vosges. Before me, southward and eastward, was a great plain with the fortress of Belfort in the midst of it. This plain is called by soldiers 'the Gap of Belfort', and is the only break in the hill frontier that covers France all the way from the Mediterranean to Flanders. On the farther side of this plain ran the Jura mountains, which are like a northern wall to Switzerland, and just before you reach them is the Frontier. The Jura are fold on fold of high limestone ridges, thousands of feet high, all parallel, with deep valleys, thousands of feet deep, between them; and beyond their last abrupt escarpment is the wide plain of the river Aar.

Now the straight line to Rome ran from where I stood, right across that plain of Belfort, right across the ridges of the Jura, and cut the plain of the Aar a few miles to the west of a town called Solothurn or Soleure, which stands upon that river.

It was impossible to follow that line exactly, but one could average it closely enough by following the high road down the mountain through Belfort to a Swiss town called Porrentruy or Portrut--so far one was a little to the west of the direct line.

From Portrut, by picking one's way through forests, up steep banks, over open downs, along mule paths, and so forth, one could cross the first ridge called the 'Terrible Hill', and so reach the profound gorge of the river Doubs, and a town called St Ursanne. From St Ursanne, by following a mountain road and then climbing some rocks and tracking through a wood, one could get straight over the second ridge to Glovelier. From Glovelier a highroad took one through a gap to Undervelier and on to a town called Moutier or Munster. Then from Munster, the road, still following more or less the line to Rome but now somewhat to the east of it, went on southward till an abrupt turn in it forced one to leave it. Then there was another rough climb by a difficult path up over the last ridge, called the Weissenstein, and from its high edge and summit it was but a straight fall of a mile or two on to Soleure.

So much my map told me, and this mixture of roads and paths and rock climbs that I had planned out, I exactly followed, so as to march on as directly as possible towards Rome, which was my goal. For if I had not so planned it, but had followed the highroads, I should have been compelled to zig-zag enormously for days, since these ridges of the Jura are but little broken, and the roads do not rise above the crests, but follow the parallel valleys, taking advantage only here and there of the rare gaps to pass from one to another.

Here is a sketch of the way I went, where my track is a white line, and the round spots in it are the towns and villages whose names are written at the side. In this sketch the plains and low valleys are marked dark, and the crests of the mountains left white. The shading is lighter

47

according to the height, and the contour lines (which are very far from accurate) represent, I suppose, about a thousand feet between each, or perhaps a little more; and as for the distance, from the Ballon d'Alsace to Soleure might be two long days' march on a flat road, but over mountains and up rocks it was all but three, and even that was very good going. My first stage was across the plain of Belfort, and I had determined to sleep that night in Switzerland.

I wandered down the mountain. A little secret path, one of many, saved me the long windings of the road. It followed down the central hollow of the great cleft and accompanied the stream. All the way for miles the water tumbled in fall after fall over a hundred steps of rock, and its noise mixed with the freshness of the air, and its splashing weighted the overhanging branches of the trees. A little rain that fell from time to time through the clear morning seemed like a sister to the spray of the waterfalls; and what with all this moisture and greenery, and the surrounding silence, all the valley was inspired with content. It was a repose to descend through its leaves and grasses, and find the lovely pastures at the foot of the descent, a narrow floor between the hills. Here there were the first houses of men; and, from one, smoke was already going up thinly into the morning. The air was very pure and cold; it was made more nourishing and human by the presence and noise of the waters, by the shining wet grasses and the beaded leaves all through that umbrageous valley. The shreds of clouds which, high above the calm, ran swiftly in the upper air, fed it also with soft rains from time to time as fine as dew; and through those clear and momentary showers one could see the sunlight.

When I had enjoyed the descent through this place for but a few miles, everything changed. The road in front ran straight and bordered-- it led out and onwards over a great flat, set here and there with hillocks. The Vosges ended abruptly. Houses came more thickly, and by the ceaseless culture of the fields, by the flat slate roofs, the white-washed walls, and the voices, and the glare, I knew myself to be once more in France of the plains; and the first town I came to was Giromagny.

Here, as I heard a bell, I thought I would go up and hear Mass; and I did so, but my attention at the holy office was distracted by the enormous number of priests that I found in the church, and I have wondered painfully ever since how so many came to be in a little place like Giromagny. There were three priests at the high altar, and nearly one for each chapel, and there was such a buzz of Masses going on, beginning and ending, that I am sure I need not have gone without my breakfast in my hurry to get one. With all this there were few people at Mass so early; nothing but these priests going in and out, and continual little bells. I am still wondering. Giromagny is no place for relics or for a pilgrimage, it cures no one, and has nothing of a holy look about it, and all these priests--

LECTOR. Pray dwell less on your religion, and--

AUCTOR. Pray take books as you find them, and treat travel as travel. For you, when you go to a foreign country, see nothing but what you expect to see. But I am astonished at a thousand accidents, and always find things twenty-fold as great as I supposed they would be, and far more curious; the whole covered by a strange light of adventure. And that is the peculiar value of this book. Now, if you can explain these priests---

LECTOR. I can. It was the season of the year, and they were swarming.

AUCTOR. So be it. Then if you will hear nothing of what interests me, I see no reason for setting down with minute care what interests you, and I may leave out all mention of the Girl who could only speak German, of the Arrest of the Criminal, and even of the House of Marshal Turenne--- this last something quite exceptionally entertaining. But do not let us continue thus, nor push things to an open quarrel. You must imagine for yourself about six miles of road, and then--then in the increasing heat, the dust rising in spite of the morning rain, and the road most wearisome, I heard again the sound of bugles and the sombre excitement of the drums.

It is a thought-provoking thing, this passing from one great garrison to another all the way down the frontier. I had started from the busy order of Toul; I had passed through the silence and peace of all that Moselle country, the valley like a long garden, and I had come to the guns and the tramp of Epinal. I had left Epinal and counted the miles and miles of silence in the forests, I had crossed the great hills and come down into quite another plain draining to another sea, and I heard again all the clamour that goes with soldiery, and looking backward then over my four days, one felt--one almost saw--the new system of fortification, the vast entrenched camps each holding an army, the ungarnished gaps between.

As I came nearer to Belfort, I saw the guns going at a trot down a side road, and, a little later, I saw marching on my right, a long way off, the irregular column, the dust and the invincible gaiety of the French line. The sun here and there glinted on the ends of rifle-barrels and the polished pouches. Their heavy pack made their tramp loud and thudding. They were singing a song.

I had already passed the outer forts; I had noted a work close to the road; I had gone on a mile or so and had entered the long and ugly suburb where the tramway lines began, when, on one of the ramshackle houses of that burning, paved, and noisy endless street, I saw written up the words,

Wine; shut or open.

As it is a great rule to examine every new thing, and to suck honey out of every flower, I did not--as some would--think the phrase odd and pass on. I stood stock-still gazing at the house and imagining a hundred explanations. I had never in my life heard wine divided into shut and open wine. I determined to acquire yet one more great experience, and going in I found a great number of tin cans, such as the French carry up water in, without covers, tapering to the top, and standing about three feet high; on these were pasted large printed labels, '30', '40', and '50', and they were brimming with wine. I spoke to the woman, and pointing at the tin cans, said--

'Is this what you call open wine?'

'Why, yes,' said she. 'Cannot you see for yourself that it is open?'

That was true enough, and it explained a great deal. But it did not explain how--seeing that if you leave a bottle of wine uncorked for ten minutes you spoil it--you can keep gallons of it in a great wide can, for all the world like so much milk, milked from the Panthers of the God. I determined to test the prodigy yet further, and choosing the middle price, at fourpence a quart, I said--

'Pray give me a hap'orth in a mug.'

This the woman at once did, and when I came to drink it, it was delicious. Sweet, cool, strong, lifting the heart, satisfying, and full of all those things wine-merchants talk of, bouquet, and body, and flavour. It was what I have heard called a very pretty wine.

I did not wait, however, to discuss the marvel, but accepted it as one of those mysteries of which this pilgrimage was already giving me examples, and of which more were to come--(wait till you hear about the brigand of Radicofani). I said to myself--

'When I get out of the Terre Majeure, and away from the strong and excellent government of the Republic, when I am lost in the Jura Hills to-morrow there will be no such wine as this.'

So I bought a quart of it, corked it up very tight, put it in my sack, and held it in store against the wineless places on the flanks of the hill called Terrible, where there are no soldiers, and where Swiss is the current language. Then I went on into the centre of the town.

As I passed over the old bridge into the market-place, where I proposed to lunch (the sun was terrible--it was close upon eleven), I saw them building parallel with that old bridge a new one to replace it. And the way they build a bridge in Belfort is so wonderfully simple, and yet so new, that it is well worth telling.

50

In most places when a bridge has to be made, there is an infinite pother and worry about building the piers, coffer-dams, and heaven knows what else. Some swing their bridges to avoid this trouble, and some try to throw an arch of one span from side to side. There are a thousand different tricks. In Belfort they simply wait until the water has run away. Then a great brigade of workmen run down into the dry bed of the river and dig the foundations feverishly, and begin building the piers in great haste. Soon the water comes back, but the piers are already above it, and the rest of the work is done from boats. This is absolutely true. Not only did I see the men in the bed of the river, but a man whom I asked told me that it seemed to him the most natural way to build bridges, and doubted if they were ever made in any other fashion.

There is also in Belfort a great lion carved in rock to commemorate the siege of 1870. This lion is part of the precipice under the castle, and is of enormous size--- how large I do not know, but I saw that a man looked quite small by one of his paws. The precipice was first smoothed like a stone slab or tablet, and then this lion was carved into and out of it in high relief by Bartholdi, the same man that made the statue of Liberty in New York Harbour.

The siege of 1870 has been fixed for history in yet another way, and one that shows you how the Church works on from one stem continually. For there is a little church somewhere near or in Belfort (I do not know where, I only heard of it) which, a local mason and painter being told to decorate for so much, he amused himself by painting all round it little pictures of the siege--of the cold, and the wounds, and the heroism. This is indeed the way such things should be done, I mean by men doing them for pleasure and of their own thought. And I have a number of friends who agree with me in thinking this, that art should not be competitive or industrial, but most of them go on to the very strange conclusion that one should not own one's garden, nor one's beehive, nor one's great noble house, nor one's pigsty, nor one's railway shares, nor the very boots on one's feet. I say, out upon such nonsense. Then they say to me, what about the concentration of the means of production? And I say to them, what about the distribution of the ownership of the concentrated means of production? And they shake their heads sadly, and say it would never endure; and I say, try it first and see. Then they fly into a rage.

When I lunched in Belfort (and at lunch, by the way, a poor man asked me to use *all my influence* for his son, who was an engineer in the navy, and this he did because I had been boasting of my travels, experiences, and grand acquaintances throughout the world)--when, I say, I had lunched in a workman's cafe at Belfort, I set out again on my road, and was very much put out to find that showers still kept on falling.

In the early morning, under such delightful trees, up in the mountains, the branches had given me a roof, the wild surroundings made me part of the out-of-doors, and the rain had seemed to marry itself to the pastures and the foaming beck. But here, on a road and in a town, all its tradition of discomfort came upon me. I was angry, therefore, with the weather and the road for some miles, till two things came to comfort me. First it cleared, and a glorious sun showed me from a little eminence the plain of Alsace and the mountains of the Vosges all in line; secondly, I came to a vast powder-magazine.

To most people there is nothing more subtle or pleasing in a powder-magazine than in a reservoir. They are both much the same in the mere exterior, for each is a flat platform, sloping at the sides and covered with grass, and each has mysterious doors. But, for my part, I never see a powder-magazine without being filled at once with two very good feelings--- laughter and companionship. For it was my good fortune, years and years ago, to be companion and friend to two men who were on sentry at a powder-magazine just after there had been some anarchist attempts (as they call them) upon such depots--and for the matter of that I can imagine nothing more luscious to the anarchist than seven hundred and forty-two cases of powder and fifty cases of melinite all stored in one place. And to prevent the enormous noise, confusion, and waste that would have resulted from the over-attraction of this base of operations to the anarchists, my two friends, one of whom was a duty-doing Burgundian, but the other a loose Parisian man, were on sentry that night. They had strict orders to challenge once and then to fire.

Now, can you imagine anything more exquisite to a poor devil of a conscript, fagged out with garrison duty and stale sham-fighting, than an order of that kind? So my friends took it, and in one summer night they killed a donkey and wounded two mares, and broke the thin stem of a growing tree.

This powder-magazine was no exception to my rule, for as I approached it I saw a round-faced corporal and two round-faced men looking eagerly to see who might be attacking their treasure, and I became quite genial in my mind when I thought of how proud these boys felt, and of how I was of the 'class of ninety, rifled and mounted on its carriage' (if you don't see the point of the allusion, I can't stop to explain it. It was a good gun in its time--now they have the seventy-five that doesn't recoil--*requiescat),* and of how they were longing for the night, and a chance to shoot anything on the sky line.

Full of these foolish thoughts, but smiling in spite of their folly, I went down the road.

Shall I detail all that afternoon? My leg horrified me with dull pain, and made me fear I should never hold out, I do not say to Rome, but even to the frontier. I rubbed it from time to time with balm, but, as always happens to miraculous things, the virtue had gone out of it with the lapse of time. At last I found a side road going off from the main way, and my map told me it was on the whole a short cut to the frontier. I determined to take it for those few last miles, because, if one is suffering, a winding lane is more tolerable than a wide turnpike.

Just as I came to the branching of the roads I saw a cross put up, and at its base the motto that is universal to French crosses--

Ave Crux Spes Unica.

I thought it a good opportunity for recollection, and sitting down, I looked backward along the road I had come.

There were the high mountains of the Vosges standing up above the plain of Alsace like sloping cliffs above a sea. I drew them as they stood, and wondered if that frontier were really permanent. The mind of man is greater than such accidents, and can easily overleap even the high hills.

Then having drawn them, and in that drawing said a kind of farewell to the influences that had followed me for so many miles--the solemn quiet, the steady industry, the self-control, the deep woods, of Lorraine--1 rose up stiffly from the bank that had been my desk, and pushed along the lane that ran devious past neglected villages.

The afternoon and the evening followed as I put one mile after another behind me. The frontier seemed so close that I would not rest. I left my open wine, the wine I had found outside Belfort, untasted, and I plodded on and on as the light dwindled. I was in a grand wonderment for Switzerland, and I wished by an immediate effort to conquer the last miles before night, in spite of my pain. Also, I will confess to a silly pride in distances, and a desire to be out of France on my fourth day.

The light still fell, and my resolution stood, though my exhaustion undermined it. The line of the mountains rose higher against the sky, and there entered into my pilgrimage for the first time the loneliness and the mystery of meres. Something of what a man feels in East England belonged to this last of the plain under the guardian hills. Everywhere I passed ponds and reeds, and saw the level streaks of sunset reflected in stagnant waters.

The marshy valley kept its character when I had left the lane and regained the highroad. Its isolation dominated the last effort with which I made for the line of the Jura in that summer twilight, and as I blundered on my whole spirit was caught or lifted in the influence of the waste waters and of the birds of evening.

I wished, as I had often wished in such opportunities of recollection and of silence, for a complete barrier that might isolate the mind. With that wish came in a puzzling thought, very proper to a pilgrimage, which was: 'What do men mean by the desire to be dissolved and to enjoy the spirit free and without attachments?' That many men have so desired there can be no doubt, and the best men, whose holiness one recognizes at once, tell us that the joys of the soul are incomparably higher than those of the living man. In India, moreover, there are great numbers of men who do the most fantastic things with the object of thus unprisoning the soul, and Milton talks of the same thing with evident conviction, and the Saints all praise it in chorus. But what is it? For my part I cannot understand so much as the meaning of the words, for every pleasure I know comes from an intimate union between my body and my very human mind, which last receives, confirms, revives, and can summon up again what my body has experienced. Of pleasures, however, in which my senses have had no part I know nothing, so I have determined to take them upon trust and see whether they could make the matter clearer in Rome.

But when it comes to the immortal mind, the good spirit in me that is so cunning at forms and colours and the reasons of things, that is a very different story. *That*, I do indeed desire to have to myself at whiles, and the waning light of a day or the curtains of autumn closing in the year are often to me like a door shutting after one, as one comes in home. For I find that with less and less impression from without the mind seems to take on a power of creation, and by some mystery it can project songs and landscapes and faces much more desirable than the music or the shapes one really hears and sees. So also memory can create. But it is not the soul that does this, for the songs, the landscapes, and the faces are of a kind that have come in by the senses, nor have I ever understood what could be higher than these pleasures, nor indeed how in anything formless and immaterial there could be pleasure at all. Yet the wisest people assure us that our souls are as superior to our minds as are our minds to our inert and merely material bodies. I cannot understand it at all.

As I was pondering on these things in this land of pastures and lonely ponds, with the wall of the Jura black against the narrow bars of evening--(my pain seemed gone for a moment, yet I was hobbling slowly)--I say as I was considering this complex doctrine, I felt my sack suddenly much lighter, and I had hardly time to rejoice at the miracle when I heard immediately a very loud crash, and turning half round I saw on the blurred white of the twilit road my quart of Open Wine all broken to atoms. My disappointment was so great that I sat down on a milestone to consider the accident and to see if a little thought would not lighten my acute annoyance. Consider that I had carefully cherished this bottle and had not drunk throughout a painful march all that afternoon, thinking that there would be no wine worth drinking after I had passed the frontier.

I consoled myself more or less by thinking about torments and evils to which even such a loss as this was nothing, and then I rose to go on into the night. As it turned out I was to find beyond the frontier a wine in whose presence this wasted wine would have seemed a wretched jest, and whose wonderful taste was to colour all my memories of the Mount Terrible. It is always thus with sorrows if one will only wait.

So, lighter in the sack but heavier in the heart, I went forward to cross the frontier in the dark. I did not quite know where the point came: I only knew that it was about a mile from Delle, the last French town. I supped there and held on my way. When I guessed that I had covered this mile I saw a light in the windows on my left, a trellis and the marble tables of a cafe. I put my head in at the door and said--

'Am I in Switzerland?'

A German-looking girl, a large heavy man, a Bavarian commercial traveller, and a colleague of his from Marseilles, all said together in varying accents: 'Yes.'

'Why then,' I said, 'I will come in and drink.'

This book would never end if I were to attempt to write down so much as the names of a quarter of the extraordinary things that I saw and heard on my enchanted pilgrimage, but let me at least mention the Commercial Traveller from Marseilles.

He talked with extreme rapidity for two hours. He had seen all the cities in the world and he remembered their minutest details. He was extremely accurate, his taste was abominable, his patriotism large, his wit crude but continual, and to his German friend, to the host of the inn, and to the blonde serving-girl, he was a familiar god. He came, it seems, once a year, and for a day would pour out the torrent of his travels like a waterfall of guide-books (for he gloried in dates, dimensions, and the points of the compass in his descriptions); then he disappeared for another year, and left them to feast on the memory of such a revelation.

For my part I sat silent, crippled with fatigue, trying to forget my wounded feet, drinking stoup after stoup of beer and watching the Phocean. He was of the old race you see on vases in red and black; slight, very wiry, with a sharp, eager, but well-set face, a small, black, pointed beard, brilliant eyes like those of lizards, rapid gestures, and a vivacity that played all over his features as sheet lightning does over the glow of midnight in June.

That delta of the Rhone is something quite separate from the rest of France. It is a wedge of Greece and of the East thrust into the Gauls. It came north a hundred years ago and killed the monarchy. It caught the value in, and created, the great war song of the Republic.

I watched the Phocean. I thought of a man of his ancestry three thousand years ago sitting here at the gates of these mountains talking

55

of his travels to dull, patient, and admiring northerners, and travelling for gain up into the Germanics, and I felt the changeless form of Europe under me like a rock.

When he heard I was walking to Rome, this man of information turned off his flood into another channel, as a miller will send the racing water into a side sluice, and he poured out some such torrent as this:

'Do not omit to notice the famous view S.E. from the Villa So and So on Monte Mario; visit such and such a garden, and hear Mass in such and such a church. Note the curious illusion produced on the piazza of St Peter's by the interior measurements of the trapezium, which are so many years and so many yards, ...' &c., and so forth ... exactly like a mill.

I meanwhile sat on still silent, still drinking beer and watching the Phocean; gradually suffering the fascination that had captured the villagers and the German friend. He was a very wonderful man.

He was also kindly, for I found afterwards that he had arranged with the host to give me up his bed, seeing my weariness. For this, most unluckily, I was never able to thank him, since the next morning I was off before he or any one else was awake, and I left on the table such money as I thought would very likely satisfy the innkeeper.

It was broad day, but not yet sunrise (there were watery thin clouds left here and there from the day before, a cold wind drove them) when, with extreme pain, going slowly one step after the other and resting continually, I started for Porrentruy along a winding road, and pierced the gap in the Jura. The first turn cut me off from France, and I was fairly in a strange country.

The valley through which I was now passing resembled that of the lovely river Jed where it runs down from the Cheviots, and leads like a road into the secret pastures of the lowlands. Here also, as there, steep cliffs of limestone bounded a very level dale, all green grass and plenty; the plateau above them was covered also with perpetual woods, only here, different from Scotland, the woods ran on and upwards till they became the slopes of high mountains; indeed, this winding cleft was a natural passage through the first ridge of the Jura; the second stood up southward before me like a deep blue storm.

I had, as I passed on along this turning way, all the pleasures of novelty; it was quite another country from the governed and ordered France which I had left. The road was more haphazard, less carefully tended, and evidently less used. The milestones were very old, and marked leagues instead of kilometres. There was age in everything. Moss grew along the walls, and it was very quiet under the high trees. I did not know the name of the little river that went slowly through the meadows, nor whether it followed the custom of its French neighbours on the watershed, and was called by some such epithet as hangs to all the waters in that gap of Belfort, that plain of ponds and marshes: for they are called 'the Sluggish', 'the Muddy', or 'the Laggard'. Even the name of the Saone, far off, meant once 'Slow Water'.

I was wondering what its name might be, and how far I stood from Porrentruy (which I knew to be close by), when I saw a tunnel across the valley, and I guessed by the trend of the higher hills that the river was about to make a very sharp angle. Both these signs, I had been told, meant that I was quite close to the town; so I took a short cut up through the forest over a spur of hill--a short cut most legitimate, because it was trodden and very manifestly used--and I walked up and then on a level for a mile, along a lane of the woods and beneath small, dripping trees. When this short silence of the forest was over, I saw an excellent sight.

There, below me, where the lane began to fall, was the first of the German cities.

LECTOR. How 'German'?

AUCTOR. Let me explain. There is a race that stretches vaguely, without defined boundaries, from the Baltic into the high hills of the south. I will not include the Scandinavians among them, for the Scandinavians (from whom we English also in part descend) are long-headed, lean, and fierce, with a light of adventure in their pale eyes. But beneath them, I say, there stretches from the Baltic to the high hills a race which has a curious unity. Yes; I know that great patches of it are Catholic, and that other great patches hold varying philosophies; I know also that within them are counted long-headed and round-headed men, dark and fair, violent and silent; I know also that they have continually fought among themselves and called in Welch allies; still I go somewhat by the language, for I am concerned here with the development of a modern European people, and I say that the Germans run from the high hills to the northern sea. In all of them you find (it is not race, it is something much more than race, it is the type of culture) a dreaminess and a love of ease. In all of them you find music. They are those Germans whose countries I had seen a long way off, from the Ballon d'Alsace, and whose language and traditions I now first touched in the town that stood before me.

LECTOR. But in Porrentruy they talk French!

AUCTOR. They are welcome; it is an excellent tongue. Nevertheless, they are Germans. Who but Germans would so preserve--would so rebuild the past? Who but Germans would so feel the mystery of the hills, and so fit their town to the mountains? I was to pass through but a narrow wedge of this strange and diffuse people. They began at Porrentruy, they ended at the watershed of the Adriatic, in the high passes of the Alps; but in that little space of four days I made acquaintance with their influence, and I owe them a perpetual gratitude for their architecture and their tales. I had come from France, which is full of an active memory of Rome. I was to debouch into those larger plains of Italy, which keep about them an atmosphere of Rome in decay. Here in Switzerland, for four marches, I touched a northern, exterior, and barbaric people; for though these mountains spoke a distorted Latin tongue, and only after the first day began to give me a Teutonic dialect, yet it was evident from the first that they had about them neither the Latin order nor the Latin power to create, but were contemplative and easily absorbed by a little effort.

The German spirit is a marvel. There lay Porrentruy. An odd door with Gothic turrets marked the entry to the town. To the right of this gateway a tower, more enormous than anything I remembered to have seen, even in dreams, flanked the approach to the city. How vast it was, how protected, how high, how eaved, how enduring! I was told later that some part of that great bastion was Roman, and I can believe it. The Germans hate to destroy. It overwhelmed me as visions overwhelm, and I felt in its presence as boys feel when they first see the mountains. Had I not been a Christian, I would have worshipped and propitiated this obsession, this everlasting thing.

As it was I entered Porrentruy soberly. I passed under its deep gateway and up its steep hill. The moment I was well into the main street, something other of the Middle Ages possessed me, and I began to think of food and wine. I went to the very first small guest-house I could find, and asked them if they could serve me food. They said that at such an early hour (it was not yet ten) they could give me nothing but bread, yesterday's meat, and wine. I said that would do very well, and all these things were set before me, and by a custom of the country I paid before I ate. (A bad custom. Up in the Limousin, when I was a boy, in the noisy valley of the Torrent, on the Vienne, I remember a woman that did not allow me to pay till she had held the bottle up to the light, measured the veal with her finger, and estimated the bread with her eye; also she charged me double. God rest her soul!) I say I paid. And had I had to pay twenty or twenty-three times as much it would have been worth it for the wine.

I am hurrying on to Rome, and I have no time to write a georgic. But, oh! my little friends of the north; my struggling, strenuous, introspective, self-analysing, autoscopic, and generally reentrant friends, who spout the 'Hue! Pater, oh! Lenae!' without a ghost of an idea what you are talking about, do you know what is meant by the god? Bacchus is everywhere, but if he has special sites to be ringed in and kept sacred, I say let these be Brule, and the silent vineyard that lies under the square wood by Tournus, the hollow underplace of Heltz le Maurupt, and this town of Porrentruy. In these places if I can get no living friends to help me, I will strike the foot alone on the genial ground, and I know of fifty maenads and two hundred little attendant gods by name that will come to the festival.

What a wine!

I was assured it would not travel. 'Nevertheless,' said I, 'give me a good quart bottle of it, for I have to go far, and I see there is a providence for pilgrims.'

So they charged me fourpence, and I took my bottle of this wonderful stuff, sweet, strong, sufficient, part of the earth, desirable, and went up on my way to Rome.

Could this book be infinite, as my voyage was infinite, I would tell you about the shifty priest whom I met on the platform of the church where a cliff overhangs the valley, and of the anarchist whom I met when I recovered the highroad--- he was a sad, good man, who had committed some sudden crime and so had left France, and his hankering for France all those years had soured his temper, and he said he wished there were no property, no armies, and no governments.

But I said that we live as parts of a nation, and that there was no fate so wretched as to be without a country of one's own--what else was exile which so many noble men have thought worse than death, and which all have feared? I also told him that armies fighting in a just cause were the happiest places for living, and that a good battle for justice was the beginning of all great songs; and that as for property, a man on his own land was the nearest to God.

He therefore not convinced, and I loving and pitying him, we separated; I had not time to preach my full doctrine, but gave him instead a deep and misty glass of cool beer, and pledged him brotherhood, freedom, and an equal law. Then I went on my way, praying God that all these rending quarrels might be appeased. For they would certainly be appeased if we once again had a united doctrine in Europe, since economics are but an expression of the mind and do not (as the poor blind slaves of the great cities think) mould the mind. What is more, nothing makes property run into a few hands but the worst of the capital sins, and you who say it is 'the modern facilities of distribution' are like men who cannot read large print without spectacles; or again, you are like men who should say that their drunkenness was due to their drink, or that arson was caused by matches.

But, frankly, do you suppose I came all this way over so many hills to talk economics? Very far from it! I will pray for all poor men when I get to St Peter's in Rome (I should like to know what capital St Peter had in that highly capitalistic first century), and, meanwhile, do you discuss the margin of production while I go on the open way; there are no landlords here, and if you would learn at least one foreign language, and travel but five miles off a railway, you town-talkers, you would find how much landlordism has to do with your 'necessities' and your 'laws'.

LECTOR. I thought you said you were not going to talk economics?

AUCTOR. Neither am I. It is but the backwash of a wave ... Well, then, I went up the open way, and came in a few miles of that hot afternoon to the second ridge of the Jura, which they call 'the Terrible Hill', or 'the Mount Terrible'--and, in truth, it is very jagged. A steep, long crest of very many miles lies here between the vale of Porrentruy and the deep gorge of the Doubs. The highroad goes off a long way westward, seeking for a pass or neck in the chain, but I determined to find a straight road across, and spoke to some wood-cutters who were felling trees just where the road began to climb. They gave me this curious indication. They said--

'Go you up this muddy track that has been made athwart the woods and over the pastures by our sliding logs' (for they had cut their trunks higher up the mountains), 'and you will come to the summit easily. From thence you will see the Doubs running below you in a very deep and dark ravine.'

I thanked them, and soon found that they had told me right. There, unmistakable, a gash in the forest and across the intervening fields of grass, was the run of the timber.

When I had climbed almost to the top, I looked behind me to take my last view of the north. I saw just before me a high isolated rock; between me and it was the forest. I saw beyond it the infinite plain of Alsace and the distant Vosges. The cliff of limestone that bounded that height fell sheer upon the tree-tops; its sublimity arrested me, and compelled me to record it.

'Surely,' I said, 'if Switzerland has any gates on the north they are these.' Then, having drawn the wonderful outline of what I had seen, I went up, panting, to the summit, and, resting there, discovered beneath me the curious swirl of the Doubs, where it ran in a dark gulf thousands of feet below. The shape of this extraordinary turn I will describe in a moment. Let me say, meanwhile, that there was no precipice or rock between me and the river, only a down, down, down through other trees and pastures, not too steep for a man to walk, but steeper than our steep downs and fells in England, where a man hesitates and picks his way. It was so much of a descent, and so long, that one looked above the tree-tops. It was a place where no one would care to ride.

I found a kind of path, sideways on the face of the mountain, and followed it till I came to a platform with a hut perched thereon, and men building. Here a good woman told me just how to go. I was not to attempt the road to Brune-Farine--that is, 'Whole-Meal Farm'--as I had first intended, foolishly trusting a map, but to take a gully she would show me, and follow it till I reached the river. She came out, and led me steeply across a hanging pasture; all the while she had knitting in her hands, and I noticed that on the levels she went on with her knitting. Then, when we got to the gully, she said I had but to follow it. I thanked her, and she climbed up to her home.

This gully was the precipitous bed of a stream; I clanked down it--thousands of feet--warily; I reached the valley, and at last, very gladly, came to a drain, and thus knew that I approached a town or village. It was St Ursanne.

The very first thing I noticed in St Ursanne was the extraordinary shape of the lower windows of the church. They lighted a crypt and ran along the ground, which in itself was sufficiently remarkable, but much more remarkable was their shape, which seemed to me to approach that of a horseshoe; I never saw such a thing before. It looked as though the weight of the church above had bulged these little windows out, and that is the way I explain it. Some people would say it was a man coming home from the Crusades that had made them this eastern way, others that it was a symbol of something or other. But I say--

LECTOR. What rhodomontade and pedantry is this talk about the shape of a window?

AUCTOR. Little friend, how little you know! To a building windows are everything; they are what eyes are to a man. Out of windows a building takes its view; in windows the outlook of its human inhabitants is framed. If you were the lord of a very high tower overlooking a town, a plain, a river, and a distant hill (I doubt if you will ever have such luck!), would you not call your architect up before you and say--

'Sir, see that the windows of my house are *tall, narrow, thick*, and have a *round top to them*'?

Of course you would, for thus you would best catch in separate pictures the sunlit things outside your home.

Never ridicule windows. It is out of windows that many fall to their deaths. By windows love often enters. Through a window went the bolt that killed King Richard. King William's father spied Arlette from a window (I have looked through it myself, but not a soul did I see washing below). When a mob would rule England, it breaks windows, and when a patriot would save her, he taxes them. Out of windows we walk on to lawns in summer and meet men and women, and in winter windows are drums for the splendid music of storms that makes us feel so masterly round our fires. The windows of the great cathedrals are all their meaning. But for windows we should have to go out-of-doors to see daylight. After the sun, which they serve, I know of nothing so beneficent as windows. Fie upon the ungrateful man that has no window-god in his house, and thinks himself too great a philosopher to bow down to windows! May he live in a place without windows for a while to teach him the value of windows. As for me, I will keep up the

61

high worship of windows till I come to the windowless grave. Talk to me of windows!

Yes. There are other things in St Ursanne. It is a little tiny town, and yet has gates. It is full of very old houses, people, and speech. It was founded (or named) by a Bear Saint, and the statue of the saint with his bear is carved on the top of a column in the market-place. But the chief thing about it, so it seemed to me, was its remoteness.

The gorge of the Doubs, of which I said a word or two above, is of that very rare shape which isolates whatever may be found in such valleys. It turns right back upon itself, like a very narrow U, and thus cannot by any possibility lead any one anywhere; for though in all times travellers have had to follow river valleys, yet when they come to such a long and sharp turn as this, they have always cut across the intervening bend.

Here is the shape of this valley with the high hills round it and in its core, which will show better than description what I mean. The little picture also shows what the gorge looked like as I came down on it from the heights above.

In the map the small white 'A' shows where the railway bridge was, and in this map, as in the others, the dark is for the depth and the light is for the heights. As for the picture, it is what one sees when one is coming over the ridge at the north or top of the map, and when one first catches the river beneath one.

I thought a good deal about what the Romans did to get through the Mont Terrible, and how they negotiated this crook in the Doubs (for they certainly passed into Gaul through the gates of Porrentruy, and by that obvious valley below it). I decided that they probably came round eastward by Delemont. But for my part, I was on a straight path to Rome, and as that line lay just along the top of the river bend I was bound to take it.

Now outside St Ursanne, if one would go along the top of the river bend and so up to the other side of the gorge, is a kind of subsidiary ravine--awful, deep, and narrow--and this was crossed, I could see, by a very high railway bridge.

Not suspecting any evil, and desiring to avoid the long descent into the ravine, the looking for a bridge or ford, and the steep climb up the other side, I made in my folly for the station which stood just where the railway left solid ground to go over this high, high bridge. I asked leave of the stationmaster to cross it, who said it was strictly forbidden, but that he was not a policeman, and that I might do it at my own risk. Thanking him, therefore, and considering how charming was the loose habit of small uncentralized societies, I went merrily on to the bridge, meaning to walk across it by stepping from sleeper to sleeper. But it was not to be so simple. The powers of the air, that hate to have their kingdom disturbed, watched me as I began.

I had not been engaged upon it a dozen yards when I was seized with terror.

I have much to say further on in this book concerning terror: the panic that haunts high places and the spell of many angry men. This horrible affection of the mind is the delight of our modern scribblers; it is half the plot of their insane 'short stories', and is at the root of their worship of what they call 'strength', a cowardly craving for protection, or the much more despicable fascination of brutality. For my part I have always disregarded it as something impure and devilish, unworthy of a Christian. Fear I think, indeed, to be in the nature of things, and it is as much part of my experience to be afraid of the sea or of an untried horse as it is to eat and sleep; but terror, which is a sudden madness and paralysis of the soul, that I say is from hell, and not to be played with or considered or put in pictures or described in stories. All this I say to preface what happened, and especially to point out how terror is in the nature of a possession and is unreasonable.

For in the crossing of this bridge there was nothing in itself perilous. The sleepers lay very close together--I doubt if a man could have slipped between them; but, I know not how many hundred feet below, was the flashing of the torrent, and it turned my brain. For the only parapet there was a light line or pipe, quite slender and low down, running from one spare iron upright to another. These rather emphasized than encouraged my mood. And still as I resolutely put one foot in front of the other, and resolutely kept my eyes off the abyss and fixed on the opposing hill, and as the long curve before me was diminished by successive sharp advances, still my heart was caught half-way in every breath, and whatever it is that moves a man went uncertainly within me, mechanical and half-paralysed. The great height with that narrow unprotected ribbon across it was more than I could bear.

I dared not turn round and I dared not stop. Words and phrases began repeating themselves in my head as they will under a strain: so I know at sea a man perilously hanging on to the tiller makes a kind of litany of his instructions. The central part was passed, the three-quarters; the tension of that enduring effort had grown intolerable, and I doubted my ability to complete the task. Why? What could prevent me? I cannot say; it was all a bundle of imaginaries. Perhaps at bottom what I feared was sudden giddiness and the fall--

At any rate at this last supreme part I vowed one candle to Our Lady of Perpetual Succour if she would see that all went well, and this candle I later paid in Rome; finding Our Lady of Succour not hung up in a public place and known to all, as I thought She would be, but peculiar to a little church belonging to a Scotchman and standing above his high altar. Yet it is a very famous picture, and extremely old.

Well, then, having made this vow I still went on, with panic aiding me, till I saw that the bank beneath had risen to within a few feet of the bridge, and that dry land was not twenty yards away. Then my resolution left me and I ran, or rather stumbled, rapidly from sleeper to sleeper till I could take a deep breath on the solid earth beyond.

I stood and gazed back over the abyss; I saw the little horrible strip between heaven and hell--the perspective of its rails. I was made ill by the relief from terror. Yet I suppose railway-men cross and recross it twenty times a day. Better for them than for me!

There is the story of the awful bridge of the Mont Terrible, and it lies to a yard upon the straight line--*quid dicam*--the segment of the Great Circle uniting Toul and Rome.

The high bank or hillside before me was that which ends the gorge of the Doubs and looks down either limb of the sharp bend. I had here not to climb but to follow at one height round the curve. My way ran by a rather ill-made lane and passed a village. Then it was my business to make straight up the farther wall of the gorge, and as there was wood upon this, it looked an easy matter.

But when I came to it, it was not easy. The wood grew in loose rocks and the slope was much too steep for anything but hands and knees, and far too soft and broken for true climbing. And no wonder this ridge seemed a wall for steepness and difficulty, since it was the watershed between the Mediterranean and the cold North Sea. But I did not know this at the time. It must have taken me close on an hour before I had covered the last thousand feet or so that brought me to the top of the ridge, and there, to my great astonishment, was a road. Where could such a road lead, and why did it follow right along the highest edge of the mountains? The Jura with their unique parallels provide twenty such problems.

Wherever it led, however, this road was plainly perpendicular to my true route, and I had but to press on my straight line. So I crossed it, saw for a last time through the trees the gorge of the Doubs, and then got upon a path which led down through a field more or less in the direction of my pilgrimage.

Here the country was so broken that one could make out but little of its general features, but of course, on the whole, I was following down yet another southern slope, the southern slope of the *third* chain of the Jura, when, after passing through many glades and along a stony path, I found a kind of gate between two high rocks, and emerged somewhat suddenly upon a wide down studded with old trees and also many stunted yews, and this sank down to a noble valley which lay all before me.

The open down or prairie on which I stood I afterwards found to be called the 'Pasturage of Common Right', a very fine name; and, as a gallery will command a great hall, so this field like a platform commanded the wide and fading valley below.

It was a very glad surprise to see this sight suddenly unrolled as I stood on the crest of the down. The Jura had hitherto been either lonely, or somewhat awful, or naked and rocky, but here was a true vale in which one could imagine a spirit of its own; there were corn lands and no rocks. The mountains on either side did not rise so high as three thousand feet. Though of limestone they were rounded in form, and the slanting sun of the late afternoon (all the storm had left the sky) took them full and warm. The valley remaining wide and fruitful went on out eastward till the hills became mixed up with brume and distance. As I did not know its name I called it after the village immediately below me for which I was making; and I still remember it as the Valley of Glovelier, and it lies between the third and fourth ridges of the Jura.

Before leaving the field I drew what I saw but I was much too tired by the double and prodigious climb of the past hours to draw definitely or clearly. Such as it is, there it is. Then I went down over the smooth field.

There is something that distinguishes the rugged from the gracious in landscape, and in our Europe this something corresponds to the use and presence of men, especially in mountainous places. For men's habits and civilization fill the valleys and wash up the base of the hills, making, as it were, a tide mark. Into this zone I had already passed. The turf was trodden fine, and was set firm as it can only become by thousands of years of pasturing. The moisture that oozed out of the earth was not the random bog of the high places but a human spring, caught in a stone trough. Attention had been given to the trees. Below me stood a wall, which, though rough, was not the haphazard thing men pile up in the last recesses of the hills, but formed of chosen stones, and these bound together with mortar. On my right was a deep little dale with children playing in it--and this' I afterwards learned was called a 'combe': delightful memory! All our deeper hollows are called the same at home, and even the Welsh have the word, but they spell it cwm; it is their mountain way. Well, as I was saying, everything surrounding me was domestic and grateful, and I was therefore in a mood for charity and companionship when I came down the last dip and entered Glovelier. But Glovelier is a place of no excellence whatever, and if the thought did not seem extravagant I should be for putting it to the sword and burning it all down.

For just as I was going along full of kindly thoughts, and had turned into the sign of (I think it was) the 'Sun' to drink wine and leave them my benediction--

LECTOR. Why your benediction?

AUCTOR. Who else can give benedictions if people cannot when they are on pilgrimage? Learn that there are three avenues by which blessing can be bestowed, and three kinds of men who can bestow it.

(1) There is the good man, whose goodness makes him of himself a giver of blessings. His power is not conferred or of office, but is *inhaerens persona;* part of the stuff of his mind. This kind can confer the solemn benediction, or *Benedictio major*, if they choose; but besides this their every kind thought, word, or action is a *Benedictio generalise* and even their frowns, curses, angry looks and irritable gestures may be called *Benedictiones minores vel incerti*. I believe I am within the definitions. I avoid heresy. All this is sound theology. I do not smell of the faggot. And this kind of Benedictory Power is the fount or type or natural origin, as it were, of all others.

(2) There is the Official of Religion who, in the exercise of his office--

LECTOR. For Heaven's sake--

AUCTOR. Who began it? You protested my power to give benediction, and I must now prove it at length; otherwise I should fall under the accusation of lesser Simony--that is, the false assumption of particular powers. Well, then, there is the Official who *ex officio*, and when he makes it quite clear that it is *qua sponsus* and not *sicut ut ipse*, can give formal benediction. This power belongs certainly to all Bishops, mitred Abbots, and Archimandrates; to Patriarchs of course, and *a fortiori* to the Pope. In Rome they will have it that Monsignores also can so bless, and I have heard it debated whether or no the same were not true in some rustic way of parish priests. However this may be, all their power proceeds, not from themselves, but from the accumulation of goodness left as a deposit by the multitudes of exceptionally good men who have lived in times past, and who have now no use for it.

(3) Thirdly--and this is my point--any one, good or bad, official or non-official, who is for the moment engaged in an *opusfaustum* can act certainly as a conductor or medium, and the influence of what he is touching or doing passes to you from him. This is admitted by every one who worships trees, wells, and stones; and indeed it stands to reason, for it is but a branch of the well-known *'Sanctificatio ex loco, opere, tactu vel conditione.'* I will admit that this power is but vague, slight, tenuous, and dissipatory, still there it is: though of course its poor effect is to that of the *Benedictio major* what a cat's-paw in the Solent is to a north-east snorter on Lindsey Deeps.

I am sorry to have been at such length, but it is necessary to have these things thrashed out once for all. So now you see how I, being on pilgrimage, could give a kind of little creeping blessing to the people on the way, though, as St Louis said to the Hascisch-eaters, *'May it be a long time before you can kiss my bones.'*

So I entered the 'Sun' inn and saw there a woman sewing, a great dull-faced man like an ox, and a youth writing down figures in a little book. I said--

'Good morning, madam, and sirs, and the company. Could you give me a little red wine?' Not a head moved.

True I was very dirty and tired, and they may have thought me a beggar, to whom, like good sensible Christians who had no nonsense about them, they would rather have given a handsome kick than a cup of cold water. However, I think it was not only my poverty but a native churlishness which bound their bovine souls in that valley.

I sat down at a very clean table. I notice that those whom the Devil has made his own are always spick and span, just as firemen who have to go into great furnaces have to keep all their gear highly polished. I sat down at it, and said again, still gently--

'It is, indeed, a fine country this of yours. Could you give me a little red wine?'

Then the ox-faced man who had his back turned to me, and was the worst of the lot, said sulkily, not to me, but to the woman--

'He wants wine.'

The woman as sulkily said to me, not looking me in the eyes--

'How much will you pay?'

I said, 'Bring the wine. Set it here. See me drink it. Charge me your due.'

I found that this brutal way of speaking was just what was needed for the kine and cattle of this pen. She skipped off to a cupboard, and set wine before me, and a glass. I drank quite quietly till I had had enough, and asked what there was to pay. She said 'Threepence,' and I said 'Too much,' as I paid it. At this the ox-faced man grunted and frowned, and I was afraid; but hiding my fear I walked out boldly and slowly, and made a noise with my stick upon the floor of the hall without. Neither did I bid them farewell. But I made a sign at the house as I left it. Whether it suffered from this as did the house at Dorchester which the man in the boat caused to wither in one night, is more than I can tell.

The road led straight across the valley and approached the further wall of hills. These I saw were pierced by one of the curious gaps which are peculiar to limestone ranges. Water cuts them, and a torrent ran through this one also. The road through it, gap though it was, went up steeply, and the further valley was evidently higher than the one I was leaving. It was already evening as I entered this narrow ravine; the sun only caught the tops of the rock-walls. My fatigue was very great, and my walking painful to an extreme, when, having come to a place where the gorge was narrowest and where the two sides were like the posts of a giant's stile, where also the fifth ridge of the Jura stood up beyond me in the further valley, a vast shadow, I sat down wearily and drew what not even my exhaustion could render unremarkable.

While I was occupied sketching the slabs of limestone, I heard wheels coming up behind me, and a boy in a waggon stopped and hailed me.

What the boy wanted to know was whether I would take a lift, and this he said in such curious French that I shuddered to think how far I had pierced into the heart of the hills, and how soon I might come to quite strange people. I was greatly tempted to get into his cart, but though I had broken so many of my vows one remained yet whole and sound, which was that I would ride upon no wheeled thing. Remembering this, therefore, and considering that the Faith is rich in interpretation, I clung on to the waggon in such a manner that it did all my work for me, and yet could not be said to be actually carrying me. *Distinguo*. The essence of a vow is its literal meaning. The spirit and intention are for the major morality, and concern Natural Religion, but when upon a point of ritual or of dedication or special worship a man talks to you of the Spirit and Intention, and complains of the dryness of the Word, look at him askance. He is not far removed from Heresy.

I knew a man once that was given to drinking, and I made up this rule for him to distinguish between Bacchus and the Devil. To wit: that he should never drink what has been made and sold since the Reformation--I mean especially spirits and champagne. Let him (said I) drink red wine and white, good beer and mead--if he could get it--liqueurs made by monks, and, in a word, all those feeding, fortifying, and confirming beverages that our fathers drank in old time; but not whisky, nor brandy, nor sparkling wines, not absinthe, nor the kind of drink called gin. This he promised to do, and all went well. He became a merry companion, and began to write odes. His prose clarified and set, that had before been very mixed and cloudy. He slept well; he comprehended divine things; he was already half a republican, when one fatal day--it was the feast of the eleven thousand virgins, and they were too busy up in heaven to consider the needs of us poor hobbling, polyktonous and betempted wretches of men--I went with him to the Society for the Prevention of Annoyances to the Rich, where a certain usurer's son was to read a paper on the cruelty of Spaniards to their mules. As we were all seated there round a table with a staring green cloth on it, and a damnable gas pendant above, the host of that evening offered him whisky and water, and, my back being turned, he took it. Then when I would have taken it from him he used these words--

'After all, it is the intention of a pledge that matters;' and I saw that all was over, for he had abandoned definition, and was plunged back into the horrible mazes of Conscience and Natural Religion.

What do you think, then, was the consequence? Why, he had to take some nasty pledge or other to drink nothing whatever, and become a spectacle and a judgement, whereas if he had kept his exact word he might by this time have been a happy man.

Remembering him and pondering upon the advantage of strict rule, I hung on to my cart, taking care to let my feet still feel the road, and so passed through the high limestone gates of the gorge, and was in the fourth valley of the Jura, with the fifth ridge standing up black and huge before me against the last of the daylight. There were as yet no stars.

There, in this silent place, was the little village of Undervelier, and I thanked the boy, withdrew from his cart, and painfully approached the inn, where I asked the woman if she could give me something to eat, and she said that she could in about an hour, using, however, with regard to what it was I was to have, words which I did not understand. For the French had become quite barbaric, and I was now indeed lost in one of the inner places of the world.

A cigar is, however, even in Undervelier, a cigar; and the best cost a penny. One of these, therefore, I bought, and then I went out smoking it into the village square, and, finding a low wall, leaned over it and contemplated the glorious clear green water tumbling and roaring along beneath it on the other side; for a little river ran through the village.

As I leaned there resting and communing I noticed how their church, close at hand, was built along the low banks of the torrent. I admired the luxuriance of the grass these waters fed, and the generous arch of the trees beside it. The graves seemed set in a natural place of rest and home, and just beyond this churchyard was that marriage of hewn stone and water which is the source of so peculiar a satisfaction; for the church tower was built boldly right out into the stream and the current went eddying round it. But why it is that strong human building when it dips into water should thus affect the mind I cannot say, only I know that it is an emotion apart to see our device and structure where it is most enduring come up against and challenge that element which we cannot conquer, and which has always in it something of danger for men. It is therefore well to put strong mouldings on to piers and quays, and to make an architecture of them, and so it was a splendid thought of the Romans to build their villas right out to sea; so they say does Venice enthrall one, but where I have most noticed this thing is at the Mont St Michel--only one must take care to shut one's eyes or sleep during all the low tide.

As I was watching that stream against those old stones, my cigar being now half smoked, a bell began tolling, and it seemed as if the whole village were pouring into the church. At this I was very much surprised, not having been used at any time of my life to the unanimous devotion of an entire population, but having always thought of the Faith as something fighting odds, and having seen unanimity only in places where some sham religion or other glozed over our tragedies and excused our sins. Certainly to see all the men, women, and children of a place taking Catholicism for granted was a new sight, and so I put my cigar carefully down under a stone on the top of the wall and went in with them. I then saw that what they were at was vespers.

All the village sang, knowing the psalms very well, and I noticed that their Latin was nearer German than French; but what was most pleasing of all was to hear from all the men and women together that very noble good-night and salutation to God which begins--

Te, lucis ante terminum.

My whole mind was taken up and transfigured by this collective act, and I saw for a moment the Catholic Church quite plain, and I remembered Europe, and the centuries. Then there left me altogether that attitude of difficulty and combat which, for us others, is always associated with the Faith. The cities dwindled in my imagination, and I took less heed of the modern noise. I went out with them into the clear evening and the cool. I found my cigar and lit it again, and musing much more deeply than before, not without tears, I considered the nature of Belief.

Of its nature it breeds a reaction and an indifference. Those who believe nothing but only think and judge cannot understand this. Of its nature it struggles with us. And we, we, when our youth is full on us, invariably reject it and set out in the sunlight content with natural things. Then for a long time we are like men who follow down the cleft of a mountain and the peaks are hidden from us and forgotten. It takes years to reach the dry plain, and then we look back and see our home.

What is it, do you think, that causes the return? I think it is the problem of living; for every day, every experience of evil, demands a solution. That solution is provided by the memory of the great scheme which at last we remember. Our childhood pierces through again ... But I will not attempt to explain it, for I have not the power; only I know that we who return suffer hard things; for there grows a gulf between us and many companions. We are perpetually thrust into minorities, and the world almost begins to talk a strange language; we are troubled by the human machinery of a perfect and superhuman revelation; we are over-anxious for its safety, alarmed, and in danger of violent decisions.

And this is hard: that the Faith begins to make one abandon the old way of judging. Averages and movements and the rest grow uncertain. We see things from within and consider one mind or a little group as a salt or leaven. The very nature of social force seems changed to us. And this is hard when a man has loved common views and is happy only with his fellows.

And this again is very hard, that we must once more take up that awful struggle to reconcile two truths and to keep civic freedom sacred in spite of the organization of religion, and not to deny what is certainly true. It is hard to accept mysteries, and to be humble. We are tost as the great schoolmen were tost, and we dare not neglect the duty of that wrestling.

But the hardest thing of all is that it leads us away, as by a command, from all that banquet of the intellect than which there is no keener joy known to man.

I went slowly up the village place in the dusk, thinking of this deplorable weakness in men that the Faith is too great for them, and accepting it as an inevitable burden. I continued to muse with my eyes upon the ground...

There was to be no more of that studious content, that security in historic analysis, and that constant satisfaction of an appetite which never cloyed. A wisdom more imperative and more profound was to put a term to the comfortable wisdom of learning. All the balance of judgement, the easy, slow convictions, the broad grasp of things, the vision of their complexity, the pleasure in their innumerable life--all that had to be given up. Fanaticisms were no longer entirely to be despised, just appreciations and a strong grasp of reality no longer entirely to be admired.

The Catholic Church will have no philosophies. She will permit no comforts; the cry of the martyrs is in her far voice; her eyes that see beyond the world present us heaven and hell to the confusion of our human reconciliations, our happy blending of good and evil things.

By the Lord! I begin to think this intimate religion as tragic as a great love. There came back into my mind a relic that I have in my house. It is a panel of the old door of my college, having carved on it my college arms. I remembered the Lion and the Shield, *Haec fuit, Haec almae janua sacra domus*. Yes, certainly religion is as tragic as first love, and drags us out into the void away from our dear homes.

It is a good thing to have loved one woman from a child, and it is a good thing not to have to return to the Faith.

They cook worse in Undervelier than any place I was ever in, with the possible exception of Omaha, Neb.

71

LECTOR. Why do you use phrases like *'possible exception'*?

AUCTOR. Why not? I see that all the religion I have stuck into the book has no more effect on you than had Rousseau upon Sir Henry Maine. You are as full of Pride as a minor Devil. You would avoid the *cliche* and the commonplace, and the *phrase toute faite*. Why? Not because you naturally write odd prose--contrariwise, left to yourself you write pure journalese; but simply because you are swelled and puffed up with a desire to pose. You want what the Martha Brown school calls 'distinction' in prose. My little friend, I know how it is done, and I find it contemptible. People write their articles at full speed, putting down their unstudied and valueless conclusions in English as pale as a film of dirty wax--sometimes even they dictate to a typewriter. Then they sit over it with a blue pencil and carefully transpose the split infinitives, and write alternative adjectives, and take words away out of their natural place in the sentence and generally put the Queen's English--yes, the Queen's English--on the rack. And who is a penny the better for it? The silly authors get no real praise, not even in the horrible stucco villas where their clique meet on Sundays. The poor public buys the *Marvel* and gasps at the cleverness of the writing and despairs, and has to read what it can understand, and is driven back to toshy novels about problems, written by cooks. 'The hungry sheep,' as some one says somewhere, 'look up and are not fed;' and the same poet well describes your pipings as being on wretched straw pipes that are 'scrannel'--a good word.

Oh, for one man who should write healthy, hearty, straightforward English! Oh, for Cobbett! There are indeed some great men who write twistedly simply because they cannot help it, but *their* honesty is proved by the mass they turn out. What do you turn out, you higglers and sticklers? Perhaps a bad triolet every six months, and a book of criticism on something thoroughly threadbare once in five years. If I had my way--

LECTOR. I am sorry to have provoked all this.

AUCTOR. Not at all! Not at all! I trust I have made myself clear.

Well, as I was saying, they cook worse at Undervelier than any place I was ever in, with the possible exception of Omaha, Neb. However, I forgave them, because they were such good people, and after a short and bitter night I went out in the morning before the sun rose and took the Moutier road.

The valley in which I was now engaged--the phrase seems familiar--was more or less like an H. That is, there were two high parallel ranges bounding it, but across the middle a low ridge of perhaps a thousand feet. The road slowly climbed this ridge through pastures where cows with deep-toned bells were rising from the dew on the grass, and where

72

one or two little cottages and a village already sent up smoke. All the way up I was thinking of the surfeit of religion I had had the night before, and also of how I had started that morning without bread or coffee, which was a folly.

When I got to the top of the ridge there was a young man chopping wood outside a house, and I asked him in French how far it was to Moutier. He answered in German, and I startled him by a loud cry, such as sailors give when they see land, for at last I had struck the boundary of the languages, and was with pure foreigners for the first time in my life. I also asked him for coffee, and as he refused it I took him to be a heretic and went down the road making up verses against all such, and singing them loudly through the forest that now arched over me and grew deeper as I descended.

And my first verse was--

Heretics all, whoever you be,
In Tarbes or Nimes, or over the sea,
You never shall have good words from me.
Caritas non conturbat me.

If you ask me why I put a Latin line at the end, it was because I had to show that it was a song connected with the Universal Fountain and with European culture, and with all that Heresy combats. I sang it to a lively hymn-tune that I had invented for the occasion.

I then thought what a fine fellow I was, and how pleasant were my friends when I agreed with them. I made up this second verse, which I sang even more loudly than the first; and the forest grew deeper, sending back echoes--

But Catholic men that live upon wine
Are deep in the water, and frank, and fine;
Wherever I travel I find it so,
Benedicamus Domino.

There is no doubt, however, that if one is really doing a catholic work, and expressing one's attitude to the world, charity, pity, and a great sense of fear should possess one, or, at least, appear. So I made up this third verse and sang it to suit--

On childing women that are forlorn,
And men that sweat in nothing but scorn:
That is on all that ever were born,
Miserere Domine.

Then, as everything ends in death, and as that is just what Heretics least like to be reminded of, I ended thus--

73

To my poor self on my deathbed,
And all my dear companions dead,
Because of the love that I bore them,
Dona Eis Requiem.

I say 'I ended.' But I did not really end there, for I also wrote in the spirit of the rest a verse of Mea Culpa and Confession of Sin, but I shall not print it here.

So my song over and the woods now left behind, I passed up a dusty piece of road into Moutier, a detestable town, all whitewashed and orderly, down under the hills.

I was tired, for the sun was now long risen and somewhat warm, and I had walked ten miles, and that over a high ridge; and I had written a canticle and sung it--- and all that without a sup or a bite. I therefore took bread, coffee, and soup in Moutier, and then going a little way out of the town I crossed a stream off the road, climbed a knoll, and, lying under a tree, I slept.

I awoke and took the road.

The road after Moutier was not a thing for lyrics; it stirred me in no way. It was bare in the sunlight, had fields on either side; and in the fields stood houses. In the houses were articulately-speaking mortal men.

There is a school of Poets (I cannot read them myself) who treat of common things, and their admirers tell us that these men raise the things of everyday life to the plane of the supernatural. Note that phrase, for it is a shaft of light through a cloud revealing their disgusting minds.

Everyday life! As *La Croix* said in a famous leading article: *'La Presse?'* POOH!' I know that everyday life. It goes with sandals and pictures of lean ugly people all just like one another in browny photographs on the wall, and these pictures are called, one 'The House of Life', or another, 'The Place Beautiful', or yet again a third, 'The Lamp of the Valley', and when you complain and shift about uneasily before these pictures, the scrub-minded and dusty-souled owners of them tell you that of course in photographs you lose the marvellous colour of the original. This everyday life has mantelpieces made of the same stuff as cafe-tables, so that by instinct I try to make rings on them with my wine-glass, and the people who suffer this life get up every morning at eight, and the poor sad men of the house slave at wretched articles and come home to hear more literature and more appreciations, and the unholy women do nothing and attend to local government, that is, the oppression of the poor; and altogether this accursed everyday life of theirs is instinct with the four sins crying to heaven for vengeance, and there is no humanity in it, and no simplicity, and no recollection. I know whole quarters of the towns of that life where they have never heard of Virtus or Verecundia or Pietas.

LECTOR. Then--

AUCTOR. Alas! alas! Dear Lector, in these houses there is no honest dust. Not a bottle of good wine or bad; no prints inherited from one's uncle, and no children's books by Mrs Barbauld or Miss Edgeworth; no human disorder, nothing of that organic comfort which makes a man's house like a bear's fur for him. They have no debts, they do not read in bed, and they will have difficulty in saving their souls.

LECTOR. Then tell me, how would you treat of common things?

AUCTOR. Why, I would leave them alone; but if I had to treat of them I will show you how I would do it. Let us have a dialogue about this road from Moutier.

LECTOR. By all means.

AUCTOR. What a terrible thing it is to miss one's sleep. I can hardly bear the heat of the road, and my mind is empty!

LECTOR. Why, you have just slept in a wood!

AUCTOR. Yes, but that is not enough. One must sleep at night.

LECTOR. My brother often complains of insomnia. He is a policeman.

AUCTOR. Indeed? It is a sad affliction.

LECTOR. Yes, indeed.

AUCTOR. Indeed, yes.

LECTOR. I cannot go on like this.

AUCTOR. There. That is just what I was saying. One cannot treat of common things: it is not literature; and for my part, if I were the editor even of a magazine, and the author stuck in a string of dialogue, I would not pay him by the page but by the word, and I would count off 5 per cent for epigrams, 10 per cent for dialect, and some quarter or so for those stage directions in italics which they use to pad out their work.

So. I will not repeat this experiment, but next time I come to a bit of road about which there is nothing to say, I will tell a story or sing a song, and to that I pledge myself.

By the way, I am reminded of something. Do you know those books and stories in which parts of the dialogues often have no words at all?

Only dots and dashes and asterisks and interrogations? I wonder what the people are paid for it? If I knew I would earn a mint of money, for I believe I have a talent for it. Look at this--

There. That seems to me worth a good deal more money than all the modern 'delineation of character', and 'folk' nonsense ever written. What verve! What terseness! And yet how clear!

LECTOR. Let us be getting on.

AUCTOR. By all means, and let us consider more enduring things.

After a few miles the road going upwards, I passed through another gap in the hills and--

LECTOR. Pardon me, but I am still ruminating upon that little tragedy of yours. Why was the guardian a duchess?

AUCTOR. Well, it was a short play and modern, was it not?

LECTOR. Yes. And therefore, of course, you must have a title in it. I know that. I do not object to it. What I want to know is, why a duchess?

AUCTOR. On account of the reduction of scale: the concentration of the thing. You see in the full play there would have been a lord, two baronets, and say three ladies, and I could have put suitable words into their mouths. As it was I had to make absolutely sure of the element of nobility without any help, and, as it were, in one startling moment. Do you follow? Is it not art?

I cannot conceive why a pilgrimage, an adventure so naturally full of great, wonderful, far-off and holy things should breed such fantastic nonsense as all this; but remember at least the little acolyte of Rheims, whose father, in 1512, seeing him apt for religion, put him into a cassock and designed him for the Church, whereupon the youngling began to be as careless and devilish as Mercury, putting beeswax on the misericords, burning feathers in the censer, and even going round himself with the plate without leave and scolding the rich in loud whispers when they did not put in enough. So one way with another they sent him home to his father; the archbishop thrusting him out of the south porch with his own hands and giving him the Common or Ferial Malediction, which is much the same as that used by carters to stray dogs.

When his father saw him he fumed terribly, cursing like a pagan, and asking whether his son were a roysterer fit for the gallows as well as a fool fit for a cassock. On hearing which complaint the son very humbly and contritely said--

'It is not my fault but the contact with the things of the Church that makes me gambol and frisk, just as the Devil they say is a good enough fellow left to himself and is only moderately heated, yet when you put him into holy water all the world is witness how he hisses and boils.'

The boy then taking a little lamb which happened to be in the drawing-room, said--

'Father, see this little lamb; how demure he is and how simple and innocent, and how foolish and how tractable. Yet observe!' With that he whipped the cassock from his arm where he was carrying it and threw it all over the lamb, covering his head and body; and the lamb began plunging and kicking and bucking and rolling and heaving and sliding and rearing and pawing and most vigorously wrestling with the clerical and hierarchically constraining garment of darkness, and bleating all the while more and more angrily and loudly, for all the world like the great goat Baphomet himself when the witches dance about him on All-hallowe'en. But when the boy suddenly plucked off the cassock again, the lamb, after sneezing a little and finding his feet, became quite gentle once more, and looked only a little confused and dazed.

'There, father,' said the boy, 'is proof to you of how the meekest may be driven to desperation by the shackles I speak of, and which I pray you never lay upon me again.'

His father finding him so practical and wise made over his whole fortune and business to him, and thus escaped the very heavy Heriot and Death Dues of those days, for he was a Socage tenant of St Remi in Double Burgage. But we stopped all that here in England by the statute of Uses, and I must be getting back to the road before the dark catches me.

As I was saying, I came to a gap in the hills, and there was there a house or two called Gansbrunnen, and one of the houses was an inn. Just by the inn the road turned away sharply up the valley; the very last slope of the Jura, the last parallel ridge, lay straight before me all solemn, dark, and wooded, and making a high feathery line against the noon. To cross this there was but a vague path rather misleading, and the name of the mountain was Weissenstein.

So before that last effort which should lead me over those thousands of feet, and to nourish Instinct (which would be of use to me when I got into that impenetrable wood), I turned into the inn for wine.

A very old woman having the appearance of a witch sat at a dark table by the little criss-cross window of the dark room. She was crooning to herself, and I made the sign of the evil eye and asked her in French for wine; but French she did not understand. Catching, however, two words which sounded like the English 'White' and 'Red', I said 'Yaw' after the last and nodded, and she brought up a glass of exceedingly good red wine which I drank in silence, she watching me uncannily.

Then I paid her with a five-franc piece, and she gave me a quantity of small change rapidly, which, as I counted it, I found to contain one Greek piece of fifty lepta very manifestly of lead. This I held up angrily before her, and (not without courage, for it is hard to deal with the darker powers) I recited to her slowly that familiar verse which the well-known Satyricus Empiricius was for ever using in his now classical attacks on the grammarians; and without any Alexandrian twaddle of accents I intoned to her--and so left her astounded to repentance or to shame.

Then I went out into the sunlight, and crossing over running water put myself out of her power.

The wood went up darkly and the path branched here and there so that I was soon uncertain of my way, but I followed generally what seemed to me the most southerly course, and so came at last up steeply through a dip or ravine that ended high on the crest of the ridge.

Just as I came to the end of the rise, after perhaps an hour, perhaps two, of that great curtain of forest which had held the mountain side, the trees fell away to brushwood, there was a gate, and then the path was lost upon a fine open sward which was the very top of the Jura and the coping of that multiple wall which defends the Swiss Plain. I had crossed it straight from edge to edge, never turning out of my way.

It was too marshy to lie down on it, so I stood a moment to breathe and look about me.

It was evident that nothing higher remained, for though a new line of wood--firs and beeches--stood before me, yet nothing appeared above them, and I knew that they must be the fringe of the descent. I approached this edge of wood, and saw that it had a rough fence of post and rails bounding it, and as I was looking for the entry of a path (for my original path was lost, as such tracks are, in the damp grass of the little down) there came to me one of those great revelations which betray to us suddenly the higher things and stand afterwards firm in our minds.

There, on this upper meadow, where so far I had felt nothing but the ordinary gladness of The Summit, I had a vision.

What was it I saw? If you think I saw this or that, and if you think I am inventing the words, you know nothing of men.

I saw between the branches of the trees in front of me a sight in the sky that made me stop breathing, just as great danger at sea, or great

about half-way down the mountain side that its vastness most impressed me. And yet it had been but a platform as it were, from which to view the Alps and their much greater sublimity.

This vastness, even of these limestone mountains, took me especially at a place where the path bordered a steep, or rather precipitous, lift of white rock to which only here and there a tree could cling.

I was still very high up, but looking somewhat more eastward than before, and the plain went on inimitably towards some low vague hills; nor in that direction could any snow be seen in the sky. Then at last I came to the slopes which make a little bank under the mountains, and there, finding a highroad, and oppressed somewhat suddenly by the afternoon heat of those low places, I went on more slowly towards Soleure.

Beside me, on the road, were many houses, shaded by great trees, built of wood, and standing apart. To each of them almost was a little water-wheel, run by the spring which came down out of the ravine. The water-wheel in most cases worked a simple little machine for sawing planks, but in other cases it seemed used for some purpose inside the house, which I could not divine; perhaps for spinning.

All this place was full of working, and the men sang and spoke at their work in German, which I could not understand. I did indeed find one man, a young hay-making man carrying a scythe, who knew a little French and was going my way. I asked him, therefore, to teach me German, but he had not taught me much before we were at the gates of the old town and then I left him. It is thus, you will see, that for my next four days or five, which were passed among the German-speaking Swiss, I was utterly alone.

This book must not go on for ever; therefore I cannot say very much about Soleure, although there is a great deal to be said about it. It is distinguished by an impression of unity, and of civic life, which I had already discovered in all these Swiss towns; for though men talk of finding the Middle Ages here or there, I for my part never find it, save where there has been democracy to preserve it. Thus I have seen the Middle Ages especially alive in the small towns of Northern France, and I have seen the Middle Ages in the University of Paris. Here also in Switzerland. As I had seen it at St Ursanne, so I found it now at Soleure. There were huge gates flanking the town, and there was that evening a continual noise of rifles, at which the Swiss are for ever practising. Over the church, however, I saw something terribly seventeenth century, namely, Jaweh in great Hebrew letters upon its front.

Well, dining there of the best they had to give me (for this was another milestone in my pilgrimage), I became foolishly refreshed and valiant, and instead of sleeping in Soleure, as a wise man would have done, I determined, though it was now nearly dark, to push on upon the road to Burgdorf.

I therefore crossed the river Aar, which is here magnificently broad and strong, and has bastions jutting out into it in a very bold fashion. I saw the last colourless light of evening making its waters seem like dull metal between the gloomy banks; I felt the beginnings of fatigue, and half regretted my determination. But as it is quite certain that one should never go back, I went on in the darkness, I do not know how many miles, till I reached some cross roads and an inn.

This inn was very poor, and the people had never heard in their lives, apparently, that a poor man on foot might not be able to talk German, which seemed to me an astonishing thing; and as I sat there ordering beer for myself and for a number of peasants (who but for this would have me their butt, and even as it was found something monstrous in me), I pondered during my continual attempts to converse with them (for I had picked up some ten words of their language) upon the folly of those who imagine the world to be grown smaller by railways.

I suppose this place was more untouched, as the phrase goes, that is, more living, more intense, and more powerful to affect others, whenever it may be called to do so, than are even the dear villages of Sussex that lie under my downs. For those are haunted by a nearly cosmopolitan class of gentry, who will have actors, financiers, and what not to come and stay with them, and who read the paper, and from time to time address their village folk upon matters of politics. But here, in this broad plain by the banks of the Emmen, they knew of nothing but themselves and the Church which is the common bond of Europe, and they were in the right way. Hence it was doubly hard on me that they should think me such a stranger.

When I had become a little morose at their perpetual laughter, I asked for a bed, and the landlady, a woman of some talent, showed me on her fingers that the beds were 50c., 75c., and a franc. I determined upon the best, and was given indeed a very pleasant room, having in it the statue of a saint, and full of a country air. But I had done too much in this night march, as you will presently learn, for my next day was a day without salt, and in it appreciation left me. And this breakdown of appreciation was due to what I did not know at the time to be fatigue, but to what was undoubtedly a deep inner exhaustion.

When I awoke next morning it was as it always is: no one was awake, and I had the field to myself, to slip out as I chose. I looked out of the window into the dawn. The race had made its own surroundings.

These people who suffocated with laughter at the idea of one's knowing no German, had produced, as it were, a German picture by the mere influence of years and years of similar thoughts.

Out of my window I saw the eaves coming low down. I saw an apple-tree against the grey light. The tangled grass in the little garden, the dog-kennel, and the standing butt were all what I had seen in those German pictures which they put into books for children, and which are drawn in thick black lines: nor did I see any reason why tame faces should not appear in that framework. I expected the light lank hair and the heavy unlifting step of the people whose only emotions are in music.

But it was too early for any one to be about, and my German garden, *si j'ose m'exprimer ainsi*, had to suffice me for an impression of the Central Europeans. I gazed at it a little while as it grew lighter. Then I went downstairs and slipped the latch (which, being German, was of a quaint design). I went out into the road and sighed profoundly.

All that day was destined to be covered, so far as my spirit was concerned, with a motionless lethargy. Nothing seemed properly to interest or to concern me, and not till evening was I visited by any muse. Even my pain (which was now dull and chronic) was no longer a subject for my entertainment, and I suffered from an uneasy isolation that had not the merit of sharpness and was no spur to the mind. I had the feeling that every one I might see would be a stranger, and that their language would be unfamiliar to me, and this, unlike most men who travel, I had never felt before.

The reason being this: that if a man has English thoroughly he can wander over a great part of the world familiarly, and meet men with whom he can talk. And if he has French thoroughly all Italy, and I suppose Spain, certainly Belgium, are open to him. Not perhaps that he will understand what he hears or will be understood of others, but that the order and nature of the words and the gestures accompanying them are his own. Here, however, I, to whom English and French were the same, was to spend (it seemed) whole days among a people who put their verbs at the end, where the curses or the endearments come in French and English, and many of whose words stand for ideas we have not got. I had no room for good-fellowship. I could not sit at tables and expand the air with terrible stories of adventure, nor ask about their politics, nor provoke them to laughter or sadness by my tales. It seemed a poor pilgrimage taken among dumb men.

Also I have no doubt that I had experienced the ebb of some vitality, for it is the saddest thing about us that this bright spirit with which we are lit from within like lanterns, can suffer dimness. Such frailty makes one fear that extinction is our final destiny, and it saps us with numbness, and we are less than ourselves. Seven nights had I been on pilgrimage, and two of them had I passed in the open. Seven great heights had I climbed: the Forest, Archettes, the Ballon, the Mont Terrible, the Watershed, the pass by Moutier, the Weissenstein. Seven depths had I fallen to: twice to the Moselle, the gap of Belfort, the gorge of the Doubs, Glovelier valley, the hole of Moutier, and now this plain of the Aar. I had marched 180 miles. It was no wonder that on this eighth day I was oppressed and that all the light long I drank no good wine, met no one to remember well, nor sang any songs. All this part of my way was full of what they call Duty, and I was sustained only by my knowledge that the vast mountains (which had disappeared) would be part of my life very soon if I still went on steadily towards Rome.

The sun had risen when I reached Burgdorf, and I there went to a railway station, and outside of it drank coffee and ate bread. I also bought old newspapers in French, and looked at everything wearily and with sad eyes. There was nothing to draw. How can a man draw pain in the foot and knee?   And that was all there was remarkable at that moment.

I watched a train come in. It was full of tourists, who (it may have been a subjective illusion) seemed to me common and worthless people, and sad into the bargain. It was going to Interlaken; and I felt a languid contempt for people who went to Interlaken instead of driving right across the great hills to Rome.

After an hour, or so of this melancholy dawdling, I put a map before me on a little marble table, ordered some more coffee, and blew into my tepid life a moment of warmth by the effort of coming to a necessary decision. I had (for the first time since I had left Lorraine) the choice of two roads; and why this was so the following map will make clear.

Here you see that there is no possibility of following the straight way to Rome, but that one must go a few miles east or west of it. From Burgundy one has to strike a point on the sources of the Emmen, and Burgdorf is on the Emmen. Therefore one might follow the Emmen all the way up. But it seemed that the road climbed up above a gorge that way, whereas by the other (which is just as straight) the road is good (it seemed) and fairly level. So I chose this latter Eastern way, which, at the bifurcation, takes one up a tributary of the Emmen, then over a rise to the Upper Emmen again.

Do you want it made plainer than that? I should think not. And, tell me--what can it profit you to know these geographical details? Believe me, I write them down for my own gratification, not yours.

I say a day without salt. A trudge. The air was ordinary, the colours common; men, animals, and trees indifferent. Something had stopped working.

Our energy also is from God, and we should never be proud of it, even if we can cover thirty miles day after day (as I can), or bend a peony in one's hand as could Frocot, the driver in my piece--a man you never knew--or write bad verse very rapidly as can so many moderns. I say our energy also is from God, and we should never be proud of it as though it were from ourselves, but we should accept it as a kind of present, and we should be thankful for it; just as a man should thank

84

God for his reason, as did the madman in the Story of the Rose, who thanked God that he at least was sane though all the rest of the world had recently lost their reason.

Indeed, this defaillance and breakdown which comes from time to time over the mind is a very sad thing, but it can be made of great use to us if we will draw from it the lesson that we ourselves are nothing. Perhaps it is a grace. Perhaps in these moments our minds repose ... Anyhow, a day without salt.

You understand that under (or in) these circumstances--

When I was at Oxford there was a great and terrible debate that shook the Empire, and that intensely exercised the men whom we send out to govern the Empire, and which, therefore, must have had its effect upon the Empire, as to whether one should say 'under these circumstances' or 'in these circumstances'; nor did I settle matters by calling a conclave and suggesting *Quae quum ita sint* as a common formula, because a new debate arose upon when you should say *sint* and when you should say *sunt*, and they all wrangled like kittens in a basket.

Until there rose a deep-voiced man from an outlying college, who said, 'For my part I will say that under these circumstances, or in these circumstances, or in spite of these circumstances, or hovering playfully above these circumstances, or--

I take you all for Fools and Pedants, in the Chief, in the Chevron, and in the quarter Fess. Fools absolute, and Pedants lordless. Free Fools, unlanded Fools, and Fools incommensurable, and Pedants displayed and rampant of the Tierce Major. Fools incalculable and Pedants irreparable; indeed, the arch Fool-pedants in a universe of pedantic folly and foolish pedantry, O you pedant-fools of the world!'

But by this time he was alone, and thus was this great question never properly decided.

Under these circumstances, then (or in these circumstances), it would profit you but little if I were to attempt the description of the Valley of the Emmen, of the first foot-hills of the Alps, and of the very uninteresting valley which runs on from Langnau.

I had best employ my time in telling the story of the Hungry Student.

LECTOR. And if you are so worn-out and bereft of all emotions, how can you tell a story?

AUCTOR. These two conditions permit me. First, that I am writing some time after, and that I have recovered; secondly, that the story is not mine, but taken straight out of that nationalist newspaper which had served me so long to wrap up my bread and bacon in my haversack. This is the story, and I will tell it you.

Now, I think of it, it would be a great waste of time. Here am I no farther than perhaps a third of my journey, and I have already admitted so much digression that my pilgrimage is like the story of a man asleep and dreaming, instead of the plain, honest, and straightforward narrative of fact. I will therefore postpone the Story of the Hungry Student till I get into the plains of Italy, or into the barren hills of that peninsula, or among the over-well-known towns of Tuscany, or in some other place where a little padding will do neither you nor me any great harm.

On the other hand, do not imagine that I am going to give you any kind of description of this intolerable day's march. If you want some kind of visual Concept (pretty word), take all these little chalets which were beginning and make what you can of them.

LECTOR. Where are they?

AUCTOR. They are still in Switzerland; not here. They were overnumerous as I maundered up from where at last the road leaves the valley and makes over a little pass for a place called Schangnau. But though it is not a story, on the contrary, an exact incident and the truth--a thing that I would swear to in the court of justice, or quite willingly and cheerfully believe if another man told it to me; or even take as historical if I found it in a modern English history of the Anglo-Saxon Church--though, I repeat, it is a thing actually lived, yet I will tell it you.

It was at the very end of the road, and when an enormous weariness had begun to add some kind of interest to this stuffless episode of the dull day, that a peasant with a brutal face, driving a cart very rapidly, came up with me. I said to him nothing, but he said to me some words in German which I did not understand. We were at that moment just opposite a little inn upon the right hand of the road, and the peasant began making signs to me to hold his horse for him while he went in and drank.

How willing I was to do this you will not perhaps understand, unless you have that delicate and subtle pleasure in the holding of horses' heads, which is the boast and glory of some rare minds. And I was the more willing to do it from the fact that I have the habit of this kind of thing, acquired in the French manoeuvres, and had once held a horse for no less a person than a General of Division, who gave me a franc for it, and this franc I spent later with the men of my battery, purchasing wine. So to make a long story short, as the publisher said when he published the popular edition of *Pamela*, I held the horse for the peasant; always, of course, under the implicit understanding that he should allow me when he came out to have a drink, which I, of course, expected him to bring in his own hands.

86

Far from it. I can understand the anger which some people feel against the Swiss when they travel in that country, though I will always hold that it is monstrous to come into a man's country of your own accord, and especially into a country so free and so well governed as is Switzerland, and then to quarrel with the particular type of citizen that you find there.

Let us not discuss politics. The point is that the peasant sat in there drinking with his friends for a good three-quarters of an hour. Now and then a man would come out and look at the sky, and cough and spit and turn round again and say something to the people within in German, and go off; but no one paid the least attention to me as I held this horse.

I was already in a very angry and irritable mood, for the horse was restive and smelt his stable, and wished to break away from me. And all angry and irritable as I was, I turned around to see if this man were coming to relieve me; but I saw him laughing and joking with the people inside; and they were all looking my way out of their window as they laughed. I may have been wrong, but I thought they were laughing at me. A man who knows the Swiss intimately, and who has written a book upon 'The Drink Traffic: The Example of Switzerland', tells me they certainly were not laughing at me; at any rate, I thought they were, and moved by a sudden anger I let go the reins, gave the horse a great clout, and set him off careering and galloping like a whirlwind down the road from which he had come, with the bit in his teeth and all the storms of heaven in his four feet. Instantly, as you may imagine, all the scoffers came tumbling out of the inn, hullabooling, gesticulating, and running like madmen after the horse, and one old man even turned to protest to me. But I, setting my teeth, grasping my staff, and remembering the purpose of my great journey, set on up the road again with my face towards Rome.

I sincerely hope, trust, and pray that this part of my journey will not seem as dull to you as it did to me at the time, or as it does to me now while I write of it. But now I come to think of it, it cannot seem as dull, for I had to walk that wretched thirty miles or so all the day long, whereas you have not even to read it; for I am not going to say anything more about it, but lead you straight to the end.

Oh, blessed quality of books, that makes them a refuge from living! For in a book everything can be made to fit in, all tedium can be skipped over, and the intense moments can be made timeless and eternal, and as a poet who is too little known has well said in one of his unpublished lyrics, we, by the art of writing--

Can fix the high elusive hour
And stand in things divine.

And as for high elusive hours, devil a bit of one was there all the way from Burgdorf to the Inn of the Bridge, except the ecstatic flash of joy when I sent that horse careering down the road with his bad master after him and all his gang shouting among the hollow hills.

So. It was already evening. I was coming, more tired than ever, to a kind of little pass by which my road would bring me back again to the Emmen, now nothing but a torrent. All the slope down the other side of the little pass (three or four hundred feet perhaps) was covered by a village, called, if I remember right, Schangnau, and there was a large school on my right and a great number of children there dancing round in a ring and singing songs. The sight so cheered me that I determined to press on up the valley, though with no definite goal for the night. It was a foolish decision, for I was really in the heart of an unknown country, at the end of roads, at the sources of rivers, beyond help. I knew that straight before me, not five miles away, was the Brienzer Grat, the huge high wall which it was my duty to cross right over from side to side. I did not know whether or not there was an inn between me and that vast barrier.

The light was failing. I had perhaps some vague idea of sleeping out, but that would have killed me, for a heavy mist that covered all the tops of the hills and that made a roof over the valley, began to drop down a fine rain; and, as they sing in church on Christmas Eve, 'the heavens sent down their dews upon a just man'. But that was written in Palestine, where rain is a rare blessing; there and then in the cold evening they would have done better to have warmed the righteous. There is no controlling them; they mean well, but they bungle terribly.

The road stopped being a road, and became like a Californian trail. I approached enormous gates in the hills, high, precipitous, and narrow. The mist rolled over them, hiding their summits and making them seem infinitely lifted up and reaching endlessly into the thick sky; the straight, tenuous lines of the rain made them seem narrower still. Just as I neared them, hobbling, I met a man driving two cows, and said to him the word, 'Guest-house?' to which he said 'Yaw!' and pointed out a clump of trees to me just under the precipice and right in the gates I speak of. So I went there over an old bridge, and found a wooden house and went in.

It was a house which one entered without ceremony. The door was open, and one walked straight into a great room. There sat three men playing at cards. I saluted them loudly in French, English, and Latin, but they did not understand me, and what seemed remarkable in an hotel (for it was an hotel rather than an inn), no one in the house understood me--neither the servants nor any one; but the servants did not laugh at me as had the poor people near Burgdorf, they only stood round me looking at me patiently in wonder as cows do at trains. Then they brought me food, and as I did not know the names of the different kinds of food, I had to eat what they chose; and the angel of that valley protected me from boiled mutton. I knew, however, the word Wein, which is the same in all languages, and so drank a quart of it consciously and of a set purpose. Then I slept, and next morning at dawn I rose up, put on my thin, wet linen clothes, and went downstairs. No one was about. I looked around for something to fill my sack. I picked up a great hunk of bread from the dining-room table, and went out shivering into the cold drizzle that was still falling from a shrouded sky. Before me, a great forbidding wall, growing blacker as it went upwards and ending in a level line of mist, stood the Brienzer Grat.

You will observe that the straight way to Rome cuts the Lake of Brienz rather to the eastward of the middle, and then goes slap over Wetterhorn and strikes the Rhone Valley at a place called Ulrichen. That is how a bird would do it, if some High Pope of Birds lived in Rome and needed visiting, as, for instance, the Great Auk; or if some old primal relic sacred to birds was connected therewith, as, for instance, the bones of the Dodo.... But I digress. The point is that the straight line takes one over the Brienzer Grat, over the lake, and then over the Wetterhorn. That was manifestly impossible. But whatever of it was possible had to be done, and among the possible things was clambering over the high ridge of the Brienzer Grat instead of going round like a coward by Interlaken. After I had clambered over it, however, needs must I should have to take a pass called the Grimsel Pass and reach the Rhone Valley that way. It was with such a determination that I had come here to the upper waters of the Emmen, and stood now on a moist morning in the basin where that stream rises, at the foot of the mountain range that divided me from the lake.

The Brienzer Grat is an extraordinary thing. It is quite straight; its summits are, of course, of different heights, but from below they seem even, like a ridge: and, indeed, the whole mountain is more like a ridge than any other I have seen. At one end is a peak called the 'Red Horn', the other end falls suddenly above Interlaken, and wherever you should cut it you would get a section like this, for it is as steep as anything can be short of sheer rock. There are no precipices on it, though there are nasty slabs quite high enough to kill a man--I saw several of three or four hundred feet. It is about five or six thousand feet high, and it stands right up and along the northern shore of the lake of Brienz. I began the ascent.

Spongy meads, that soughed under the feet and grew steeper as one rose, took up the first few hundred feet. Little rivulets of mere dampness ran in among the under moss, and such very small hidden flowers as there were drooped with the surfeit of moisture. The rain was now indistinguishable from a mist, and indeed I had come so near to the level belt of cloud, that already its gloom was exchanged for that diffused light which fills vapours from within and lends them their mystery. A belt of thick brushwood and low trees lay before me, clinging to the slope, and as I pushed with great difficulty and many turns to right and left through its tangle a wisp of cloud enveloped me, and from that time on I was now in, now out, of a deceptive drifting fog, in which it was most difficult to gauge one's progress.

Now and then a higher mass of rock, a peak on the ridge, would showr clear through a corridor of cloud and be hidden again; also at times I would stand hesitating before a sharp wall or slab, and wait for a shifting of the fog to make sure of the best way round. I struck what might have been a loose path or perhaps only a gully; lost it again and found it again. In one place I climbed up a jagged surface for fifty feet, only to find when it cleared that it was no part of the general ascent, but a mere obstacle which might have been outflanked. At another time I stopped for a good quarter of an hour at an edge that might have been an indefinite fall of smooth rock, but that turned out to be a short drop, easy for a man, and not much longer than my body. So I went upwards always, drenched and doubting, and not sure of the height I had reached at any time.

At last I came to a place where a smooth stone lay between two pillared monoliths, as though it had been put there for a bench. Though all around me was dense mist, yet I could see above me the vague shape of a summit looming quite near. So I said to myself--

'I will sit here and wait till it grows lighter and clearer, for I must now be within two or three hundred feet of the top of the ridge, and as anything at all may be on the other side, I had best go carefully and knowing my way.'

So I sat down facing the way I had to go and looking upwards, till perhaps a movement of the air might show me against a clear sky the line of the ridge, and so let me estimate the work that remained to do. I kept my eyes fixed on the point where I judged that sky line to lie, lest I should miss some sudden gleam revealing it; and as I sat there I grew mournful and began to consider the folly of climbing this great height on an empty stomach. The soldiers of the Republic fought their battles often before breakfast, but never, I think, without having drunk warm coffee, and no one should attempt great efforts without some such refreshment before starting. Indeed, my fasting, and the rare thin air of the height, the chill and the dampness that had soaked my thin clothes through and through, quite lowered my blood and left it piano, whimpering and irresolute. I shivered and demanded the sun.

Then I bethought me of the hunk of bread I had stolen, and pulling it out of my haversack I began to munch that ungrateful breakfast. It was hard and stale, and gave me little sustenance; I still gazed upwards into the uniform meaningless light fog, looking for the ridge.

Suddenly, with no warning to prepare the mind, a faint but distinct wind blew upon me, the mist rose in a wreath backward and upward, and I was looking through clear immensity, not at any ridge, but over an awful gulf at great white fields of death. The Alps were right upon me and before me, overwhelming and commanding empty downward distances of air. Between them and me was a narrow dreadful space of nothingness and silence, and a sheer mile below us both, a floor to that prodigious hollow, lay the little lake.

My stone had not been a halting-place at all, but was itself the summit of the ridge, and those two rocks on either side of it framed a notch upon the very edge and skyline of the high hills of Brienz.

Surprise and wonder had not time to form in my spirit before both were swallowed up by fear. The proximity of that immense wall of cold, the Alps, seen thus full from the level of its middle height and comprehended as it cannot be from the depths; its suggestion of something never changing throughout eternity--yet dead--was a threat to the eager mind. They, the vast Alps, all wrapped round in ice, frozen, and their immobility enhanced by the delicate, roaming veils which (as from an attraction) hovered in their hollows, seemed to halt the process of living. And the living soul whom they thus perturbed was supported by no companionship. There were no trees or blades of grass around me, only the uneven and primal stones of that height. There were no birds in the gulf; there was no sound. And the whiteness of the glaciers, the blackness of the snow-streaked rocks beyond, was glistening and unsoftened. There had come something evil into their sublimity. I was afraid.

Nor could I bear to look downwards. The slope was in no way a danger. A man could walk up it without often using his hands, and a man could go down it slowly without any direct fall, though here and there he would have to turn round at each dip or step and hold with his hands and feel a little for his foothold. I suppose the general slope, down, down, to where the green began was not sixty degrees, but have you ever tried looking down five thousand feet at sixty degrees? It drags the mind after it, and I could not bear to begin the descent.

However I reasoned with myself. I said to myself that a man should only be afraid of real dangers. That nightmare was not for the daylight. That there was now no mist but a warm sun. Then choosing a gully where water sometimes ran, but now dry, I warily began to descend, using my staff and leaning well backwards.

There was this disturbing thing about the gully, that it went in steps, and before each step one saw the sky just a yard or two ahead: one lost the comforting sight of earth. One knew of course that it would only be a little drop, and that the slope would begin again, but it disturbed one. And it is a trial to drop or clamber down, say fourteen or fifteen feet, sometimes twenty, and then to find no flat foothold but that eternal steep beginning again. And this outline in which I have somewhat, but not much, exaggerated the slope, will show what I mean. The dotted line is the line of vision just as one got to a 'step'. The little figure is

AUCTOR. LECTOR is up in the air looking at him. Observe the perspective of the lake below, but make no comments.

I went very slowly. When I was about half-way down and had come to a place where a shoulder of heaped rock stood on my left and where little parallel ledges led up to it, having grown accustomed to the descent and easier in my mind, I sat down on a slab and drew imperfectly the things I saw: the lake below me, the first forests clinging to the foot of the Alps beyond, their higher slopes of snow, and the clouds that had now begun to gather round them and that altogether hid the last third of their enormous height.

Then I saw a steamer on the lake. I felt in touch with men. The slope grew easier. I snapped my fingers at the great devils that haunt high mountains. I sniffed the gross and comfortable air of the lower valleys, I entered the belt of wood and was soon going quite a pace through the trees, for I had found a path, and was now able to sing. So I did.

At last I saw through the trunks, but a few hundred feet below me, the highroad that skirts the lake. I left the path and scrambled straight down to it. I came to a wall which I climbed, and found myself in somebody's garden. Crossing this and admiring its wealth and order (I was careful not to walk on the lawns), I opened a little private gate and came on to the road, and from there to Brienz was but a short way along a fine hard surface in a hot morning sun, with the gentle lake on my right hand not five yards away, and with delightful trees upon my left, caressing and sometimes even covering me with their shade.

I was therefore dry, ready and contented when I entered by mid morning the curious town of Brienz, which is all one long street, and of which the population is Protestant. I say dry, ready and contented; dry in my clothes, ready for food, contented with men and nature. But as I entered I squinted up that interminable slope, I saw the fog wreathing again along the ridge so infinitely above me, and I considered myself a fool to have crossed the Brienzer Grat without breakfast. But I could get no one in Brienz to agree with me, because no one thought I had done it, though several people there could talk French.

The Grimsel Pass is the valley of the Aar; it is also the eastern flank of that great *massif*, or bulk and mass of mountains called the Bernese Oberland. Western Switzerland, you must know, is not (as I first thought it was when I gazed down from the Weissenstein) a plain surrounded by a ring of mountains, but rather it is a plain in its northern half (the plain of the lower Aar), and in its southern half it is two enormous parallel lumps of mountains. I call them 'lumps', because they are so very broad and tortuous in their plan that they are hardly ranges. Now these two lumps are the Bernese Oberland and the Pennine Alps, and between them runs a deep trench called the valley of the Rhone. Take Mont Blanc in the west and a peak called the Crystal Peak over the Val Bavona on the east, and they are the flanking bastions of one great wall, the Pennine Alps. Take the Diablerets on the west, and the Wetterhorn on the east, and they are the flanking bastions of another great wall, the Bernese Oberland. And these two walls are parallel, with the Rhone in between.

Now these two walls converge at a point where there is a sort of knot of mountain ridges, and this point may be taken as being on the boundary between Eastern and Western Switzerland. At this wonderful point the Ticino, the Rhone, the Aar, and the Reuss all begin, and it is here that the simple arrangement of the Alps to the west turns into the confused jumble of the Alps to the east.

When you are high up on either wall you can catch the plan of all this, but to avoid a confused description and to help you to follow the marvellous, Hannibalian and never-before-attempted charge and march which I made, and which, alas! ended only in a glorious defeat--to help you to picture faintly to yourselves the mirific and horripilant adventure whereby I nearly achieved superhuman success in spite of all the powers of the air, I append a little map which is rough but clear and plain, and which I beg you to study closely, for it will make it easy for you to understand what next happened in my pilgrimage.

The dark strips are the deep cloven valleys, the shaded belt is that higher land which is yet passable by any ordinary man. The part left white you may take to be the very high fields of ice and snow with great peaks which an ordinary man must regard as impassable, unless, indeed, he can wait for his weather and take guides and go on as a tourist instead of a pilgrim.

You will observe that I have marked five clefts or valleys. A is that of the *Aar*, and the little white patch at the beginning is the lake of Brienz. B is that of the *Reuss*. C is that of the *Rhone*; and all these three are *north* of the great watershed or main chain, and all three are full of German-speaking people.

On the other hand, D is the valley of the *Toccia*, E of the *Maggia*, and F of the *Ticino*. All these three are *south* of the great watershed, and are inhabited by Italian-speaking people. All these three lead down at last to Lake Major, and so to Milan and so to Rome.

The straight line to Rome is marked on my map by a dotted line ending in an arrow, and you will see that it was just my luck that it should cross slap over that knot or tangle of ranges where all the rivers spring. The problem was how to negotiate a passage from the valley of the Aar to one of the three Italian valleys, without departing too far from my straight line. To explain my track I must give the names of all the high passes between the valleys. That between A and C is called the *Grimsel*; that between B and C the *Furka*. That between D and C is the *Gries* Pass, that between F and C the *Nufenen*, and that between E and F is not the easy thing it looks on the map; indeed it is hardly a pass at all but a scramble over very high peaks, and it is called the Crystalline Mountain. Finally, on the far right of my map, you see a high passage between B and F. This is the famous St Gothard.

The straightest way of all was (1) over the *Grimsel*, then, the moment I got into the valley of the Rhone (2), up out of it again over the *Nufenen*, then the moment I was down into the valley of the *Ticino* (F), up out of it again (3) over the Crystalline to the valley of the *Maggia* (E). Once in the Maggia valley (the top of it is called the *Val Bavona),* it is a straight path for the lakes and Rome. There were also these advantages: that I should be in a place very rarely visited--all the guide-books are doubtful on it; that I should be going quite straight; that I should be accomplishing a feat, viz. the crossing of those high passes one after the other (and you must remember that over the Nufenen there is no road at all).

But every one I asked told me that thus early in the year (it was not the middle of June) I could not hope to scramble over the Crystalline. No one (they said) could do it and live. It was all ice and snow and cold mist and verglas, and the precipices were smooth--a man would never get across; so it was not worth while crossing the Nufenen Pass if I was to be balked at the Crystal, and I determined on the Gries Pass. I said to myself: 'I will go on over the Grimsel, and once in the valley of the Rhone, I will walk a mile or two down to where the Gries Pass opens, and I will go over it into Italy.' For the Gries Pass, though not quite in the straight line, had this advantage, that once over it you are really in Italy. In the Ticino valley or in the Val Bavona, though the people are as Italian as Catullus, yet politically they count as part of Switzerland; and therefore if you enter Italy thereby, you are not suddenly introduced to that country, but, as it were, inoculated, and led on by degrees, which is a pity. For good things should come suddenly, like the demise of that wicked man, Mr *(deleted by the censor)*, who had oppressed the poor for some forty years, when he was shot dead from behind a hedge, and died in about the time it takes to boil an egg, and there was an end of him.

Having made myself quite clear that I had a formed plan to go over the Grimsel by the new road, then up over the Gries, where there is no road at all, and so down into the vale of the Tosa, and having calculated that on the morrow I should be in Italy, I started out from Brienz after eating a great meal, it being then about midday, and I having already, as you know, crossed the Brienzer Grat since dawn.

The task of that afternoon was more than I could properly undertake, nor did I fulfil it. From Brienz to the top of the Grimsel is, as the crow flies, quite twenty miles, and by the road a good twenty-seven. It is true I had only come from over the high hills; perhaps six miles in a straight line. But what a six miles! and all without food. Not certain, therefore, how much of the pass I could really do that day, but aiming at crossing it, like a fool, I went on up the first miles.

For an hour or more after Brienz the road runs round the base of and then away from a fine great rock. There is here an alluvial plain like a continuation of the lake, and the Aar runs through it, canalized and banked and straight, and at last the road also becomes straight. On either side rise gigantic cliffs enclosing the valley, and (on the day I passed there) going up into the clouds, which, though high, yet made a roof for the valley. From the great mountains on the left the noble rock jutted out alone and dominated the little plain; on the right the buttresses of the main Alps all stood in a row, and between them went whorls of vapour high, high up--just above the places where snow still clung to the slopes. These whorls made the utmost steeps more and more misty, till at last they were lost in a kind of great darkness, in which the last and highest banks of ice seemed to be swallowed up. I often stopped to gaze straight above me, and I marvelled at the silence.

It was the first part of the afternoon when I got to a place called Meiringen, and I thought that there I would eat and drink a little more. So I steered into the main street, but there I found such a yelling and roaring as I had never heard before, and very damnable it was; as though men were determined to do common evil wherever God has given them a chance of living in awe and worship.

For they were all bawling and howling, with great placards and tickets, and saying, 'This way to the Extraordinary Waterfall; that way to the Strange Cave. Come with me and you shall see the never-to-be-forgotten Falls of the Aar,' and so forth. So that my illusion of being alone in the roots of the world dropped off me very quickly, and I wondered how people could be so helpless and foolish as to travel about in Switzerland as tourists and meet with all this vulgarity and beastliness.

If a man goes to drink good wine he does not say, 'So that the wine be good I do not mind eating strong pepper and smelling hartshorn as I drink it,' and if a man goes to read a good verse, for instance, Jean Richepin, he does not say, 'Go on playing on the trombone, go on banging the cymbals; so long as I am reading good verse I am content.' Yet men now go into the vast hills and sleep and live in their recesses, and pretend to be indifferent to all the touts and shouters and hurry and hotels and high prices and abominations. Thank God, it goes in grooves! I say it again, thank God, the railways are trenches that drain our modern marsh, for you have but to avoid railways, even by five miles, and you can get more peace than would fill a nosebag. All the world is my garden since they built railways, and gave me leave to keep off them.

Also I vowed a franc to the Black Virgin of La Delivrande (next time I should be passing there) because I was delivered from being a tourist, and because all this horrible noise was not being dinned at me (who was a poor and dirty pilgrim, and no kind of prey for these cabmen, and

95

busmen, and guides and couriers), but at a crowd of drawn, sad, jaded tourists that had come in by a train.

Soon I had left them behind. The road climbed the first step upwards in the valley, going round a rock on the other side of which the Aar had cut itself a gorge and rushed in a fall and rapids. Then the road went on and on weary mile after weary mile, and I stuck to it, and it rose slowly all the time, and all the time the Aar went dashing by, roaring and filling the higher valley with echoes.

I got beyond the villages. The light shining suffused through the upper mist began to be the light of evening. Rain, very fine and slight, began to fall. It was cold. There met and passed me, going down the road, a carriage with a hood up, driving at full speed. It could not be from over the pass, for I knew that it was not yet open for carriages or carts. It was therefore from a hotel somewhere, and if there was a hotel I should find it. I looked back to ask the distance, but they were beyond earshot, and so I went on.

My boots in which I had sworn to walk to Rome were ruinous. Already since the Weissenstein they had gaped, and now the Brienzer Grat had made the sole of one of them quite free at the toe. It flapped as I walked. Very soon I should be walking on my uppers. I limped also, and I hated the wet cold rain. But I had to go on. Instead of flourishing my staff and singing, I leant on it painfully and thought of duty, and death, and dereliction, and every other horrible thing that begins with a D. I had to go on. If I had gone back there was nothing for miles.

Before it was dark--indeed one could still read--I saw a group of houses beyond the Aar, and soon after I saw that my road would pass them, going over a bridge. When I reached them I went into the first, saying to myself, 'I will eat, and if I can go no farther I will sleep here.'

There were in the house two women, one old, the other young; and they were French-speaking, from the Vaud country. They had faces like Scotch people, and were very kindly, but odd, being Calvinist. I said, 'Have you any beans?' They said, 'Yes.' I suggested they should make me a dish of beans and bacon, and give me a bottle of wine, while I dried myself at their great stove. All this they readily did for me, and I ate heartily and drank heavily, and they begged me afterwards to stop the night and pay them for it; but I was so set up by my food and wine that I excused myself and went out again and took the road. It was not yet dark.

By some reflection from the fields of snow, which were now quite near at hand through the mist, the daylight lingered astonishingly late. The cold grew bitter as I went on through the gloaming. There were no trees save rare and stunted pines. The Aar was a shallow brawling torrent, thick with melting ice and snow and mud. Coarse grass grew on the rocks sparsely; there were no flowers. The mist overhead was now quite near, and I still went on and steadily up through the half-light. It was as lonely as a calm at sea, except for the noise of the river. I had overworn myself, and that sustaining surface which hides from us in our health the abysses below the mind--I felt it growing weak and thin. My fatigue bewildered me. The occasional steeps beside the road, one especially beneath a high bridge where a tributary falls into the Aar in a cascade, terrified me. They were like the emptiness of dreams. At last it being now dark, and I having long since entered the upper mist, or rather cloud (for I was now as high as the clouds), I saw a light gleaming through the fog, just off the road, through pine-trees. It was time. I could not have gone much farther.

To this I turned and found there one of those new hotels, not very large, but very expensive. They knew me at once for what I was, and welcomed me with joy. They gave me hot rum and sugar, a fine warm bed, told me I was the first that had yet stopped there that year, and left me to sleep very deep and yet in pain, as men sleep who are stunned. But twice that night I woke suddenly, staring at darkness. I had outworn the physical network upon which the soul depends, and I was full of terrors.

Next morning I had fine coffee and bread and butter and the rest, like a rich man; in a gilded dining-room all set out for the rich, and served by a fellow that bowed and scraped. Also they made me pay a great deal, and kept their eyes off my boots, and were still courteous to me, and I to them. Then I bought wine of them--the first wine not of the country that I had drunk on this march, a Burgundy--and putting it in my haversack with a nice white roll, left them to wait for the next man whom the hills might send them.

The clouds, the mist, were denser than ever in that early morning; one could only see the immediate road. The cold was very great; my clothes were not quite dried, but my heart was high, and I pushed along well enough, though stiffly, till I came to what they call the Hospice, which was once a monk-house, I suppose, but is now an inn. I had brandy there, and on going out I found that it stood at the foot of a sharp ridge which was the true Grimsel Pass, the neck which joins the Bernese Oberland to the eastern group of high mountains. This ridge or neck was steep like a pitched roof--very high I found it, and all of black glassy rock, with here and there snow in sharp, even, sloping sheets just holding to it. I could see but little of it at a time on account of the mist.

Hitherto for all these miles the Aar had been my companion, and the road, though rising always, had risen evenly and not steeply. Now the Aar was left behind in the icy glen where it rises, and the road went in an artificial and carefully built set of zig-zags up the face of the cliff. There is a short cut, but I could not find it in the mist. It is the old mule-path. Here and there, however, it was possible to cut off long corners by scrambling over the steep black rock and smooth ice, and all the while the cold, soft mist wisped in and out around me. After a thousand feet of this I came to the top of the Grimsel, but not before I had passed a place where an avalanche had destroyed the road and where planks were laid. Also before one got to the very summit, no short cuts or climbing were possible. The road ran deep in a cutting like a Devonshire lane. Only here the high banks were solid snow.

Some little way past the summit, on the first zig-zag down, I passed the Lake of the Dead in its mournful hollow. The mist still enveloped all the ridge-side, and moved like a press of spirits over the frozen water, then--as suddenly as on the much lower Brienzer Grat, and (as on the Brienzer Grat) to the southward and the sun, the clouds lifted and wreathed up backward and were gone, and where there had just been fulness was only an immensity of empty air and a sudden sight of clear hills beyond and of little strange distant things thousands and thousands of feet below.

LECTOR. Pray are we to have any more of that fine writing?

AUCTOR. I saw there as in a cup things that I had thought (when I first studied the map at home) far too spacious and spread apart to go into the view. Yet here they were all quite contained and close together, on so vast a scale was the whole place conceived. It was the comb of mountains of which I have written; the meeting of all the valleys.

There, from the height of a steep bank, as it were (but a bank many thousands of feet high), one looked down into a whole district or little world. On the map, I say, it had seemed so great that I had thought one would command but this or that portion of it; as it was, one saw it all.

And this is a peculiar thing I have noticed in all mountains, and have never been able to understand--- namely, that if you draw a plan or section to scale, your mountain does not seem a very important thing. One should not, in theory, be able to dominate from its height, nor to feel the world small below one, nor to hold a whole countryside in one's hand--yet one does. The mountains from their heights reveal to us two truths. They suddenly make us feel our insignificance, and at the same time they free the immortal Mind, and let it feel its greatness, and they release it from the earth. But I say again, in theory, when one considers the exact relation of their height to the distances one views from them, they ought to claim no such effect, and that they can produce that effect is related to another thing--the way in which they exaggerate their own steepness.

For instance, those noble hills, my downs in Sussex, when you are upon them overlooking the weald, from Chanctonbury say, feel like this--or even lower. Indeed, it is impossible to give them truly, so insignificant are they; if the stretch of the Weald were made nearly a yard long, Chanctonbury would not, in proportion, be more than a fifth of an inch high! And yet, from the top of Chanctonbury, how one seems to overlook it and possess it all!

Well, so it was here from the Grimsel when I overlooked the springs of the Rhone. In true proportion the valley I gazed into and over must have been somewhat like this--

It felt for all the world as deep and utterly below me as this other--

Moreover, where there was no mist, the air was so surprisingly clear that I could see everything clean and sharp wherever I turned my eyes. The mountains forbade any very far horizons to the view, and all that I could see was as neat and vivid as those coloured photographs they sell with bright green grass and bright white snow, and blue glaciers like precious stones.

I scrambled down the mountain, for here, on the south side of the pass, there was no snow or ice, and it was quite easy to leave the road and take the old path cutting off the zig-zags. As the air got heavier, I became hungry, and at the very end of my descent, two hundred feet or so above the young Rhone, I saw a great hotel. I went round to their front door and asked them whether I could eat, and at what price. 'Four francs,' they said.

'What!' said I, 'four francs for a meal! Come, let me eat in the kitchen, and charge me one.' But they became rude and obstinate, being used only to deal with rich people, so I cursed them, and went down the road. But I was very hungry.

The road falls quite steeply, and the Rhone, which it accompanies in that valley, leaps in little falls. On a bridge I passed a sad Englishman reading a book, and a little lower down, two American women in a carriage, and after that a priest (it was lucky I did not see him first. Anyhow, I touched iron at once, to wit, a key in my pocket), and after that a child minding a goat. Altogether I felt myself in the world again, and as I was on a good road, all down hill, I thought myself capable of pushing on to the next village. But my hunger was really excessive, my right boot almost gone, and my left boot nothing to exhibit or boast of, when I came to a point where at last one looked down the Rhone valley for miles. It is like a straight trench, and at intervals there are little villages, built of most filthy chalets, the said chalets raised on great stones. There are pine-trees up, up on either slope, into the clouds, and beyond the clouds I could not see. I left on my left a village called 'Between the Waters'. I passed through another called 'Ehringen', but it has no inn. At last, two miles farther, faint from lack of food, I got into Ulrichen, a village a little larger than the rest, and the place where I believed one should start to go either over the Gries or Nufenen Pass. In Ulrichen was a warm, wooden, deep-eaved, frousty, comfortable, ramshackle, dark, anyhow kind of a little inn called 'The Bear'. And entering, I saw one of the women whom god loves.

99

She was of middle age, very honest and simple in the face, kindly and good. She was messing about with cooking and stuff, and she came up to me stooping a little, her eyes wide and innocent, and a great spoon in her hand. Her face was extremely broad and flat, and I have never seen eyes set so far apart. Her whole gait, manner, and accent proved her to be extremely good, and on the straight road to heaven. I saluted her in the French tongue. She answered me in the same, but very broken and rustic, for her natural speech was a kind of mountain German. She spoke very slowly, and had a nice soft voice, and she did what only good people do, I mean, looked you in the eyes as she spoke to you.

Beware of shifty-eyed people. It is not only nervousness, it is also a kind of wickedness. Such people come to no good. I have three of them now in my mind as I write. One is a Professor.

And, by the way, would you like to know why universities suffer from this curse of nervous disease? Why the great personages stammer or have St Vitus' dance, or jabber at the lips, or hop in their walk, or have their heads screwed round, or tremble in the fingers, or go through life with great goggles like a motor car? Eh? I will tell you. It is the punishment of their *intellectual pride*, than which no sin is more offensive to the angels.

What! here are we with the jolly world of God all round us, able to sing, to draw, to paint, to hammer and build, to sail, to ride horses, to run, to leap; having for our splendid inheritance love in youth and memory in old age, and we are to take one miserable little faculty, our one-legged, knock-kneed, gimcrack, purblind, rough-skinned, underfed, and perpetually irritated and grumpy intellect, or analytical curiosity rather (a diseased appetite), and let it swell till it eats up every other function? Away with such foolery.

LECTOR. When shall we get on to ...

AUCTOR. Wait a moment. I say, away with such foolery. Note that pedants lose all proportion. They never can keep sane in a discussion. They will go wild on matters they are wholly unable to judge, such as Armenian Religion or the Politics of Paris or what not. Never do they use one of those three phrases which keep a man steady and balance his mind, I mean the words (1) After all it is not my business. (2) Tut! tut! You don't say so! and (3) Credo in Unum Deum Patrem Omnipotentem, Factorem omnium visibilium atque invisibilium; in which last there is a power of synthesis that can jam all their analytical dust-heap into such a fine, tight, and compact body as would make them stare to see. I understand that they need six months' holiday a year. Had I my way they should take twelve, and an extra day on leap years.

LECTOR. Pray, pray return to the woman at the inn.

AUCTOR. I will, and by this road: to say that on the day of Judgement, when St Michael weighs souls in his scales, and the wicked are led off by the Devil with a great rope, as you may see them over the main porch of Notre Dame (I will heave a stone after them myself I hope), all the souls of the pedants together will not weigh as heavy and sound as the one soul of this good woman at the inn.

She put food before me and wine. The wine was good, but in the food was some fearful herb or other I had never tasted before--a pure spice or scent, and a nasty one. One could taste nothing else, and it was revolting; but I ate it for her sake.

Then, very much refreshed, I rose, seized my great staff, shook myself and said, 'Now it is about noon, and I am off for the frontier.'

At this she made a most fearful clamour, saying that it was madness, and imploring me not to think of it, and running out fetched from the stable a tall, sad, pale-eyed man who saluted me profoundly and told me that he knew more of the mountains than any one for miles. And this by asking many afterwards I found out to be true. He said that he had crossed the Nufenen and the Gries whenever they could be crossed since he was a child, and that if I attempted it that day I should sleep that night in Paradise. The clouds on the mountain, the soft snow recently fallen, the rain that now occupied the valleys, the glacier on the Gries, and the pathless snow in the mist on the Nufenen would make it sheer suicide for him, an experienced guide, and for me a worse madness. Also he spoke of my boots and wondered at my poor coat and trousers, and threatened me with intolerable cold.

It seems that the books I had read at home, when they said that the Nufenen had no snow on it, spoke of a later season of the year; it was all snow now, and soft snow, and hidden by a full mist in such a day from the first third of the ascent. As for the Gries, there was a glacier on the top which needed some kind of clearness in the weather. Hearing all this I said I would remain--but it was with a heavy heart. Already I felt a shadow of defeat over me. The loss of time was a thorn. I was already short of cash, and my next money was Milan. My return to England was fixed for a certain date, and stronger than either of these motives against delay was a burning restlessness that always takes men when they are on the way to great adventures.

I made him promise to wake me next morning at three o'clock, and, short of a tempest, to try and get me across the Gries. As for the Nufenen and Crystalline passes which I had desired to attempt, and which were (as I have said) the straight line to Rome, he said (and he was right), that let alone the impassability of the Nufenen just then, to climb the Crystal Mountain in that season would be as easy as flying to the moon. Now, to cross the Nufenen alone, would simply land me in the upper valley of the Ticino, and take me a great bend out of my way by Bellinzona. Hence my bargain that at least he should show me over the Gries Pass, and this he said, if man could do it, he would do the next day; and I, sending my boots to be cobbled (and thereby breaking another vow), crept up to bed, and all afternoon read the school-books of the children. They were in French, from lower down the valley, and very Genevese and heretical for so devout a household. But the Genevese civilization is the standard for these people, and they combat the Calvinism of it with missions, and have statues in their rooms, not to speak of holy water stoups.

The rain beat on my window, the clouds came lower still down the mountain. Then (as is finely written in the Song of Roland), 'the day passed and the night came, and I slept.' But with the coming of the small hours, and with my waking, prepare yourselves for the most extraordinary and terrible adventure that befell me out of all the marvels and perils of this pilgrimage, the most momentous and the most worthy of perpetual record, I think, of all that has ever happened since the beginning of the world.

At three o'clock the guide knocked at my door, and I rose and came out to him. We drank coffee and ate bread. We put into our sacks ham and bread, and he white wine and I brandy. Then we set out. The rain had dropped to a drizzle, and there was no wind. The sky was obscured for the most part, but here and there was a star. The hills hung awfully above us in the night as we crossed the spongy valley. A little wooden bridge took us over the young Rhone, here only a stream, and we followed a path up into the tributary ravine which leads to the Nufenen and the Gries. In a mile or two it was a little lighter, and this was as well, for some weeks before a great avalanche had fallen, and we had to cross it gingerly. Beneath the wide cap of frozen snow ran a torrent roaring. I remembered Colorado, and how I had crossed the Arkansaw on such a bridge as a boy. We went on in the uneasy dawn. The woods began to show, and there was a cross where a man had slipped from above that very April and been killed. Then, most ominous and disturbing, the drizzle changed to a rain, and the guide shook his head and said it would be snowing higher up. We went on, and it grew lighter. Before it was really day (or else the weather confused and darkened the sky), we crossed a good bridge, built long ago, and we halted at a shed where the cattle lie in the late summer when the snow is melted. There we rested a moment.

But on leaving its shelter we noticed many disquieting things. The place was a hollow, the end of the ravine--a bowl, as it were; one way out of which is the Nufenen, and the other the Gries.

Here it is in a sketch map. The heights are marked lighter and lighter, from black in the valleys to white in the impassable mountains. E is where we stood, in a great cup or basin, having just come up the ravine B. C is the Italian valley of the Tosa, and the neck between it and E is the Gries. D is the valley of the Ticino, and the neck between E and it is the Nufenen. A is the Crystal Mountain. You may take the necks or passes to be about 8000, and the mountains 10,000 or 11,000 feet above the sea.

We noticed, I say, many disquieting things. First, all, that bowl or cup below the passes was a carpet of snow, save where patches of black water showed, and all the passes and mountains, from top to bottom, were covered with very thick snow; the deep surface of it soft and fresh fallen. Secondly, the rain had turned into snow. It was falling thickly all around. Nowhere have I more perceived the immediate presence of great Death. Thirdly, it was far colder, and we felt the beginning of a wind. Fourthly, the clouds had come quite low down.

The guide said it could not be done, but I said we must attempt it. I was eager, and had not yet felt the awful grip of the cold. We left the Nufenen on our left, a hopeless steep of new snow buried in fog, and we attacked the Gries. For half-an-hour we plunged on through snow above our knees, and my thin cotton clothes were soaked. So far the guide knew we were more or less on the path, and he went on and I panted after him. Neither of us spoke, but occasionally he looked back to make sure I had not dropped out.

The snow began to fall more thickly, and the wind had risen somewhat. I was afraid of another protest from the guide, but he stuck to it well, and I after him, continually plunging through soft snow and making yard after yard upwards. The snow fell more thickly and the wind still rose.

We came to a place which is, in the warm season, an alp; that is, a slope of grass, very steep but not terrifying; having here and there sharp little precipices of rock breaking it into steps, but by no means (in summer) a matter to make one draw back. Now, however, when everything was still Arctic it was a very different matter. A sheer steep of snow whose downward plunge ran into the driving storm and was lost, whose head was lost in the same mass of thick cloud above, a slope somewhat hollowed and bent inwards, had to be crossed if we were to go any farther; and I was terrified, for I knew nothing of climbing. The guide said there was little danger, only if one slipped one might slide down to safety, or one might (much less probably) get over rocks and be killed. I was chattering a little with cold; but as he did not propose a return, I followed him. The surface was alternately slabs of frozen snow and patches of soft new snow. In the first he cut steps, in the second we plunged, and once I went right in and a mass of snow broke off beneath me and went careering down the slope. He showed me how to hold my staff backwards as he did his alpenstock, and use it as a kind of brake in case I slipped.

We had been about twenty minutes crawling over that wall of snow and ice; and it was more and more apparent that we were in for danger. Before we had quite reached the far side, the wind was blowing a very full gale and roared past our ears. The surface snow was whirring furiously like dust before it: past our faces and against them drove the snow-flakes, cutting the air: not falling, but making straight darts and streaks. They seemed like the form of the whistling wind; they blinded us. The rocks on the far side of the slope, rocks which had been our goal when we set out to cross it, had long ago disappeared in the increasing rush of the blizzard. Suddenly as we were still painfully moving on, stooping against the mad wind, these rocks loomed up over as large as houses, and we saw them through the swarming snow-flakes as great hulls are seen through a fog at sea. The guide crouched under the lee of the nearest; I came up close to him and he put his hands to my ear and shouted to me that nothing further could be done--he had so to shout because in among the rocks the hurricane made a roaring sound, swamping the voice.

I asked how far we were from the summit. He said he did not know where we were exactly, but that we could not be more than 800 feet from it. I was but that from Italy and I would not admit defeat. I offered him all I had in money to go on, but it was folly in me, because if I had had enough to tempt him and if he had yielded we should both have died. Luckily it was but a little sum. He shook his head. He would not go on, he broke out, for all the money there was in the world. He shouted me to eat and drink, and so we both did.

Then I understood his wisdom, for in a little while the cold began to seize me in my thin clothes. My hands were numb, my face already gave me intolerable pain, and my legs suffered and felt heavy. I learnt another thing (which had I been used to mountains I should have known), that it was not a simple thing to return. The guide was hesitating whether to stay in this rough shelter, or to face the chances of the descent. This terror had not crossed my mind, and I thought as little of it as I could, needing my courage, and being near to breaking down from the intensity of the cold.

It seems that in a *tourmente* (for by that excellent name do the mountain people call such a storm) it is always a matter of doubt whether to halt or go back. If you go back through it and lose your way, you are done for. If you halt in some shelter, it may go on for two or three days, and then there is an end of you.

After a little he decided for a return, but he told me honestly what the chances were, and my suffering from cold mercifully mitigated my fear. But even in that moment, I felt in a confused but very conscious way that I was defeated. I had crossed so many great hills and rivers, and pressed so well on my undeviating arrow-line to Rome, and I had charged this one great barrier manfully where the straight path of my pilgrimage crossed the Alps--and I had failed! Even in that fearful cold I felt it, and it ran through my doubt of return like another and deeper current of pain. Italy was there, just above, right to my hand. A lifting of a cloud, a little respite, and every downward step would have been towards the sunlight. As it was, I was being driven back northward, in retreat and ashamed. The Alps had conquered me.

Let us always after this combat their immensity and their will, and always hate the inhuman guards that hold the gates of Italy, and the powers that lie in wait for men on those high places. But now I know that Italy will always stand apart. She is cut off by no ordinary wall, and Death has all his army on her frontiers.

Well, we returned. Twice the guide rubbed my hands with brandy, and once I had to halt and recover for a moment, failing and losing my hold. Believe it or not, the deep footsteps of our ascent were already quite lost and covered by the new snow since our halt, and even had they been visible, the guide would not have retraced them. He did what I did not at first understand, but what I soon saw to be wise. He took a steep slant downward over the face of the snow-slope, and though such a pitch of descent a little unnerved me, it was well in the end. For when we had gone down perhaps 900 feet, or a thousand, in perpendicular distance, even I, half numb and fainting, could feel that the storm was less violent. Another two hundred, and the flakes could be seen not driving in flashes past, but separately falling. Then in some few minutes we could see the slope for a very long way downwards quite clearly; then, soon after, we saw far below us the place where the mountain-side merged easily into the plain of that cup or basin whence we had started.

When we saw this, the guide said to me, 'Hold your stick thus, if you are strong enough, and let yourself slide.' I could just hold it, in spite of the cold. Life was returning to me with intolerable pain. We shot down the slope almost as quickly as falling, but it was evidently safe to do so, as the end was clearly visible, and had no break or rock in it.

So we reached the plain below, and entered the little shed, and thence looking up, we saw the storm above us; but no one could have told it for what it was. Here, below, was silence, and the terror and raging above seemed only a great trembling cloud occupying the mountain. Then we set our faces down the ravine by which we had come up, and so came down to where the snow changed to rain. When we got right down into the valley of the Rhone, we found it all roofed with cloud, and the higher trees were white with snow, making a line like a tide mark on the slopes of the hills.

I re-entered 'The Bear', silent and angered, and not accepting the humiliation of that failure. Then, having eaten, I determined in equal silence to take the road like any other fool; to cross the Furka by a fine highroad, like any tourist, and to cross the St Gothard by another fine highroad, as millions had done before me, and not to look heaven in the face again till I was back after my long detour, on the straight road again for Rome.

But to think of it! I who had all that planned out, and had so nearly done it! I who had cut a path across Europe like a shaft, and seen so many strange places!--now to have to recite all the litany of the vulgar; Bellinzona, Lugano, and this and that, which any railway travelling fellow can tell you. Not till Como should I feel a man again ...

Indeed it is a bitter thing to have to give up one's sword.

I had not the money to wait; my defeat had lowered me in purse as well as in heart. I started off to enter by the ordinary gates--not Italy even, but a half-Italy, the canton of the Ticino. It was very hard.

This book is not a tragedy, and I will not write at any length of such pain. That same day, in the latter half of it, I went sullenly over the Furka; exactly as easy a thing as going up St James' Street and down Piccadilly. I found the same storm on its summit, but on a highroad it was a different affair. I took no short cuts. I drank at all the inns--at the base, half-way up, near the top, and at the top. I told them, as the snow beat past, how I had attacked and all but conquered the Gries that wild morning, and they took me for a liar; so I became silent even within my own mind. I looked sullenly at the white ground all the way. And when on the far side I had got low enough to be rid of the snow and wind and to be in the dripping rain again, I welcomed the rain, and let it soothe like a sodden friend my sodden uncongenial mind.

I will not write of Hospenthal. It has an old tower, and the road to it is straight and hideous. Much I cared for the old tower! The people of the inn (which I chose at random) cannot have loved me much.

I will not write of the St Gothard. Get it out of a guide-book. I rose when I felt inclined; I was delighted to find it still raining. A dense mist above the rain gave me still greater pleasure. I had started quite at my leisure late in the day, and I did the thing stolidly, and my heart was like a dully-heated mass of coal or iron because I was acknowledging defeat. You who have never taken a straight line and held it, nor seen strange men and remote places, you do not know what it is to have to go round by the common way.

Only in the afternoon, and on those little zig-zags which are sharper than any other in the Alps (perhaps the road is older), something changed.

A warm air stirred the dense mist which had mercifully cut me off from anything but the mere road and from the contemplation of hackneyed sights.

A hint or memory of gracious things ran in the slight breeze, the wreaths of fog would lift a little for a few yards, and in their clearings I thought to approach a softer and more desirable world. I was soothed as though with caresses and when I began to see somewhat farther and

106

felt a vigour and fulness in the outline of the Trees, I said to myself suddenly--

'I know what it is! It is the South, and a great part of my blood. They may call it Switzerland still, but I know now that I am in Italy, and this is the gate of Italy lying in groves.'

Then and on till evening I reconciled myself with misfortune, and when I heard again at Airolo the speech of civilized men, and saw the strong Latin eyes and straight forms of the Race after all those days of fog and frost and German speech and the north, my eyes filled with tears and I was as glad as a man come home again, and I could have kissed the ground.

The wine of Airolo and its songs, how greatly they refreshed me! To see men with answering eyes and to find a salute returned; the noise of careless mouths talking all together; the group at cards, and the laughter that is proper to mankind; the straight carriage of the women, and in all the people something erect and noble as though indeed they possessed the earth. I made a meal there, talking to all my companions left and right in a new speech of my own, which was made up, as it were, of the essence of all the Latin tongues, saying--

'Ha! Si jo a traversa li montagna no erat facile! Nenni! Il san Gottardo? Nil est! pooh! poco! Ma hesterna jo ha voulu traversar in Val Bavona, e credi non ritornar, namfredo, fredo erat in alto! La tourmente ma prise...'

And so forth, explaining all fully with gestures, exaggerating, emphasizing, and acting the whole matter, so that they understood me without much error. But I found it more difficult to understand them, because they had a regular formed language with terminations and special words.

It went to my heart to offer them no wine, but a thought was in me of which you shall soon hear more. My money was running low, and the chief anxiety of a civilized man was spreading over my mind like the shadow of a cloud over a field of corn in summer. They gave me a number of 'good-nights', and at parting I could not forbear from boasting that I was a pilgrim on my way to Rome. This they repeated one to another, and one man told me that the next good halting-place was a town called Faido, three hours down the road. He held up three fingers to explain, and that was the last intercourse I had with the Airolans, for at once I took the road.

I glanced up the dark ravine which I should have descended had I crossed the Nufenen. I thought of the Val Bavona, only just over the great wall that held the west; and in one place where a rift (you have just seen its picture) led up to the summits of the hills I was half tempted to go back to Airolo and sleep and next morning to attempt a crossing. But I had accepted my fate on the Gries and the falling road also held me, and so I continued my way.

Everything was pleasing in this new valley under the sunlight that still came strongly from behind the enormous mountains; everything also was new, and I was evidently now in a country of a special kind. The slopes were populous, I had come to the great mother of fruits and men, and I was soon to see her cities and her old walls, and the rivers that glide by them. Church towers also repeated the same shapes up and up the wooded hills until the villages stopped at the line of the higher slopes and at the patches of snow. The houses were square and coloured; they were graced with arbours, and there seemed to be all around nothing but what was reasonable and secure, and especially no rich or poor.

I noticed all these things on the one side and the other till, not two hours from Airolo, I came to a step in the valley. For the valley of the Ticino is made up of distinct levels, each of which might have held a lake once for the way it is enclosed: and each level ends in high rocks with a gorge between them. Down this gorge the river tumbles in falls and rapids and the road picks its way down steeply, all banked and cut, and sometimes has to cross from side to side by a bridge, while the railway above one overcomes the sharp descent by running round into the heart of the hills through circular tunnels and coming out again far below the cavern where it plunged in. Then when all three--the river, the road, and the railway--- have got over the great step, a new level of the valley opens. This is the way the road comes into the south, and as I passed down to the lower valley, though it was darkening into evening, something melted out of the mountain air, there was content and warmth in the growing things, and I found it was a place for vineyards. So, before it was yet dark, I came into Faido, and there I slept, having at last, after so many adventures, crossed the threshold and occupied Italy.

Next day before sunrise I went out, and all the valley was adorned and tremulous with the films of morning.

Now all of you who have hitherto followed the story of this great journey, put out of your minds the Alps and the passes and the snows-- postpone even for a moment the influence of the happy dawn and of that South into which I had entered, and consider only this truth, that I found myself just out of Faido on this blessed date of God with eight francs and forty centimes for my viaticum and temporal provision wherewith to accomplish the good work of my pilgrimage.

Now when you consider that coffee and bread was twopence and a penny for the maid, you may say without lying that I had left behind me the escarpment of the Alps and stood upon the downward slopes of the first Italian stream and at the summit of the entry road with *eight francs ten centimes* in my pocket--my body hearty and my spirit light, for the

108

arriving sun shot glory into the sky. The air was keen, and a fresh day came radiant over the high eastern walls of the valley.

And what of that? Why, one might make many things of it. For instance, eight francs and ten centimes is a very good day's wages; it is a lot to spend in cab fares but little for a *coupe*. It is a heavy price for Burgundy but a song for Tokay. It is eighty miles third-class and more; it is thirty or less first-class; it is a flash in a train *de luxe*, and a mere fleabite as a bribe to a journalist. It would be enormous to give it to an apostle begging at a church door, but nothing to spend on luncheon.

Properly spent I can imagine it saving five or six souls, but I cannot believe that so paltry a sum would damn half an one.

Then, again, it would be a nice thing to sing about. Thus, if one were a modern fool one might write a dirge with 'Huit francs et dix centimes' all chanted on one low sad note, and coming in between brackets for a 'motif, and with a lot about autumn and Death--which last, Death that is, people nowadays seem to regard as something odd, whereas it is well known to be the commonest thing in the world. Or one might make the words the Backbone of a triolet, only one would have to split them up to fit it into the metre; or one might make it the decisive line in a sonnet; or one might make a pretty little lyric of it, to the tune of 'Madame la Marquise'--

'Huit francs et dix centimes, Tra la la, la la la.'

Or one might put it rhetorically, fiercely, stoically, finely, republicanly into the Heroics of the Great School. Thus--

HERNANI *(with indignation)... dans ces efforts sublimes* 'Qu'avez vous a offrir?'

RUY BLAS *(simply) Huit francs et dix centimes!*

Or finally (for this kind of thing cannot go on for ever), one might curl one's hair and dye it black, and cock a dirty slouch hat over one ear and take a guitar and sit on a flat stone by the roadside and cross one's legs, and, after a few pings and pongs on the strings, strike up a Ballad with the refrain--

Car j'ai toujours huit francs et dix centimes! a jocular, sub-sardonic, a triumphant refrain!

But all this is by the way; the point is, why was the eight francs and ten centimes of such importance just there and then?

For this reason, that I could get no more money before Milan; and I think a little reflection will show you what a meaning lies in that phrase. Milan was nearer ninety miles than eighty miles off. By the strict road it was over ninety. And so I was forced to consider and to be anxious, for how would this money hold out?

There was nothing for it but forced marches, and little prospect of luxuries. But could it be done?

I thought it could, and I reasoned this way.

'It is true I need a good deal of food, and that if a man is to cover great distances he must keep fit. It is also true that many men have done more on less. On the other hand, they were men who were not pressed for time--I am; and I do not know the habits of the country. Ninety miles is three good days; two very heavy days. Indeed, whether it can be done at all in two is doubtful. But it can be done in two days, two nights, and half the third day. So if I plan it thus I shall achieve it; namely, to march say forty-five miles or more to-day, and to sleep rough at the end of it. My food may cost me altogether three francs. I march the next day twenty-five to thirty, my food costing me another three francs. Then with the remaining two francs and ten centimes I will take a bed at the end of the day, and coffee and bread next morning, and will march the remaining twenty miles or less (as they may be) into Milan with a copper or two in my pocket. Then in Milan, having obtained my money, I will eat.'

So I planned with very careful and exact precision, but many accidents and unexpected things, diverting my plans, lay in wait for me among the hills.

And to cut a long story short, as the old sailor said to the young fool--

LECTOR. What did the old sailor say to the young fool?

AUCTOR. Why, the old sailor was teaching the young fool his compass, and he said---

'Here we go from north, making round by west, and then by south round by east again to north. There are thirty-two points of the compass, namely, first these four, N., W., S., and E., and these are halved, making four more, viz., NW., S W., SE., and NE. I trust I make myself clear,' said the old sailor.

'That makes eight divisions, as we call them. So look smart and follow. Each of these eight is divided into two symbolically and symmetrically divided parts, as is most evident in the nomenclature of the same,' said the old sailor. 'Thus between N. and NE. is NNE., between NE. and E. is ENE., between E. and SE. is...'

'I see,' said the young fool.

The old sailor, frowning at him, continued--

'Smart you there. Heels together, and note you well. Each of these sixteen divisions is separated quite reasonably and precisely into two. Thus between N. and NNE. we get N. by E.,' said the old sailor; 'and between NNE. and NE. we get NE. by E., and between NE. and ENE. we get NE. by E.,' said the old sailor; 'and between ENE. and E. we get E. by N., and then between E. and ESE. we get...'

But here he noticed something dangerous in the young fool's eyes, and having read all his life Admiral Griles' 'Notes on Discipline', and knowing that discipline is a subtle bond depending 'not on force but on an attitude of the mind,' he continued--

'And so TO CUT A LONG STORY SHORT we come round to the north again.' Then he added, 'It is customary also to divide each of these points into quarters. Thus NNE. 3/4 E. signifies...'

But at this point the young fool, whose hands were clasped behind him and concealed a marlin-spike, up and killed the old sailor, and so rounded off this fascinating tale.

Well then, to cut a long story short, I had to make forced marches. With eight francs and ten centimes, and nearer ninety than eighty-five miles before the next relief, it was necessary to plan and then to urge on heroically. Said I to myself, 'The thing can be done quite easily. What is ninety miles? Two long days! Who cannot live on four francs a day? Why, lots of men do it on two francs a day.'

But my guardian angel said to me, 'You are an ass! Ninety miles is a great deal more than twice forty-five. Besides which' (said he) 'a great effort needs largeness and ease. Men who live on two francs a day or less are not men who attempt to march forty-five miles a day. Indeed, my friend, you are pushing it very close.'

'Well,' thought I, 'at least in such a glorious air, with such Hills all about one, and such a race, one can come to no great harm.'

But I knew within me that Latins are hard where money is concerned, and I feared for my strength. I was determined to push forward and to live on little. I filled my lungs and put on the spirit of an attempt and swung down the valley.

Alas! I may not linger on that charge, for if I did I should not give you any measure of its determination and rapidity. Many little places passed me off the road on the flanks of that valley, and mostly to the left. While the morning was yet young, I came to the packed little town of Bodio, and passed the eight franc limit by taking coffee, brandy, and bread. There also were a gentleman and a lady in a carriage who wondered where I was going, and I told them (in French) 'to Rome'. It was nine in the morning when I came to Biasca. The sun was glorious, and not yet warm: it was too early for a meal. They gave me a little cold meat and bread and wine, and seven francs stood out dry above the falling tide of my money.

Here at Biasca the valley took on a different aspect. It became wider and more of a countryside; the vast hills, receding, took on an appearance of less familiar majesty, and because the trend of the Ticino turned southerly some miles ahead the whole place seemed enclosed from the world. One would have said that a high mountain before me closed it in and rendered it unique and unknown, had not a wide cleft in the east argued another pass over the hills, and reminded me that there were various routes over the crest of the Alps.

Indeed, this hackneyed approach to Italy which I had dreaded and despised and accepted only after a defeat was very marvellous, and this valley of the Ticino ought to stand apart and be a commonwealth of its own like Andorra or the Gresivaudan: the noble garden of the Isere within the first gates of the Dauphine.

I was fatigued, and my senses lost acuteness. Still I noticed with delight the new character of the miles I pursued. A low hill just before me, jutting out apparently from the high western mountains, forbade me to see beyond it. The plain was alluvial, while copses and wood and many cultivated fields now found room where, higher up, had been nothing but the bed of a torrent with bare banks and strips of grass immediately above them; it was a place worthy of a special name and of being one lordship and a countryside. Still I went on towards that near boundary of the mountain spur and towards the point where the river rounded it, the great barrier hill before me still seeming to shut in the valley.

It was noon, or thereabouts, the heat was increasing (I did not feel it greatly, for I had eaten and drunk next to nothing), when, coming round the point, there opened out before me the great fan of the lower valley and the widening and fruitful plain through which the Ticino rolls in a full river to reach Lake Major, which is its sea.

Weary as I was, the vision of this sudden expansion roused me and made me forget everything except the sight before me. The valley turned well southward as it broadened. The Alps spread out on either side like great arms welcoming the southern day; the wholesome and familiar haze that should accompany summer dimmed the more distant mountains of the lakes and turned them amethystine, and something of repose and of distance was added to the landscape; something I had not seen for many days. There was room in that air and space for dreams and for many living men, for towns perhaps on the slopes, for the boats of happy men upon the waters, and everywhere for crowded and contented living. History might be in all this, and I remembered it was the entry and introduction of many armies. Singing therefore a song of Charlemagne, I swung on in a good effort to where, right under the sun, what seemed a wall and two towers on a sharp little hillock set in the bosom of the valley showed me Bellinzona. Within the central street of that city, and on its shaded side, I sank down upon a bench before the curtained door of a drinking booth and boasted that I had covered in that morning my twenty-five miles.

The woman of the place came out to greet me, and asked me a question. I did not catch it (for it was in a foreign language), but guessing her to mean that I should take something, I asked for vermouth, and seeing before me a strange door built of red stone, I drew it as I sipped my glass and the woman talked to me all the while in a language I could not understand. And as I drew I became so interested that I forgot my poverty and offered her husband a glass, and then gave another to a lounging man that had watched me at work, and so from less than seven francs my money fell to six exactly, and my pencil fell from my hand, and I became afraid.

'I have done a foolish thing,' said I to myself, 'and have endangered the success of my endeavour. Nevertheless, that cannot now be remedied, and I must eat; and as eating is best where one has friends I will ask a meal of this woman.'

Now had they understood French I could have bargained and chosen; as it was I had to take what they were taking, and so I sat with them as they all came out and ate together at the little table. They had soup and flesh, wine and bread, and as we ate we talked, not understanding each other, and laughing heartily at our mutual ignorance. And they charged me a franc, which brought my six francs down to five. But I, knowing my subtle duty to the world, put down twopence more, as I would have done anywhere else, for a *pour boire;* and so with four francs and eighty centimes left, and with much less than a third of my task accomplished I rose, now drowsy with the food and wine, and saluting them, took the road once more.

But as I left Bellinzona there was a task before me which was to bring my poverty to the test; for you must know that my map was a bad one, and on a very small scale, and the road from Bellinzona to Lugano has a crook in it, and it was essential to find a short cut. So I thought to myself, 'I will try to see a good map as cheaply as possible,' and I slunk off to the right into a kind of main square, and there I found a proud stationer's shop, such as would deal with rich men only, or tourists of the coarser and less humble kind. I entered with some assurance, and said in French--

'Sir, I wish to know the hills between here and Lugano, but I am too poor to buy a map. If you will let me look at one for a few moments, I will pay you what you think fit.'

The wicked stationer became like a devil for pride, and glaring at me, said--

'Look! Look for yourself. I do not take pence. I sell maps; I do not hire them!'

Then I thought, 'Shall I take a favour from such a man?' But I yielded, and did. I went up to the wall and studied a large map for some moments. Then as I left, I said to him--

'Sir, I shall always hold in remembrance the day on which you did me this signal kindness; nor shall I forget your courtesy and goodwill.'

And what do you think he did at that?

Why, he burst into twenty smiles, and bowed and seemed beatified, and said: 'Whatever I can do for my customers and for visitors to this town, I shall always be delighted to do. Pray, sir, will you not look at other maps for a moment?'

Now, why did he say this and grin happily like a gargoyle appeased? Did something in my accent suggest wealth? or was he naturally kindly? I do not know; but of this I am sure, one should never hate human beings merely on a first, nor on a tenth, impression. Who knows? This map-seller of Bellinzona may have been a good man; anyhow, I left him as rich as I had found him, and remembering that the true key to a forced march is to break the twenty-four hours into three pieces, and now feeling the extreme heat, I went out along the burning straight road until I found a border of grass and a hedge, and there, in spite of the dust and the continually passing carts, I lay at full length in the shade and fell into the sleep of men against whom there is no reckoning. Just as I forgot the world I heard a clock strike two.

I slept for hours beneath that hedge, and when I woke the air was no longer a trembling furnace, but everything about me was wrapped round as in a cloak of southern afternoon, and was still. The sun had fallen midway, and shone in steady glory through a haze that overhung Lake Major, and the wide luxuriant estuary of the vale. There lay before me a long straight road for miles at the base of high hills; then, far off, this road seemed to end at the foot of a mountain called, I believe, Ash Mount or Cinder Hill. But my imperfect map told me that here it went sharp round to the left, choosing a pass, and then at an angle went down its way to Lugano.

Now Lugano was not fifteen miles as the crow flies from where I stood, and I determined to cut off that angle by climbing the high hills just above me. They were wooded only on their slopes; their crest and much of their sides were a down-land of parched grass, with rocks appearing here and there. At the first divergent lane I made off eastward from the road and began to climb.

114

In under the chestnut trees the lane became a number of vague beaten paths; I followed straight upwards. Here and there were little houses standing hidden in leaves, and soon I crossed the railway, and at last above the trees I saw the sight of all the Bellinzona valley to the north; and turning my eyes I saw it broaden out between its walls to where the lake lay very bright, in spite of the slight mist, and this mist gave the lake distances, and the mountains round about it were transfigured and seemed part of the mere light.

The Italian lakes have that in them and their air which removes them from common living. Their beauty is not the beauty which each of us sees for himself in the world; it is rather the beauty of a special creation; the expression of some mind. To eyes innocent, and first freshly noting our great temporal inheritance--1 mean to the eyes of a boy and girl just entered upon the estate of this glorious earth, and thinking themselves immortal, this shrine of Europe might remain for ever in the memory; an enchanted experience, in which the single sense of sight had almost touched the boundary of music. They would remember these lakes as the central emotion of their youth. To mean men also who, in spite of years and of a full foreknowledge of death, yet attempt nothing but the satisfaction of sense, and pride themselves upon the taste and fineness with which they achieve this satisfaction, the Italian lakes would seem a place for habitation, and there such a man might build his house contentedly. But to ordinary Christians I am sure there is something unnatural in this beauty of theirs, and they find in it either a paradise only to be won by a much longer road to a bait and veil of sorcery, behind which lies great peril. Now, for all we know, beauty beyond the world may not really bear this double aspect; but to us on earth--if we are ordinary men--beauty of this kind has something evil. Have you not read in books how men when they see even divine visions are terrified? So as I looked at Lake Major in its halo I also was afraid, and I was glad to cross the ridge and crest of the hill and to shut out that picture framed all round with glory.

But on the other side of the hill I found, to my great disgust, not as I had hoped, a fine slope down leading to Lugano, but a second interior valley and another range just opposite me. I had not the patience to climb this so I followed down the marshy land at the foot of it, passed round the end of the hill and came upon the railway, which had tunnelled under the range I had crossed. I followed the railway for a little while and at last crossed it, penetrated through a thick brushwood, forded a nasty little stream, and found myself again on the main road, wishing heartily I had never left it.

It was still at least seven miles to Lugano, and though all the way was downhill, yet fatigue threatened me. These short cuts over marshy land and through difficult thickets are not short cuts at all, and I was just wondering whether, although it was already evening, I dared not rest a while, when there appeared at a turn in the road a little pink house with a yard all shaded over by a vast tree; there was also a trellis making a roof over a plain bench and table, and on the trellis grew vines.

'Into such houses,' I thought, 'the gods walk when they come down and talk with men, and such houses are the scenes of adventures. I will go in and rest.'

So I walked straight into the courtyard and found there a shrivelled brown-faced man with kindly eyes, who was singing a song to himself. He could talk a little French, a little English, and his own Italian language. He had been to America and to Paris; he was full of memories; and when I had listened to these and asked for food and drink, and said I was extremely poor and would have to bargain, he made a kind of litany of 'I will not cheat you; I am an honest man; I also am poor,' and so forth. Nevertheless I argued about every item-- the bread, the sausage, and the beer. Seeing that I was in necessity, he charged me about three times their value, but I beat him down to double, and lower than that he would not go. Then we sat down together at the table and ate and drank and talked of far countries; and he would interject remarks on his honesty compared with the wickedness of his neighbours, and I parried with illustrations of my poverty and need, pulling out the four francs odd that remained to me, and jingling them sorrowfully in my hand. 'With these,' I said, 'I must reach Milan.'

Then I left him, and as I went down the road a slight breeze came on, and brought with it the coolness of evening.

At last the falling plateau reached an edge, many little lights glittered below me, and I sat on a stone and looked down at the town of Lugano. It was nearly dark. The mountains all around had lost their mouldings, and were marked in flat silhouettes against the sky. The new lake which had just appeared below me was bright as water is at dusk, and far away in the north and east the high Alps still stood up and received the large glow of evening. Everything else was full of the coming night, and a few stars shone. Up from She town came the distant noise of music; otherwise there was no sound. I could have rested there a long time, letting my tired body lapse into the advancing darkness, and catching in my spirit the inspiration of the silence--had it not been for hunger. I knew by experience that when it is very late one cannot be served in the eating-houses of poor men, and I had not the money or any other. So I rose and shambled down the steep road into the town, and there I found a square with arcades, and in the south-eastern corner of this square just such a little tavern as I required. Entering, therefore, and taking off my hat very low, I said in French to a man who was sitting there with friends, and who was the master, 'Sir, what is the least price at which you can give me a meal?'

He said, 'What do you want?'

116

I answered, 'Soup, meat, vegetables, bread, and a little wine.'

He counted on his fingers, while all his friends stared respectfully at him and me. He then gave orders, and a very young and beautiful girl set before me as excellent a meal as I had eaten for days on days, and he charged me but a franc and a half. He gave me also coffee and a little cheese, and I, feeling hearty, gave threepence over for the service, and they all very genially wished me a good-night; but their wishes were of no value to me, for the night was terrible.

I had gone over forty miles; how much over I did not know. I should have slept at Lugano, but my lightening purse forbade me. I thought, 'I will push on and on; after all, I have already slept, and so broken the back of the day. I will push on till I am at the end of my tether, then I will find a wood and sleep.' Within four miles my strength abandoned me. I was not even so far down the lake as to have lost the sound of the band at Lugano floating up the still water, when I was under an imperative necessity for repose. It was perhaps ten o'clock, and the sky was open and glorious with stars. I climbed up a bank on my right, and searching for a place to lie found one under a tree near a great telegraph pole. Here was a little parched grass, and one could lie there and see the lake and wait for sleep. It was a benediction to stretch out all supported by the dry earth, with my little side-bag for pillow, and to look at the clear night above the hills, and to listen to the very distant music, and to wonder whether or not, in this strange southern country, there might not be snakes gliding about in the undergrowth. Caught in such a skein of influence I was soothed and fell asleep.

For a little while I slept dreamlessly.

Just so much of my living self remained as can know, without understanding, the air around. It is the life of trees. That under-part, the barely conscious base of nature which trees and sleeping men are sunk in, is not only dominated by an immeasurable calm, but is also beyond all expression contented. And in its very stuff there is a complete and changeless joy. This is surely what the great mind meant when it said to the Athenian judges that death must not be dreaded since no experience in life was so pleasurable as a deep sleep; for being wise and seeing the intercommunion of things, he could not mean extinction, which is nonsense, but a lapse into that under-part of which I speak. For there are gods also below the earth.

But a dream came into my sleep and disturbed me, increasing life, and therefore bringing pain. I dreamt that I was arguing, at first easily, then violently, with another man. More and more he pressed me, and at last in my dream there were clearly spoken words, and he said to me, 'You must be wrong, because you are so cold; if you were right you would not be so cold.' And this argument seemed quite reasonable to me in my foolish dream, and I muttered to him, 'You are right, I must be in the wrong. It is very cold ...' Then I half opened my eyes and saw

117

the telegraph pole, the trees, and the lake. Far up the lake, where the Italian Frontier cuts it, the torpedo-boats, looking for smugglers, were casting their search-lights. One of the roving beams fell full on me and I became broad awake. I stood up. It was indeed cold, with a kind of clinging and grasping chill that was not to be expressed in degrees of heat, but in dampness perhaps, or perhaps in some subtler influence of the air.

I sat on the bank and gazed at the lake in some despair. Certainly I could not sleep again without a covering cloth, and it was now past midnight, nor did I know of any house, whether if I took the road I should find one in a mile, or in two, or in five. And, note you, I was utterly exhausted. That enormous march from Faido, though it had been wisely broken by the siesta at Bellinzona, needed more than a few cold hours under trees, and I thought of the three poor francs in my pocket, and of the thirty-eight miles remaining to Milan.

The stars were beyond the middle of their slow turning, and I watched them, splendid and in order, for sympathy, as I also regularly, but slowly and painfully, dragged myself along my appointed road. But in a very short time a great, tall, square, white house stood right on the roadway, and to my intense joy I saw a light in one of its higher windows. Standing therefore beneath, I cried at the top of my voice, 'Hola!' five or six times. A woman put her head out of the window into the fresh night, and said, 'You cannot sleep here; we have no rooms,' then she remained looking out of her window and ready to analyse the difficulties of the moment; a good-natured woman and fat.

In a moment another window at the same level, but farther from me, opened, and a man leaned out, just as those alternate figures come in and out of the toys that tell the weather. 'It is impossible,' said the man; 'we have no rooms.'

Then they talked a great deal together, while I shouted, *Quid vis? Non e possibile dormire in la foresta! e troppo fredo! Vis ne me assassinare? Veni de Lugano--e piu--non e possibile ritornare!'* and so forth.

They answered in strophe and antistrophe, sometimes together in full chorus, and again in semichorus, and with variations, that it was impossible. Then a light showed in the chinks of their great door; the lock grated, and it opened. A third person, a tall youth, stood in the hall. I went forward into the breach and occupied the hall. He blinked at me above a candle, and murmured, as a man apologizing 'It is not possible.'

Whatever I have in common with these southerners made me understand that I had won, so I smiled at him and nodded; he also smiled, and at once beckoned to me. He led me upstairs, and showed me a charming bed in a clean room, where there was a portrait of the Pope, looking cunning; the charge for that delightful and human place was sixpence, and as I said good-night to the youth, the man and

118

woman from above said good-night also. And this was my first introduction to the most permanent feature in the Italian character. The good people!

When I woke and rose I was the first to be up and out. It was high morning. The sun was not yet quite over the eastern mountains, but I had slept, though so shortly yet at great ease, and the world seemed new and full of a merry mind. The sky was coloured like that high metal work which you may see in the studios of Paris; there was gold in it fading into bronze, and above, the bronze softened to silver. A little morning breeze, courageous and steady, blew down the lake and provoked the water to glad ripples, and there was nothing that did not move and take pleasure in the day.

The Lake of Lugano is of a complicated shape, and has many arms. It is at this point very narrow indeed, and shallow too; a mole, pierced at either end with low arches, has here been thrown across it, and by this mole the railway and the road pass over to the eastern shore. I turned in this long causeway and noticed the northern view. On the farther shore was an old village and some pleasure-houses of rich men on the shore; the boats also were beginning to go about the water. These boats were strange, unlike other boats; they were covered with hoods, and looked like floating waggons. This was to shield the rowers from the sun. Far off a man was sailing with a little brown sprit-sail. It was morning, and all the world was alive.

Coffee in the village left me two francs and two pennies. I still thought the thing could be done, so invigorating and deceiving are the early hours, and coming farther down the road to an old and beautiful courtyard on the left, I drew it, and hearing a bell at hand I saw a tumble-down church with trees before it, and went in to Mass; and though it was a little low village Mass, yet the priest had three acolytes to serve it, and (true and gracious mark of a Catholic country!) these boys were restless and distracted at their office.

You may think it trivial, but it was certainly a portent. One of the acolytes had half his head clean shaved! A most extraordinary sight! I could not take my eyes from it, and I heartily wished I had an Omen-book with me to tell me what it might mean.

When there were oracles on earth, before Pan died, this sight would have been of the utmost use. For I should have consulted the oracle woman for a Lira--at Biasca for instance, or in the lonely woods of the Cinder Mountain; and, after a lot of incense and hesitation, and wrestling with the god, the oracle would have accepted Apollo and, staring like one entranced, she would have chanted verses which, though ambiguous, would at least have been a guide. Thus:

Matutinus adest ubi Vesper, et accipiens te
Saepe recusatum voces intelligit hospes

Rusticus ignotas notas, ac flumina tellus
Occupat--In sancto tum, tum, stans
Aede caveto Tonsuram Hirsuti
Capitis, via namque pedestrem
Ferrea praeveniens cursum, peregrine, laborem
Pro pietate tua inceptum frustratur, amore
Antiqui Ritus alto sub Numine Romae.

LECTOR. What Hoggish great Participles!

AUCTOR. Well, well, you see it was but a rustic oracle at 9 3/4 d. the revelation, and even that is supposing silver at par. Let us translate it for the vulgar:

When early morning seems but eve And they that still refuse receive: When speech unknown men understand; And floods are crossed upon dry land. Within the Sacred Walls beware The Shaven Head that boasts of Hair, For when the road attains the rail The Pilgrim's great attempt shall fail.

Of course such an oracle might very easily have made me fear too much. The 'shaven head' I should have taken for a priest, especially if it was to be met with 'in a temple'--it might have prevented me entering a church, which would have been deplorable. Then I might have taken it to mean that I should never have reached Rome, which would have been a monstrous weight upon my mind. Still, as things unfolded themselves, the oracle would have become plainer and plainer, and I felt the lack of it greatly. For, I repeat, I had certainly received an omen.

The road now neared the end of the lake, and the town called Capo di Lago, or 'Lake-head', lay off to my right. I saw also that in a very little while I should abruptly find the plains. A low hill some five miles ahead of me was the last roll of the mountains, and just above me stood the last high crest, a precipitous peak of bare rock, up which there ran a cog-railway to some hotel or other. I passed through an old town under the now rising heat; I passed a cemetery in the Italian manner, with marble figures like common living men. The road turned to the left, and I was fairly on the shoulder of the last glacis. I stood on the Alps at their southern bank, and before me was Lombardy.

Also in this ending of the Swiss canton one was more evidently in Italy than ever. A village perched upon a rock, deep woods and a ravine below it, its houses and its church, all betrayed the full Italian spirit.

The frontier town was Chiasso. I hesitated with reverence before touching the sacred soil which I had taken so long to reach, and I longed to be able to drink its health; but though I had gone, I suppose, ten miles, and though the heat was increasing, I would not stop; for I remembered the two francs, and my former certitude of reaching Milan was shaking and crumbling. The great heat of midday would soon be on me, I had yet nearly thirty miles to go, and my bad night began to oppress me.

I crossed the frontier, which is here an imaginary line. Two slovenly customs-house men asked me if I had anything dutiable on me. I said No, and it was evident enough, for in my little sack or pocket was nothing but a piece of bread. If they had applied the American test, and searched me for money, then indeed they could have turned me back, and I should have been forced to go into the fields a quarter of a mile or so and come into their country by a path instead of a highroad.

This necessity was spared me. I climbed slowly up the long slope that hides Como, then I came down upon that lovely city and saw its frame of hills and its lake below me.

These things are not like things seen by the eyes. I say it again, they are like what one feels when music is played.

I entered Como between ten and eleven faint for food, and then a new interest came to fill my mind with memories of this great adventure. The lake was in flood, and all the town was water.

Como dry must be interesting enough; Como flooded is a marvel. What else is Venice? And here is a Venice at the foot of high mountains, and *all* in the water, no streets or squares; a fine even depth of three feet and a half or so for navigators, much what you have in the Spitway in London River at low spring tides.

There were a few boats about, but the traffic and pleasure of Como was passing along planks laid on trestles over the water here and there like bridges; and for those who were in haste, and could afford it (such as take cabs in London), there were wheelbarrows, coster carts, and what not, pulled about by men for hire; and it was a sight to remember all one's life to see the rich men of Como squatting on these carts and barrows, and being pulled about over the water by the poor men of Como, being, indeed, an epitome of all modern sociology and economics and religion and organized charity and strenuousness and liberalism and sophistry generally.

For my part I was determined to explore this curious town in the water, and I especially desired to see it on the lake side, because there one would get the best impression of its being really an aquatic town; so I went northward, as I was directed, and came quite unexpectedly upon the astonishing cathedral. It seemed built of polished marble, and it was in every way so exquisite in proportion, so delicate in sculpture, and so triumphant in attitude, that I thought to myself--

'No wonder men praise Italy if this first Italian town has such a building as this.'

121

But, as you will learn later, many of the things praised are ugly, and are praised only by certain followers of charlatans.

So I went on till I got to the lake, and there I found a little port about as big as a dining-room (for the Italian lakes play at being little seas. They have little ports, little lighthouses, little fleets for war, and little custom-houses, and little storms and little lines of steamers. Indeed, if one wanted to give a rich child a perfect model or toy, one could not give him anything better than an Italian lake), and when I had long gazed at the town, standing, as it seemed, right in the lake, I felt giddy, and said to myself, 'This is the lack of food,' for I had eaten nothing but my coffee and bread eleven miles before, at dawn.

So I pulled out my two francs, and going into a little shop, I bought bread, sausage, and a very little wine for fourpence, and with one franc eighty left I stood in the street eating and wondering what my next step should be.

It seemed on the map perhaps twenty-five, perhaps twenty-six miles to Milan. It was now nearly noon, and as hot as could be. I might, if I held out, cover the distance in eight or nine hours, but I did not see myself walking in the middle heat on the plain of Lombardy, and even if I had been able I should only have got into Milan at dark or later, when the post office (with my money in it) would be shut; and where could I sleep, for my one franc eighty would be gone? A man covering these distances must have one good meal a day or he falls ill. I could beg, but there was the risk of being arrested, and that means an indefinite waste of time, perhaps several days; and time, that had defeated me at the Gries, threatened me here again. I had nothing to sell or to pawn, and I had no friends. The Consul I would not attempt; I knew too much of such things as Consuls when poor and dirty men try them. Besides which, there was no Consul I pondered.

I went into the cool of the cathedral to sit in its fine darkness and think better. I sat before a shrine where candles were burning, put up for their private intentions by the faithful. Of many, two had nearly burnt out. I watched them in their slow race for extinction when a thought took me.

'I will,' said I to myself, 'use these candles for an ordeal or heavenly judgement. The left hand one shall be for attempting the road at the risk of illness or very dangerous failure; the right hand one shall stand for my going by rail till I come to that point on the railway where one franc eighty will take me, and thence walking into Milan:--and heaven defend the right.'

They were a long time going out, and they fell evenly. At last the right hand one shot up the long flame that precedes the death of candles; the contest took on interest, and even excitement, when, just as I thought the left hand certain of winning, it went out without guess or warning, like a second-rate person leaving this world for another. The right hand candle waved its flame still higher, as though in triumph, outlived its colleague just the moment to enjoy glory, and then in its turn went fluttering down the dark way from which they say there is no return.

None may protest against the voice of the Gods. I went straight to the nearest railway station (for there are two), and putting down one franc eighty, asked in French for a ticket to whatever station that sum would reach down the line. The ticket came out marked Milan, and I admitted the miracle and confessed the finger of Providence. There was no change, and as I got into the train I had become that rarest and ultimate kind of traveller, the man without any money whatsoever-- without passport, without letters, without food or wine; it would be interesting to see what would follow if the train broke down.

I had marched 378 miles and some three furlongs, or thereabouts.

Thus did I break--but by a direct command--the last and dearest of my vows, and as the train rumbled off, I took luxury in the rolling wheels.

I thought of that other medieval and papistical pilgrim hobbling along rather than 'take advantage of any wheeled thing', and I laughed at him. Now if Moroso-Malodoroso or any other Non-Aryan, Antichristian, over-inductive, statistical, brittle-minded man and scientist, sees anything remarkable in one self laughing at another self, let me tell him and all such for their wide-eyed edification and astonishment that I knew a man once that had fifty-six selves (there would have been fifty-seven, but for the poet in him that died young)--he could evolve them at will, and they were very useful to lend to the parish priest when he wished to make up a respectable Procession on Holy-days. And I knew another man that could make himself so tall as to look over the heads of the scientists as a pine-tree looks over grasses, and again so small as to discern very clearly the thick coating or dust of wicked pride that covers them up in a fine impenetrable coat. So much for the moderns.

The train rolled on. I noticed Lombardy out of the windows. It is flat. I listened to the talk of the crowded peasants in the train. I did not understand it. I twice leaned out to see if Milan were not standing up before me out of the plain, but I saw nothing. Then I fell asleep, and when I woke suddenly it was because we were in the terminus of that noble great town, which I then set out to traverse in search of my necessary money and sustenance. It was yet but early in the afternoon.

What a magnificent city is Milan! The great houses are all of stone, and stand regular and in order, along wide straight streets. There are swift cars, drawn by electricity, for such as can afford them. Men are brisk and alert even in the summer heats, and there are shops of a very good kind, though a trifle showy. There are many newspapers to help the Milanese to be better men and to cultivate charity and humility; there are banks full of paper money; there are soldiers, good pavements, and all that man requires to fulfil him, soul and body; cafes, arcades, mutoscopes, and every sign of the perfect state. And the whole centres in a splendid open square, in the midst of which is the cathedral, which is justly the most renowned in the world.

My pilgrimage is to Rome, my business is with lonely places, hills, and the recollection of the spirit. It would be waste to describe at length this mighty capital. The mists and the woods, the snows and the interminable way, had left me ill-suited for the place, and I was ashamed. I sat outside a cafe, opposite the cathedral, watching its pinnacles of light; but I was ashamed. Perhaps I did the master a hurt by sitting there in his fine great cafe, unkempt, in such clothes, like a tramp; but he was courteous in spite of his riches, and I ordered a very expensive drink for him also, in order to make amends. I showed him my sketches, and told him of my adventures in French, and he was kind enough to sit opposite me, and to take that drink with me. He talked French quite easily, as it seems do all such men in the principal towns of north Italy. Still, the broad day shamed me, and only when darkness came did I feel at ease.

I wandered in the streets till I saw a small eating shop, and there I took a good meal. But when one is living the life of the poor, one sees how hard are the great cities. Everything was dearer, and worse, than in the simple countrysides. The innkeeper and his wife were kindly, but their eyes showed that they had often to suspect men. They gave me a bed, but it was a franc and more, and I had to pay before going upstairs to it. The walls were mildewed, the place ramshackle and evil, the rickety bed not clean, the door broken and warped, and that night I was oppressed with the vision of poverty. Dirt and clamour and inhuman conditions surrounded me. Yet the people meant well.

With the first light I got up quietly, glad to find the street again and the air. I stood in the crypt of the cathedral to hear the Ambrosian Mass, and it was (as I had expected) like any other, save for a kind of second *lavabo* before the Elevation. To read the distorted stupidity of the north one might have imagined that in the Ambrosian ritual the priest put a *non* before the *credo*, and *nec's* at each clause of it, and renounced his baptismal vows at the *kyrie*; but the Milanese are Catholics like any others, and the northern historians are either liars or ignorant men. And I know three that are both together.

Then I set out down the long street that leads south out of Milan, and was soon in the dull and sordid suburb of the Piacenzan way. The sky was grey, the air chilly, and in a little while--alas!--it rained.

Lombardy is an alluvial plain.

That is the pretty way of putting it. The truth is more vivid if you say that Lombardy is as flat as a marsh, and that it is made up of mud. Of course this mud dries when the sun shines on it, but mud it is and mud it will remain; and that day, as the rain began falling, mud it rapidly revealed itself to be; and the more did it seem to be mud when one saw how the moistening soil showed cracks from the last day's heat.

Lombardy has no forests, but any amount of groups of trees; moreover (what is very remarkable), it is all cultivated in fields more or less square. These fields have ditches round them, full of mud and water running slowly, and some of them are themselves under water in order to cultivate rice. All these fields have a few trees bordering them, apart from the standing clumps; but these trees are not very high. There are no open views in Lombardy, and Lombardy is all the same. Irregular large farmsteads stand at random all up and down the country; no square mile of Lombardy is empty. There are many, many little villages; many straggling small towns about seven to eight miles apart, and a great number of large towns from thirty to fifty miles apart. Indeed, this very road to Piacenza, which the rain now covered with a veil of despair, was among the longest stretches between any two large towns, although it was less than fifty miles.

On the map, before coming to this desolate place, there seemed a straighter and a better way to Rome than this great road. There is a river called the Lambro, which comes east of Milan and cuts the Piacenzan road at a place called Melegnano. It seemed to lead straight down to a point on the Po, a little above Piacenza. This stream one could follow (so it seemed), and when it joined the Po get a boat or ferry, and see on the other side the famous Trebbia, where Hannibal conquered and Joubert fell, and so make straight on for the Apennine.

Since it is always said in books that Lombardy is a furnace in summer, and that whole great armies have died of the heat there, this river bank would make a fine refuge. Clear and delicious water, more limpid than glass, would reflect and echo the restless poplars, and would make tolerable or even pleasing the excessive summer. Not so. It was a northern mind judging by northern things that came to this conclusion. There is not in all Lombardy a clear stream, but every river and brook is rolling mud. In the rain, not heat, but a damp and penetrating chill was the danger. There is no walking on the banks of the rivers; they are cliffs of crumbling soil, jumbled anyhow.

Man may, as Pinkerton (Sir Jonas Pinkerton) writes, be master of his fate, but he has a precious poor servant. It is easier to command a lapdog or a mule for a whole day than one's own fate for half-an-hour.

Nevertheless, though it was apparent that I should have to follow the main road for a while, I determined to make at last to the right of it, and to pass through a place called 'Old Lodi', for I reasoned thus: 'Lodi is the famous town. How much more interesting must Old Lodi be which is the mothertown of Lodi?' Also, Old Lodi brought me back again on the straight line to Rome, and I foolishly thought it might be possible to hear there of some straight path down the Lambro (for that river still possessed me somewhat).

Therefore, after hours and hours of trudging miserably along the wide highway in the wretched and searching rain, after splashing through tortuous Melegnano, and not even stopping to wonder if it was the place of the battle, after noting in despair the impossible Lambro, I came, caring for nothing, to the place where a secondary road branches off to the right over a level crossing and makes for Lodi Vecchio.

It was not nearly midday, but I had walked perhaps fifteen miles, and had only rested once in a miserable Trattoria. In less than three miles I came to that unkempt and lengthy village, founded upon dirt and living in misery, and through the quiet, cold, persistent rain I splashed up the main street. I passed wretched, shivering dogs and mournful fowls that took a poor refuge against walls; passed a sad horse that hung its head in the wet and stood waiting for a master, till at last I reached the open square where the church stood, then I knew that I had seen all Old Lodi had to offer me. So, going into an eating-house, or inn, opposite the church, I found a girl and her mother serving, and I saluted them, but there was no fire, and my heart sank to the level of that room, which was, I am sure, no more than fifty-four degrees.

Why should the less gracious part of a pilgrimage be specially remembered? In life were remember joy best--that is what makes us sad by contrast; pain somewhat, especially if it is acute; but dulness never. And a book--which has it in its own power to choose and to emphasize--has no business to record dulness. What did I at Lodi Vecchio? I ate; I dried my clothes before a tepid stove in a kitchen. I tried to make myself understood by the girl and her mother. I sat at a window and drew the ugly church on principle. Oh, the vile sketch!

Worthy of that Lombard plain, which they had told me was so full of wonderful things. I gave up all hope of by-roads, and I determined to push back obliquely to the highway again--obliquely in order to save time! Nepios!

These 'by-roads' of the map turned out in real life to be all manner of abominable tracks. Some few were metalled, some were cart-ruts merely, some were open lanes of rank grass; and along most there went a horrible ditch, and in many fields the standing water proclaimed desolation. IN so far as I can be said to have had a way at all, I lost it. I could not ask my way because my only ultimate goal was Piacenza, and that was far off. I did not know the name of any place between. Two or three groups of houses I passed, and sometimes church towers glimmered through the rain. I passed a larger and wider road than the rest, but obviously not my road; I pressed on and passed another; and by this time, having ploughed up Lombardy for some four hours, I was utterly lost. I no longer felt the north, and, for all I knew, I might be going backwards. The only certain thing was that I was somewhere in the belt between the highroad and the Lambro, and that was little enough to know at the close of such a day. Grown desperate, I clamoured within my mind for a miracle; and it was not long before I saw a little bent man sitting on a crazy cart and going ahead of me at a pace much slower than a walk--the pace of a horse crawling. I caught him up, and, doubting much whether he would understand a word, I said to him repeatedly--

'La granda via? La via a Piacenza?'

He shook his head as though to indicate that this filthy lane was not the road. Just as I had despaired of learning anything, he pointed with his arm away to the right, perpendicularly to the road we were on, and nodded. He moved his hand up and down. I had been going north!

On getting this sign I did not wait for a cross road, but jumped the little ditch and pushed through long grass, across further ditches, along the side of patches of growing corn, heedless of the huge weight on my boots and of the oozing ground, till I saw against the rainy sky a line of telegraph poles. For the first time since they were made the sight of them gave a man joy. There was a long stagnant pond full of reeds between me and the railroad; but, as I outflanked it, I came upon a road that crossed the railway at a level and led me into the great Piacenzan way. Almost immediately appeared a village. It was a hole called Secugnano, and there I entered a house where a bush hanging above the door promised entertainment, and an old hobbling woman gave me food and drink and a bed. The night had fallen, and upon the roof above me I could hear the steady rain.

The next morning--Heaven preserve the world from evil!--it was still raining.

LECTOR. It does not seem to me that this part of your book is very entertaining.

AUCTOR. I know that; but what am I to do?

LECTOR. Why, what was the next point in the pilgrimage that was even tolerably noteworthy?

AUCTOR. I suppose the Bridge of Boats.

LECTOR. And how far on was that?

AUCTOR. About fourteen miles, more or less ... I passed through a town with a name as long as my arm, and I suppose the Bridge of Boats must have been nine miles on after that.

LECTOR. And it rained all the time, and there was mud?

AUCTOR. Precisely.

LECTOR. Well, then, let us skip it and tell stories.

AUCTOR. With all my heart. And since you are such a good judge of literary poignancy, do you begin.

LECTOR. I will, and I draw my inspiration from your style.

Once upon a time there was a man who was born in Croydon, and whose name was Charles Amieson Blake. He went to Rugby at twelve and left it at seventeen. He fell in love twice and then went to Cambridge till he was twenty-three. Having left Cambridge he fell in love more mildly, and was put by his father into a government office, where he began at *180* pounds a year. At thirty-five he was earning 500 pounds a year, and perquisites made 750 pounds a year. He met a pleasant lady and fell in love quite a little compared with the other times. She had 250 pounds a year. That made *1000* pounds a year. They married and had three children--Richard, Amy, and Cornelia. He rose to a high government position, was knighted, retired at sixty-three, and died at sixty-seven. He is buried at Kensal Green...

AUCTOR. Thank you, Lector, that is a very good story. It is simple and full of plain human touches. You know how to deal with the facts of everyday life ... It requires a master-hand. Tell me, Lector, had this man any adventures?

LECTOR. None that I know of.

AUCTOR. Had he opinions?

LECTOR. Yes. I forgot to tell you he was a Unionist. He spoke two foreign languages badly. He often went abroad to Assisi, Florence, and Boulogne... He left 7,623 pounds 6s. 8d., and a house and garden at Sutton. His wife lives there still.

AUCTOR. Oh!

LECTOR. It is the human story ... the daily task!

AUCTOR. Very true, my dear Lector ... the common lot... Now let me tell my story. It is about the Hole that could not be Filled Up.

LECTOR. Oh no! Auctor, no! That is the oldest story in the--

AUCTOR. Patience, dear Lector, patience! I will tell it well. Besides which I promise you it shall never be told again. I will copyright it.

Well, once there was a Learned Man who had a bargain with the Devil that he should warn the Devil's emissaries of all the good deeds done around him so that they could be upset, and he in turn was to have all those pleasant things of this life which the Devil's allies usually get, to wit a Comfortable Home, Self-Respect, good health, 'enough money for one's rank', and generally what is called 'a happy useful life'--*till* midnight of All-Hallowe'en in the last year of the nineteenth century.

So this Learned Man did all he was required, and daily would inform the messenger imps of the good being done or prepared in the neighbourhood, and they would upset it; so that the place he lived in from a nice country town became a great Centre of Industry, full of wealth and desirable family mansions and street property, and was called in hell 'Depot B' (Depot A you may guess at). But at last toward the 15th of October 1900, the Learned Man began to shake in his shoes and to dread the judgement; for, you see, he had not the comfortable ignorance of his kind, and was compelled to believe in the Devil willy-nilly, and, as I say, he shook in his shoes.

So he bethought him of a plan to cheat the Devil, and the day before All-Hallowe'en he cut a very small round hole in the floor of his study, just near the fireplace, right through down to the cellar. Then he got a number of things that do great harm (newspapers, legal documents, unpaid bills, and so forth) and made ready for action.

Next morning when the little imps came for orders as usual, after prayers, he took them down into the cellar, and pointing out the hole in the ceiling, he said to them:

'My friends, this little hole is a mystery. It communicates, I believe, with the chapel; but I cannot find the exit. All I know is, that some pious person or angel, or what not, desirous to do good, slips into it every day whatever he thinks may be a cause of evil in the neighbourhood, hoping thus to destroy it' (in proof of which statement he showed them a scattered heap of newspapers on the floor of the cellar beneath the hole). 'And the best thing you can do,' he added, 'is to stay here and take them away as far as they come down and put them back into circulation again. Tut! tut!' he added, picking up a moneylender's threatening letter to a widow, 'it is astonishing how these people interfere with the most sacred rights! Here is a letter actually stolen from the post! Pray see that it is delivered.'

So he left the little imps at work, and fed them from above with all manner of evil-doing things, which they as promptly drew into the cellar, and at intervals flew away with, to put them into circulation again.

That evening, at about half-past eleven, the Devil came to fetch the Learned Man, and found him seated at his fine great desk, writing. The

Learned Man got up very affably to receive the Devil, and offered him a chair by the fire, just near the little round hole.

'Pray don't move,' said the Devil; 'I came early on purpose not to disturb you.'

'You are very good,' replied the Learned Man. 'The fact is, I have to finish my report on Lady Grope's Settlement among our Poor in the Bull Ring--it is making some progress. But their condition is heart-breaking, my dear sir; heart-breaking!'

'I can well believe it,' said the Devil sadly and solemnly, leaning back in his chair, and pressing his hands together like a roof. 'The poor in our great towns, Sir Charles' (for the Learned Man had been made a Baronet), 'the condition, I say, of the--Don't I feel a draught?' he added abruptly. For the Devil can't bear draughts.

'Why,' said the Learned Man, as though ashamed, 'just near your chair there *is* a little hole that I have done my best to fill up, but somehow it seemed impossible to fill it... I don't know...'

The Devil hates excuses, and is above all practical, so he just whipped the soul of a lawyer out of his side-pocket, tied a knot in it to stiffen it, and shoved it into the hole.

'There!' said the Devil contentedly; 'if you had taken a piece of rag, or what not, you might yourself... Hulloa!...' He looked down and saw the hole still gaping, and he felt a furious draught coming up again. He wondered a little, and then muttered: 'It's a pity I have on my best things. I never dare crease them, and I have nothing in my pockets to speak of, otherwise I might have brought something bigger.' He felt in his left-hand trouser pocket, and fished out a pedant, crumpled him carefully into a ball, and stuffed him hard into the hole, so that he suffered agonies. Then the Devil watched carefully. The soul of the pedant was at first tugged as if from below, then drawn slowly down, and finally shot off out of sight.

'This is a most extraordinary thing!' said the Devil.

'It is the draught. It is very strong between the joists,' ventured the Learned Man.

'Fiddle-sticks ends!' shouted the Devil. 'It is a trick! But I've never been caught yet, and I never will be.'

He clapped his hands, and a whole host of his followers poured in through the windows with mortgages, Acts of Parliament, legal decisions, declarations of war, charters to universities, patents for medicines, naturalization orders, shares in gold mines, specifications, prospectuses, water companies' reports, publishers' agreements, letters patent, freedoms of cities, and, in a word, all that the Devil controls in the way of hole-stopping rubbish; and the Devil, kneeling on the floor, stuffed them into the hole like a madman. But as fast as he stuffed, the little imps below (who had summoned a number of their kind to their aid also) pulled it through and carted it away. And the Devil, like one possessed, lashed the floor with his tail, and his eyes glared like coals of fire, and the sweat ran down his face, and he breathed hard, and pushed every imaginable thing he had into the hole so swiftly that at last his documents and parchments looked like streaks and flashes. But the loyal little imps, not to be beaten, drew them through into the cellar as fast as machinery, and whirled them to their assistants; and all the poor lost souls who had been pressed into the service were groaning that their one holiday in the year was being filched from them, when, just as the process was going on so fast that it roared like a printing-machine in full blast, the clock in the hall struck twelve.

The Devil suddenly stopped and stood up.

'Out of my house,' said the Learned Man; 'out of my house! I've had enough of you, and I've no time for fiddle-faddle! It's past twelve, and I've won!'

The Devil, though still panting, smiled a diabolical smile, and pulling out his repeater (which he had taken as a perquisite from the body of a member of Parliament), said, 'I suppose you keep Greenwich time?'

'Certainly!' said Sir Charles.

'Well,' said the Devil, 'so much the worse for you to live in Suffolk. You're four minutes fast, so I'll trouble you to come along with me; and I warn you that any words you now say may be used against...'

At this point the Learned Man's patron saint, who thought things had gone far enough, materialized himself and coughed gently. They both looked round, and there was St Charles sitting in the easy chair.

'So far,' murmured the Saint to the Devil suavely, 'so far from being four minutes too early, you are exactly a year too late.' On saying this, the Saint smiled a genial, priestly smile, folded his hands, twiddled his thumbs slowly round and round, and gazed in a fatherly way at the Devil.

'What do you mean?' shouted the Devil.

'What I say,' said St Charles calmly; '1900 is not the last year of the nineteenth century; it is the first year of the twentieth.'

'Oh!' sneered the Devil, 'are you an anti-vaccinationist as well? Now, look here' (and he began counting on his fingers); 'supposing in the year 1 B.C. ...'

131

'I never argue,' said St Charles.

'Well, all I know is,' answered the Devil with some heat, 'that in this matter as in most others, thank the Lord, I have on my side all the historians and all the scientists, all the universities, all the...'

'And I,' interrupted St Charles, waving his hand like a gentleman (he is a Borromeo), 'I have the Pope!'

At this the Devil gave a great howl, and disappeared in a clap of thunder, and was never seen again till his recent appearance at Brighton.

So the Learned Man was saved; but hardly; for he had to spend five hundred years in Purgatory catechizing such heretics and pagans as got there, and instructing them in the true faith. And with the more muscular he passed a knotty time.

You do not see the river Po till you are close to it. Then, a little crook in the road being passed, you come between high trees, and straight out before you, level with you, runs the road into and over a very wide mass of tumbling water. It does not look like a bridge, it looks like a quay. It does not rise; it has all the appearance of being a strip of road shaved off and floated on the water.

All this is because it passes over boats, as do some bridges over the Rhine. (At Cologne, I believe, and certainly at Kiel--for I once sat at the end of that and saw a lot of sad German soldiers drilling, a memory which later made me understand (1) why they can be out-marched by Latins; (2) why they impress travellers and civilians; (3) why the governing class in Germany take care to avoid common service; (4) why there is no promotion from the ranks; and (5) why their artillery is too rigid and not quick enough. It also showed me something intimate and fundamental about the Germans which Tacitus never understood and which all our historians miss--they are *of necessity* histrionic. Note I do not say it is a vice of theirs. It is a necessity of theirs, an appetite. They must see themselves on a stage. Whether they do things well or ill, whether it is their excellent army with its ridiculous parade, or their eighteenth-century *sans-soucis* with avenues and surprises, or their national legends with gods in wigs and strong men in tights, they *must* be play-actors to be happy and therefore to be efficient; and if I were Lord of Germany, and desired to lead my nation and to be loved by them, I should put great golden feathers on my helmet, I should use rhetorical expressions, spout monologues in public, organize wide cavalry charges at reviews, and move through life generally to the crashing of an orchestra. For by doing this even a vulgar, short, and diseased man, who dabbled in stocks and shares and was led by financiers, could become a hero, and do his nation good.)

132

LECTOR. What is all this?

AUCTOR. It is a parenthesis.

LECTOR. It is good to know the names of the strange things one meets with on one's travels.

AUCTOR. So I return to where I branched off, and tell you that the river Po is here crossed by a bridge of boats.

It is a very large stream. Half-way across, it is even a trifle uncomfortable to be so near the rush of the water on the trembling pontoons. And on that day its speed and turbulence were emphasized by the falling rain. For the marks of the rain on the water showed the rapidity of the current, and the silence of its fall framed and enhanced the swirl of the great river.

Once across, it is a step up into Piacenza--a step through mud and rain. On my right was that plain where Barbarossa received, and was glorified by, the rising life of the twelfth century; there the renaissance of our Europe saw the future glorious for the first time since the twilight of Rome, and being full of morning they imagined a new earth and gave it a Lord. It was at Roncaglia, I think in spring, and I wish I had been there. For in spring even the Lombard plain they say is beautiful and generous, but in summer I know by experience that it is cold, brutish, and wet.

And so in Piacenza it rained and there was mud, till I came to a hotel called the Moor's Head, in a very narrow street, and entering it I discovered a curious thing: the Italians live in palaces: I might have known it.

They are the impoverished heirs of a great time; its garments cling to them, but their rooms are too large for the modern penury. I found these men eating in a great corridor, in a hall, as they might do in a palace. I found high, painted ceilings and many things of marble, a vast kitchen, and all the apparatus of the great houses--at the service of a handful of contented, unknown men. So in England, when we have worked out our full fate, happier but poorer men will sit in the faded country-houses (a community, or an inn, or impoverished squires), and rough food will be eaten under mouldering great pictures, and there will be offices or granaries in the galleries of our castles; and where Lord Saxonthorpe (whose real name is Hauptstein) now plans our policy, common Englishmen will return to the simpler life, and there will be dogs, and beer, and catches upon winter evenings. For Italy also once gathered by artifice the wealth that was not of her making.

He was a good man, the innkeeper of this palace. He warmed me at his fire in his enormous kitchen, and I drank Malaga to the health of the cooks. I ate of their food, I bought a bottle of a new kind of sweet wine called 'Vino Dolce', and--I took the road.

LECTOR. And did you see nothing of Piacenza?

AUCTOR. Nothing, Lector; it was raining, and there was mud. I stood in front of the cathedral on my way out, and watched it rain. It rained all along the broad and splendid Emilian Way. I had promised myself great visions of the Roman soldiery passing up that eternal road; it still was stamped with the imperial mark, but the rain washed out its interest, and left me cold. The Apennines also, rising abruptly from the plain, were to have given me revelations at sunset; they gave me none. Their foothills appeared continually on my right, they themselves were veiled. And all these miles of road fade into the confused memory of that intolerable plain. The night at Firenzuola, the morning (the second morning of this visitation) still cold, still heartless, and sodden with the abominable weather, shall form no part of this book.

Things grand and simple of their nature are possessed, as you know, of a very subtle flavour. The larger music, the more majestic lengths of verse called epics, the exact in sculpture, the classic drama, the most absolute kinds of wine, require a perfect harmony of circumstance for their appreciation. Whatever is strong, poignant, and immediate in its effect is not so difficult to suit; farce, horror, rage, or what not, these a man can find in the arts, even when his mood may be heavy or disturbed; just as (to take their parallel in wines) strong Beaune will always rouse a man. But that which is cousin to the immortal spirit, and which has, so to speak, no colour but mere light, *that* needs for its recognition so serene an air of abstraction and of content as makes its pleasure seem rare in this troubled life, and causes us to recall it like a descent of the gods.

For who, having noise around him, can strike the table with pleasure at reading the Misanthrope, or in mere thirst or in fatigue praise Chinon wine? Who does not need for either of these perfect things Recollection, a variety of according conditions, and a certain easy Plenitude of the Mind?

So it is with the majesty of Plains, and with the haunting power of their imperial roads.

All you that have had your souls touched at the innermost, and have attempted to release yourselves in verse and have written trash--(and who know it)--be comforted. You shall have satisfaction at last, and you shall attain fame in some other fashion--perhaps in private theatricals or perhaps in journalism. You will be granted a prevision of complete success, and your hearts shall be filled--but you must not expect to find this mood on the Emilian Way when it is raining.

All you that feel youth slipping past you and that are desolate at the approach of age, be merry; it is not what it looks like from in front and from outside. There is a glory in all completion, and all good endings are but shining transitions. There will come a sharp moment of revelation when you shall bless the effect of time. But this divine moment--- it is not on the Emilian Way in the rain that you should seek it.

All you that have loved passionately and have torn your hearts asunder in disillusions, do not imagine that things broken cannot be mended by the good angels. There is a kind of splice called 'the long splice' which makes a cut rope seem what it was before; it is even stronger than before, and can pass through a block. There will descend upon you a blessed hour when you will be convinced as by a miracle, and you will suddenly understand the *redintegratio amoris (amoris redintegratio,* a Latin phrase). But this hour you will not receive in the rain on the Emilian Way.

Here then, next day, just outside a town called Borgo, past the middle of morning, the rain ceased.

Its effect was still upon the slippery and shining road, the sky was still fast and leaden, when, in a distaste for their towns, I skirted the place by a lane that runs westward of the houses, and sitting upon a low wall, I looked up at the Apennines, which were now plain above me, and thought over my approaching passage through those hills.

But here I must make clear by a map the mass of mountains which I was about to attempt, and in which I forded so many rivers, met so many strange men and beasts, saw such unaccountable sights, was imprisoned, starved, frozen, haunted, delighted, burnt up, and finally refreshed in Tuscany--in a word, where I had the most extraordinary and unheard-of adventures that ever diversified the life of man.

The straight line to Rome runs from Milan not quite through Piacenza, but within a mile or two of that city. Then it runs across the first folds of the Apennines, and gradually diverges from the Emilian Way. It was not possible to follow this part of the line exactly, for there was no kind of track. But by following the Emilian Way for several miles (as I had done), and by leaving it at the right moment, it was possible to strike the straight line again near a village called Medesano.

Now on the far side of the Apennines, beyond their main crest, there happens, most providentially, to be a river called the Serchio, whose valley is fairly straight and points down directly to Rome. To follow this valley would be practically to follow the line to Rome, and it struck the Tuscan plain not far from Lucca.

But to get from the Emilian Way over the eastern slope of the Apennines' main ridge and crest, to where the Serchio rises on the western side, is a very difficult matter. The few roads across the

Apennines cut my track at right angles, and were therefore useless. In order to strike the watershed at the sources of the Serchio it was necessary to go obliquely across a torrent and four rivers (the Taro, the Parma, the Enza, and the Secchia), and to climb the four spurs that divided them; crossing each nearer to the principal chain as I advanced until, after the Secchia, the next climb would be that of the central crest itself, on the far side of which I should find the Serchio valley.

Perhaps in places roads might correspond to this track. Certainly the bulk of it would be mule-paths or rough gullies--how much I could not tell. The only way I could work it with my wretched map was to note the names of towns' or hamlets more or less on the line, and to pick my way from one to another. I wrote them down as follows: Fornovo, Calestano, Tizzano, Colagna--the last at the foot of the final pass. The distance to that pass as the crow flies was only a little more than thirty miles. So exceedingly difficult was the task that it took me over two days. Till I reached Fornovo beyond the Taro, I was not really in the hills.

By country roads, picking my way, I made that afternoon for Medesano. The lanes were tortuous; they crossed continual streams that ran from the hills above, full and foaming after the rain, and frothing with the waste of the mountains. I had not gone two miles when the sky broke; not four when a new warmth began to steal over the air and a sense of summer to appear in the earth about me. With the greatest rapidity the unusual weather that had accompanied me from Milan was changing into the normal brilliancy of the south; but it was too late for the sun to tell, though he shone from time to time through clouds that were now moving eastwards more perceptibly and shredding as they moved.

Quite tired and desiring food, keen also for rest after those dispiriting days, I stopped, before reaching Medesano, at an inn where three ways met; and there I purposed to eat and spend the night, for the next day, it was easy to see, would be tropical, and I should rise before dawn if I was to save the heat. I entered.

The room within was of red wood. It had two tables, a little counter with a vast array of bottles, a woman behind the counter, and a small, nervous man in a strange hat serving. And all the little place was filled and crammed with a crowd of perhaps twenty men, gesticulating, shouting, laughing, quarrelling, and one very big man was explaining to another the virtues of his knife; and all were already amply satisfied with wine. For in this part men do not own, but are paid wages, so that they waste the little they have.

I saluted the company, and walking up to the counter was about to call for wine. They had all become silent, when one man asked me a question in Italian. I did not understand it, and attempted to say so, when another asked the same question; then six or seven--and there

136

was a hubbub. And out of the hubbub I heard a similar sentence rising all the time. To this day I do not know what it meant, but I thought (and think) it meant 'He is a Venetian,' or 'He is the Venetian.' Something in my broken language had made them think this, and evidently the Venetians (or a Venetian) were (or was) gravely unpopular here. Why, I cannot tell. Perhaps the Venetians were blacklegs. But evidently a Venetian, or the whole Venetian nation, had recently done them a wrong.

At any rate one very dark-haired man put his face close up to mine, unlipped his teeth, and began a great noise of cursing and threatening, and this so angered me that it overmastered my fear, which had till then been considerable. I remembered also a rule which a wise man once told me for guidance, and it is this: 'God disposes of victory, but, as the world is made, when men smile, smile; when men laugh, laugh; when men hit, hit; when men shout, shout; and when men curse, curse you also, my son, and in doubt let them always take the first move.'

I say my fear had been considerable, especially of the man with the knife, but I got too angry to remember it, and advancing my face also to this insulter's I shouted, '*Dio Ladro! Dios di mi alma! Sanguinamento! Nombre di Dios! Che? Che vole? Non sono da Venezia io! Sono de Francia! Je m'en fiche da vestra Venezia! Non se vede che non parlar vestra lingua? Che sono forestiere?*' and so forth. At this they evidently divided into two parties, and all began raging amongst themselves, and some at me, while the others argued louder and louder that there was an error.

The little innkeeper caught my arm over the counter, and I turned round sharply, thinking he was doing me a wrong, but I saw him nodding and winking at me, and he was on my side. This was probably because he was responsible if anything happened, and he alone could not fly from the police.

He made them a speech which, for all I know, may have been to the effect that he had known and loved me from childhood, or may have been that he knew me for one Jacques of Turin, or may have been any other lie. Whatever lie it was, it appeased them. Their anger went down to a murmur, just like soda-water settling down into a glass.

I stood wine; we drank. I showed them my book, and as my pencil needed sharpening the large man lent me his knife for courtesy. When I got it in my hand I saw plainly that it was no knife for stabbing with; it was a pruning-knife, and would have bit the hand that cherished it (as they say of serpents). On the other hand, it would have been a good knife for ripping, and passable at a slash. You must not expect too much of one article.

I took food, but I saw that in this parish it was safer to sleep out of doors than in; so in the falling evening, but not yet sunset, I wandered on, not at a pace but looking for shelter, and I found at last just what I wanted: a little shed, with dried ferns (as it seemed) strewed in a corner, a few old sacks, and a broken piece of machinery--though this last was of no use to me.

I thought: 'It will be safe here, for I shall rise before day, and the owner, if there is one, will not disturb me.'

The air was fairly warm. The place quite dry. The open side looked westward and a little south.

The sun had now set behind the Apennines, and there was a deep effulgence in the sky. I drank a little wine, lit a pipe, and watched the west in silence.

Whatever was left of the great pall from which all that rain had fallen, now was banked up on the further side of heaven in toppling great clouds that caught the full glow of evening.

The great clouds stood up in heaven, separate, like persons; and no wind blew; but everything was full of evening. I worshipped them so far as it is permitted to worship inanimate things.

They domed into the pure light of the higher air, inviolable. They seemed halted in the presence of a commanding majesty who ranked them all in order.

This vision filled me with a large calm which a travelled man may find on coming to his home, or a learner in the communion of wise men. Repose, certitude, and, as it were, a premonition of glory occupied my spirit. Before it was yet quite dark I had made a bed out of the dry bracken, covered myself with the sacks and cloths, and very soon I fell asleep, still thinking of the shapes of clouds and of the power of God.

Next morning it was as I had thought. Going out before it was fully light, a dense mist all around and a clear sky showed what the day was to be. As I reached Medesano the sun rose, and in half-an-hour the air was instinct with heat; within an hour it was blinding. An early Mass in the church below the village prepared my day, but as I took coffee afterwards in a little inn, and asked about crossing the Taro to Fornovo-- my first point--to my astonishment they shook their heads. The Taro was impassable.

Why could it not be crossed? My very broken language made it difficult for me to understand. They talked *oframi*, which I thought meant oars; but *rami*, had I known it, meant the separate branches or streams whereby these torrential rivers of Italy flow through their arid beds.

I drew a boat and asked if one could not cross in that (for I was a northerner, and my idea of a river was a river with banks and water in between), but they laughed and said 'No.' Then I made the motion of swimming. They said it was impossible, and one man hung his head to indicate drowning. It was serious. They said to-morrow, or rather next day, one might do it.

Finally, a boy that stood by said he remembered a man who knew the river better than any one, and he, if any one could, would get me across. So I took the boy with me up the road, and as we went I saw, parallel to the road, a wide plain of dazzling rocks and sand, and beyond it, shining and silhouetted like an Arab village, the group of houses that was Fornovo. This plain was their sort of river in these hills. The boy said that sometimes it was full and a mile wide, sometimes it dwindled into dirty pools. Now, as I looked, a few thin streams seemed to wind through it, and I could not understand the danger.

After a mile or two we came to a spot in the road where a patch of brushwood only separated us from the river-bed. Here the boy bade me wait, and asked a group of peasants whether the guide was in; they said they thought so, and some went up into the hillside with the boy to fetch him, others remained with me, looking at the river-bed and at Fornovo beyond, shaking their heads, and saying it had not been done for days. But I did not understand whether the rain-freshet had passed and was draining away, or whether it had not yet come down from beyond, and I waited for the guide.

They brought him at last down from his hut among the hills. He came with great strides, a kindly-looking man, extremely tall and thin, and with very pale eyes. He smiled. They pointed me out to him, and we struck the bargain by holding up three fingers each for three lira, and nodding. Then he grasped his long staff and I mine, we bade farewell to the party, and together we went in silence through thick brushwood down towards the broad river-bed. The stones of it glared like the sands of Africa; Fornovo baked under the sun all white and black; between us was this broad plain of parched shingle and rocks that could, in a night, become one enormous river, or dwindle to a chain of stagnant ponds. To-day some seven narrow streams wandered in the expanse, and again they seemed so easy to cross that again I wondered at the need of a guide.

We came to the edge of the first, and I climbed on the guide's back. He went bare-legged into the stream deeper and deeper till my feet, though held up high, just touched the water; then laboriously he climbed the further shore, and I got down upon dry land. It had been but twenty yards or so, and he knew the place well. I had seen, as we crossed, what a torrent this first little stream was, and I now knew the difficulty and understood the warnings of the inn.

The second branch was impassable. We followed it up for nearly a mile to where 'an island' (that is, a mass of high land that must have been an island in flood-time, and that had on it an old brown village) stood above the white bed of the river. Just at this 'island' my guide found a ford. And the way he found it is worth telling. He taught me the trick, and it is most useful to men who wander alone in mountains.

You take a heavy stone, how heavy you must learn to judge, for a more rapid current needs a heavier stone; but say about ten pounds. This you lob gently into mid-stream. *How*, it is impossible to describe, but when you do it it is quite easy to see that in about four feet of water, or less, the stone splashes quite differently from the way it does in five feet or more. It is a sure test, and one much easier to acquire by practice than to write about. To teach myself this trick I practised it throughout my journey in these wilds.

Having found a ford then, he again took me on his shoulders, but, in mid-stream, the water being up to his breast, his foot slipped on a stone (all the bed beneath was rolling and churning in the torrent), and in a moment we had both fallen. He pulled me up straight by his side, and then indeed, overwhelmed in the rush of water, it was easy to understand how the Taro could drown men, and why the peasants dreaded these little ribbons of water.

The current rushed and foamed past me, coming nearly to my neck; and it was icy cold. One had to lean against it, and the water so took away one's weight that at any moment one might have slipped and been carried away. The guide, a much taller man (indeed he was six foot three or so), supported me, holding my arm: and again in a moment we reached dry land.

After that adventure there was no need for carrying. The third, fourth, fifth, and sixth branches were easily fordable. The seventh was broad and deep, and I found it a heavy matter; nor should I have waded it but for my guide, for the water bore against me like a man wrestling, and it was as cold as Acheron, the river of the dead. Then on the further shore, and warning him (in Lingua Franca) of his peril, I gave him his wage, and he smiled and thanked me, and went back, choosing his plans at leisure.

Thus did I cross the river Taro; a danger for men.

Where I landed was a poor man sunning himself. He rose and walked with me to Fornovo. He knew the guide.

'He is a good man,' he said to me of this friend. 'He is as good as a little piece of bread.'

'E vero,' I answered; 'e San Cristophero.'

This pleased the peasant; and indeed it was true. For the guide's business was exactly that of St Christopher, except that the Saint took no money, and lived, I suppose, on air.

And so to Fornovo; and the heat blinded and confused, and the air was alive with flies. But the sun dried me at once, and I pressed up the road because I needed food. After I had eaten in this old town I was preparing to make for Calestano and to cross the first high spur of the Apennines that separated me from it, when I saw, as I left the place, a very old church; and I stayed a moment and looked at carvings which were in no order, but put in pell-mell, evidently chosen from some older building. They were barbaric, but one could see that they stood for the last judgement of man, and there were the good looking foolish, and there were the wicked being boiled by devils in a pot, and what was most pleasing was one devil who with great joy was carrying off a rich man's gold in a bag. But now we are too wise to believe in such follies, and when we die we take our wealth with us; in the ninth century they had no way of doing this, for no system of credit yet obtained.

Then leaving the main road which runs to Pontremoli and at last to Spezzia, my lane climbed up into the hills and ceased, little by little, to be even a lane. It became from time to time the bed of a stream, then nothing, then a lane again, and at last, at the head of the glen, I confessed to having lost it; but I noted a great rock or peak above me for a landmark, and I said to myself--

'No matter. The wall of this glen before me is obviously the ridge of the spur; the rock must be left to the north, and I have but to cross the ridge by its guidance.' By this time, however, the heat overcame me, and, as it was already afternoon, and as I had used so much of the preceding night for my journey, I remembered the wise custom of hot countries and lay down to sleep.

I slept but a little while, yet when I woke the air was cooler. I climbed the side of the glen at random, and on the summit I found, to my disgust, a road. What road could it be? To this day I do not know. Perhaps I had missed my way and struck the main highway again. Perhaps (it is often so in the Apennines) it was a road leading nowhere. At any rate I hesitated, and looked back to judge my direction.

It was a happy accident. I was now some 2000 feet above the Taro. There, before me, stood the high strange rock that I had watched from below; all around it and below me was the glen or cup of bare hills, slabs, and slopes of sand and stone calcined in the sun, and, beyond these near things, all the plain of Lombardy was at my feet.

It was this which made it worth while to have toiled up that steep wall, and even to have lost my way--to see a hundred miles of the great flat stretched out before me: all the kingdoms of the world.

141

Nor was this all. There were sharp white clouds on the far northern horizon, low down above the uncertain edge of the world. I looked again and found they did not move. Then I knew they were the Alps.

Believe it or not, I was looking back to a place of days before: over how many, many miles of road! The rare, white peaks and edges could not deceive me; they still stood to the sunlight, and sent me from that vast distance the memory of my passage, when their snows had seemed interminable and their height so monstrous; their cold such a cloak of death. Now they were as far off as childhood, and I saw them for the last time.

All this I drew. Then finding a post directing me to a side road for Calestano, I followed it down and down into the valley beyond; and up the walls of this second valley as the evening fell I heard the noise of the water running, as the Taro had run, a net of torrents from the melting snows far off. These streams I soon saw below me, winding (as those of the Taro had wound) through a floor of dry shingle and rock; but when my road ceased suddenly some hundreds of feet above the bed of the river, and when, full of evening, I had scrambled down through trees to the brink of the water, I found I should have to repeat what I had done that morning and to ford these streams. For there was no track of any kind and no bridge, and Calestano stood opposite me, a purple cluster of houses in the dusk against the farther mountain side.

Very warily, lobbing stones as I had been taught, and following up and down each branch to find a place, I forded one by one the six little cold and violent rivers, and reaching the farther shore, I reached also, as I thought, supper, companionship, and a bed.

But it is not in this simple way that human life is arranged. What awaited me in Calestano was ill favour, a prison, release, base flattery, and a very tardy meal.

It is our duty to pity all men. It is our duty to pity those who are in prison. It is our duty to pity those who are not in prison. How much more is it the duty of a Christian man to pity the rich who cannot ever get into prison? These indeed I do now specially pity, and extend to them my commiseration.

What! Never even to have felt the grip of the policeman; to have watched his bold suspicious eye; to have tried to make a good show under examination ... never to have heard the bolt grinding in the lock, and never to have looked round at the cleanly simplicity of a cell? Then what emotions have you had, unimprisonable rich; or what do you know of active living and of adventure?

It was after drinking some wine and eating macaroni and bread at a poor inn, the only one in the place, and after having to shout at the ill-natured hostess (and to try twenty guesses before I made her understand that I wanted cheese), it was when I had thus eaten and shouted, and had gone over the way to drink coffee and to smoke in a little cafe, that my adventure befell me.

In the inn there had been a fat jolly-looking man and two official-looking people with white caps dining at another table. I had taken no notice of them at the time. But as I sat smoking and thinking in the little cafe, which was bright and full of people, I noticed a first danger-signal when I was told sullenly that 'they had no bed; they thought I could get none in the town': then, suddenly, these two men in white caps came in, and they arrested me with as much ease as you or I would hold a horse.

A moment later there came in two magnificent fellows, gendarmes, with swords and cocked hats, and moustaches *a l'Abd el Kader,* as we used to say in the old days; these four, the two gendarmes and two policemen, sat down opposite me on chairs and began cross-questioning me in Italian, a language in which I was not proficient. I so far understood them as to know that they were asking for my papers.

'Niente!' said I, and poured out on the table a card-case, a sketch-book, two pencils, a bottle of wine, a cup, a piece of bread, a scrap of French newspaper, an old *Secolo*, a needle, some thread, and a flute-- but no passport.

They looked in the card-case and found 73 lira; that is, not quite three pounds. They examined the sketch-book critically, as behoved southerners who are mostly of an artistic bent: but they found no passport. They questioned me again, and as I picked about for words to reply, the smaller (the policeman, a man with a face like a fox) shouted that he had heard me speaking Italian *currently* in the inn, and that my hesitation was a blind.

This lie so annoyed me that I said angrily in French (which I made as southern as possible to suit them):

'You lie: and you can be punished for such lies, since you are an official.' For though the police are the same in all countries, and will swear black is white, and destroy men for a song, yet where there is a *droit administratif*- that is, where the Revolution has made things tolerable--you are much surer of punishing your policeman, and he is much less able to do you a damage than in England or America; for he counts as an official and is under a more public discipline and responsibility if he exceeds his powers.

Then I added, speaking distinctly, 'I can speak French and Latin. Have you a priest in Calestano, and does he know Latin?'

This was a fine touch. They winced, and parried it by saying that the Sindaco knew French. Then they led me away to their barracks while they fetched the Sindaco, and so I was imprisoned.

But not for long. Very soon I was again following up the street, and we came to the house of the Sindaco or Mayor. There he was, an old man with white hair, God bless him, playing cards with his son and daughter. To him therefore, as understanding French, I was bidden address myself. I told him in clear and exact idiom that his policemen were fools, that his town was a rabbit-warren, and his prison the only cleanly thing in it; that half-a-dozen telegrams to places I could indicate would show where I had passed; that I was a common tourist, not even an artist (as my sketch-book showed), and that my cards gave my exact address and description.

But the Sindaco, the French-speaking Sindaco, understood me not in the least, and it seemed a wicked thing in me to expose him in his old age, so I waited till he spoke. He spoke a word common to all languages, and one he had just caught from my lips.

'Tourist-e?' he said.

I nodded. Then he told them to let me go. It was as simple as that; and to this day, I suppose, he passes for a very bilingual Mayor. He did me a service, and I am willing to believe that in his youth he smacked his lips over the subtle flavour of Voltaire, but I fear to-day he would have a poor time with Anatole France.

What a contrast was there between the hour when I had gone out of the cafe a prisoner and that when I returned rejoicing with a crowd about me, proclaiming my innocence, and shouting one to another that I was a tourist and had seventy-three lira on my person! The landlady smiled and bowed: she had before refused me a bed! The men at the tables made me a god! Nor did I think them worse for this. Why should I? A man unknown, unkempt, unshaven, in tatters, covered with weeks of travel and mud, and in a suit that originally cost not ten shillings; having slept in leaves and ferns, and forest places, crosses a river at dusk and enters a town furtively, not by the road. He is a foreigner; he carries a great club. Is it not much wiser to arrest such a man? Why yes, evidently. And when you have arrested him, can you do more than let him go without proof, on his own word? Hardly!

Thus I loved the people of Calestano, especially for this strange adventure they had given me; and next day, having slept in a human room, I went at sunrise up the mountain sides beyond and above their town, and so climbed by a long cleft the *second* spur of the Apennines: the spur that separated me from the *third* river, the Parma. And my goal above the Parma (when I should have crossed it) was a place marked in the map 'Tizzano'. To climb this second spur, to reach and cross the Parma in the vale below, to find Tizzano, I left Calestano on that fragrant morning; and having passed and drawn a little hamlet called Frangi, standing on a crag, I went on up the steep vale and soon reached the top of the ridge, which here dips a little and allows a path to cross over to the southern side.

It is the custom of many, when they get over a ridge, to begin singing. Nor did I fail, early as was the hour, to sing in passing this the second of my Apennine summits. I sang easily with an open throat everything that I could remember in praise of joy; and I did not spare the choruses of my songs, being even at pains to imitate (when they were double) the various voices of either part.

Now, so much of the Englishman was in me that, coming round a corner of rock from which one first sees Beduzzo hanging on its ledge (as you know), and finding round this corner a peasant sitting at his ease, I was ashamed. For I did not like to be overheard singing fantastic songs. But he, used to singing as a solitary pastime, greeted me, and we walked along together, pointing out to each other the glories of the world before us and exulting in the morning. It was his business to show me things and their names: the great Mountain of the Pilgrimage to the South, the strange rock of Castel-Nuovo; in the far haze the plain of Parma; and Tizzano on its high hill, the ridge straight before me. He also would tell me the name in Italian of the things to hand--my boots, my staff, my hat; and I told him their names in French, all of which he was eager to learn.

We talked of the way people here tilled and owned ground, of the dangers in the hills, and of the happiness of lonely men. But if you ask how we understood each other, I will explain the matter to you.

In Italy, in the Apennines of the north, there seem to be three strata of language. In the valleys the Italian was pure, resonant, and foreign to me. There dwell the townsmen, and they deal down river with the plains. Half-way up (as at Frangi, at Beduzzo, at Tizzano) I began to understand them. They have the nasal 'n'; they clip their words. On the summits, at last, they speak like northerners, and I was easily understood, for they said not 'vino' but 'vin'; not 'duo' but 'du', and so forth. They are the Gauls of the hills. I told them so, and they were very pleased.

Then I and my peasant parted, but as one should never leave a man without giving him something to show by way of token on the Day of Judgement, I gave this man a little picture of Milan, and bade him keep it for my sake.

So he went his way, and I mine, and the last thing he said to me was about a 'molinar', but I did not know what that meant.

When I had taken a cut down the mountain, and discovered a highroad at the bottom, I saw that the river before me needed fording, like all the rest; and as my map showed me there was no bridge for many miles down, I cast about to cross directly, if possible on some man's shoulders.

I met an old woman with a heap of grass on her back; I pointed to the river, and said (in Lingua Franca) that I wished to cross. She again used that word *'molinar'*, and I had an inkling that it meant 'miller'. I said to myself--

'Where there is a miller there is a mill. For *Ubi Petrus ibi Ecclesia.* Where there is a mill there is water; a mill must have motive power: .'. (a) I must get near the stream; (b) I must look out for the noise and aspect of a mill.

I therefore (thanking the grass-bearing woman) went right over the fields till I saw a great, slow mill-wheel against a house, and a sad man standing looking at it as though it were the Procession of God's Providence. He was thinking of many things. I tapped him on the shoulder (whereat he started) and spoke the great word of that valley, *'molinar'*. It opened all the gates of his soul. He smiled at me like a man grown young again, and, beckoning me to follow, led radiantly up the sluice to where it drew from the river.

Here three men were at work digging a better entry for the water. One was an old, happy man in spectacles, the second a young man with stilts in his hands, the third was very tall and narrow; his face was sad, and he was of the kind that endure all things and conquer. I said *'Molinar?''* I had found him.

To the man who had brought me I gave 50 c., and so innocent and good are these people that he said *'Pourquoi?'* or words like it, and I said it was necessary. Then I said to the molinar, *'Quanta?'* and he, holding up a tall finger, said *'Una Lira'*. The young man leapt on to his stilts, the molinar stooped down and I got upon his shoulders, and we all attempted the many streams of the river Parma, in which I think I should by myself have drowned.

I say advisedly--'I should have been drowned.' These upper rivers of the hills run high and low according to storms and to the melting of the snows. The river of Parma (for this torrent at last fed Parma) was higher than the rest.

Even the molinar, the god of that valley, had to pick his way carefully, and the young man on stilts had to go before, much higher than mortal men, and up above the water. I could see him as he went, and I could see that, to tell the truth, there was a ford--a rare thing in upper waters, because in the torrent-sources of rivers either the upper waters run over changeless rocks or else over gravel and sand. Now if they run over rocks they have their isolated shallow places, which any man may find, and their deep--evident by the still and mysterious surface, where fish go round and round in the hollows; but no true ford continuous from side to side. So it is in Scotland. And if they run over gravel and sand, then with every storm or 'spate' they shift and change. But here by some accident there ran--perhaps a shelf or rock, perhaps a ruin of a Roman bridge--something at least that was deep enough and solid enough to be a true ford--and that we followed.

The molinar--even the molinar--was careful of his way. Twice he waited, waist high, while the man on stilts before us suddenly lost ground and plunged to his feet. Once, crossing a small branch (for the river here, like all these rivers, runs in many arms over the dry gravel), it seemed there was no foothold and we had to cast up and down. Whenever we found dry land, I came off the molinar's back to rest him, and when he took the water again I mounted again. So we passed the many streams, and stood at last on the Tizzanian side. Then I gave a lira to the molinar, and to his companion on stilts 50 c., who said, 'What is this for?' and I said, 'You also helped.'

The molinar then, with gesticulations and expression of the eyes, gave me to understand that for this 50 c. the stilt-man would take me up to Tizzano on the high ridge and show me the path up the ridge; so the stilt-man turned to me and said, 'Andiamo' which means 'Allons'. But when the Italians say 'Andiamo' they are less harsh than the northern French who say 'Allans'; for the northern French have three troubles in the blood. They are fighters; they will for ever be seeking the perfect state, and they love furiously. Hence they ferment twice over, like wine subjected to movement and breeding acidity. Therefore is it that when they say 'Allons' it is harsher than 'Andiamo'. My Italian said to me genially, 'Andiamo.

The Catholic Church makes men. By which I do not mean boasters and swaggerers, nor bullies nor ignorant fools, who, finding themselves comfortable, think that their comfort will be a boon to others, and attempt (with singular unsuccess) to force it on the world; but men, human beings, different from the beasts, capable of firmness and discipline and recognition; accepting death; tenacious. Of her effects the most gracious is the character of the Irish and of these Italians. Of such also some day she may make soldiers.

Have you ever noticed that all the Catholic Church does is thought beautiful and lovable until she comes out into the open, and then suddenly she is found by her enemies (which are the seven capital sins, and the four sins calling to heaven for vengeance) to be hateful and grinding? So it is; and it is the fine irony of her present renovation that those who were for ever belauding her pictures, and her saints, and her architecture, as we praise things dead, they are the most angered by her appearance on this modern field all armed, just as she was, with works and art and songs, sometimes superlative, often vulgar. Note you, she is still careless of art or songs, as she has always been. She lays her foundations in something other, which something other our

147

moderns hate. Yet out of that something other came the art and song of the Middle Ages. And what art or songs have you? She is Europe and all our past. She is returning. *Andiamo.*

LECTOR. But Mr *(deleted by the Censor)* does not think so?

AUCTOR. I last saw him supping at the Savoy. *Andiamo.*

We went up the hill together over a burnt land, but shaded with trees. It was very hot. I could scarcely continue, so fast did my companion go, and so much did the heat oppress me.

We passed a fountain at which oxen drank, and there I supped up cool water from the spout, but he wagged his finger before his face to tell me that this was an error under a hot sun.

We went on and met two men driving cattle up the path between the trees. These I soon found to be talking of prices and markets with my guide. For it was market-day. As we came up at last on to the little town--a little, little town like a nest, and all surrounded with walls, and a castle in it and a church--we found a thousand beasts all lowing and answering each other along the highroad, and on into the market square through the gate. There my guide led me into a large room, where a great many peasants were eating soup with macaroni in it, and some few, meat. But I was too exhausted to eat meat, so I supped up my broth and then began diapephradizing on my fingers to show the great innkeeper what I wanted.

I first pulled up the macaroni out of the dish, and said, *Fromagio, Pommodoro,* by which I meant cheese--tomato. He then said he knew what I meant, and brought me that spaghetti so treated, which is a dish for a king, a cosmopolitan traitor, an oppressor of the poor, a usurer, or any other rich man, but there is no spaghetti in the place to which such men go, whereas these peasants will continue to enjoy it in heaven.

I then pulled out my bottle of wine, drank what was left out of the neck (by way of sign), and putting it down said, *'Tale, tantum, vino rosso.'* My guide also said many things which probably meant that I was a rich man, who threw his money about by the sixpence. So the innkeeper went through a door and brought back a bottle all corked and sealed, and said on his fingers, and with his mouth and eyes, 'THIS KIND OF WINE IS SOMETHING VERY SPECIAL.'

Only in the foolish cities do men think it a fine thing to appear careless of money. So I, very narrowly watching him out of half-closed eyes, held up my five fingers interrogatively, and said, *'Cinquante?'* meaning 'Dare you ask fivepence?'

At which he and all the peasants around, even including my guide, laughed aloud as at an excellent joke, and said, *'Cinquante, Ho! ho!'* and dug each other in the ribs. But the innkeeper of Tizzano Val Parmense said in Italian a number of things which meant that I could but be joking, and added (in passing) that a lira made it a kind of gift to me. A lira was, as it were, but a token to prove that it had changed hands: a registration fee: a matter of record; at a lira it was pure charity. Then I said, 'Soixante Dix?' which meant nothing to him, so I held up seven fingers; he waved his hand about genially, and said that as I was evidently a good fellow, a traveller, and as anyhow he was practically giving me the wine, he would make it ninepence; it was hardly worth his while to stretch out his hand for so little money. So then I pulled out 80 c. in coppers, and said, 'Tutto', which means 'all'. Then he put the bottle before me, took the money, and an immense clamour rose from all those who had been watching the scene, and they applauded it as a ratified bargain. And this is the way in which bargains were struck of old time in these hills when your fathers and mine lived and shivered in a cave, hunted wolves, and bargained with clubs only.

So this being settled, and I eager for the wine, wished it to be opened, especially to stand drink to my guide. The innkeeper was in another room. The guide was too courteous to ask for a corkscrew, and I did not know the Italian for a corkscrew.

I pointed to the cork, but all I got out of my guide was a remark that the wine was very good. Then I made the emblem and sign of a corkscrew in my sketch-book with a pencil, but he pretended not to understand--such was his breeding. Then I imitated the mode, sound, and gesture of a corkscrew entering a cork, and an old man next to me said 'Tira-buchon'--a common French word as familiar as the woods of Marly! It was brought. The bottle was opened and we all drank together.

As I rose to go out of Tizzano Val Parmense my guide said to me, 'Se chiama Tira-Buchon perche E' lira il buchon' And I said to him, 'Dominus Vobiscum' and left him to his hills.

I took the road downwards from the ridge into the next dip and valley, but after a mile or so in the great heat (it was now one o'clock) I was exhausted. So I went up to a little wooded bank, and lay there in the shade sketching Tizzano Val Parmense, where it stood not much above me, and then I lay down and slept for an hour and smoked a pipe and thought of many things.

From the ridge on which Tizzano stands, which is the third of these Apennine spurs, to the next, the fourth, is but a little way; one looks across from one to the other. Nevertheless it is a difficult piece of walking, because in the middle of the valley another ridge, almost as high as the principal spurs, runs down, and this has to be climbed at its lowest part before one can get down to the torrent of the Enza, where it runs with a hollow noise in the depths of the mountains. So the whole valley looks confused, and it appears, and is, laborious.

149

Very high up above in a mass of trees stood the first of those many ruined towers and castles in which the Apennines abound, and of which Canossa, far off and indistinguishable in the haze, was the chief example. It was called 'The Tower of Rugino'. Beyond the deep trench of the Enza, poised as it seemed on its southern bank (but really much further off, in the Secchia valley), stood that strange high rock of Castel-Nuovo, which the peasant had shown me that morning and which was the landmark of this attempt. It seemed made rather by man than by nature, so square and exact was it and so cut off from the other hills.

It was not till the later afternoon, when the air was already full of the golden dust that comes before the fall of the evening, that I stood above the Enza and saw it running thousands of feet below. Here I halted for a moment irresolute, and looked at the confusion of the hills. It had been my intention to make a straight line for Collagna, but I could not tell where Collagna lay save that it was somewhere behind the high mountain that was now darkening against the sky. Moreover, the Enza (as I could see down, down from where I stood) was not fordable. It did not run in streams but in one full current, and was a true river. All the scene was wild. I had come close to the central ridge of the Apennines. It stood above me but five or six clear miles away, and on its slopes there were patches and fields of snow which were beginning to glimmer in the diminishing light.

Four peasants sat on the edge of the road. They were preparing to go to their quiet homesteads, and they were gathering their scythes together, for they had been mowing in a field. Coming up to these, I asked them how I might reach Collagna. They told me that I could not go straight, as I had wished, on account of the impassable river, but that if I went down the steep directly below me I should find a bridge; that thence a path went up the opposite ridge to where a hamlet, called Ceregio (which they showed me beyond the valley), stood in trees on the crest, and once there (they said) I could be further directed. I understood all their speech except one fatal word. I thought they told me that Ceregio was *half* the way to Collagna; and what that error cost me you shall hear.

They drank my wine, I ate their bread, and we parted: they to go to their accustomed place, and I to cross this unknown valley. But when I had left these grave and kindly men, the echo of their voices remained with me; the deep valley of the Enza seemed lonely, and as I went lower and lower down towards the noise of the river I lost the sun.

The Enza was flooded. A rough bridge, made of stout logs resting on trunks of trees that were lashed together like tripods and supported a long plank, was afforded to cross it. But in the high water it did not quite reach to the hither bank. I rolled great stones into the water and made a short causeway, and so, somewhat perilously, I attained the farther shore, and went up, up by a little precipitous path till I reached the hamlet of Ceregio standing on its hill, blessed and secluded; for no road leads in or out of it, but only mule-paths.

The houses were all grouped together round a church; it was dim between them; but several men driving oxen took me to a house that was perhaps the inn, though there was no sign; and there in a twilight room we all sat down together like Christians in perfect harmony, and the woman of the house served us.

Now when, after this communion, I asked the way to Collagna, they must have thought me foolish, and have wondered why I did not pass the night with them, for they knew how far off Collagna was. But I (by the error in language of which I have told you) believed it to be but a short way off. It was in reality ten miles. The oldest of my companions said he would put me on the way.

We went together in the half light by a lane that followed the crest of the hill, and we passed a charming thing, a little white sculpture in relief, set up for a shrine and representing the Annunciation; and as we passed it we both smiled. Then in a few hundred yards we passed another that was the Visitation, and they were gracious and beautiful to a degree, and I saw that they stood for the five joyful mysteries. Then he had to leave me, and he said, pointing to the little shrine:

'When you come to the fifth of these the path divides. Take that to the left, and follow it round the hollow of the mountain: it will become a lane. This lane crosses a stream and passes near a tower. When you have reached the tower it joins a great highroad, and that is the road to Collagna.'

And when he indicated the shrines he smiled, as though in apology for them, and I saw that we were of the same religion. Then (since people who will not meet again should give each other presents mutually) I gave him the best of my two pipes, a new pipe with letters carved on it, which he took to be the initials of my name, and he on his part gave me a hedge-rose which he had plucked and had been holding in his fingers. And I continued the path alone.

Certainly these people have a benediction upon them, granted them for their simple lives and their justice. Their eyes are fearless and kindly. They are courteous, straight, and all have in them laughter and sadness. They are full of songs, of memories, of the stories of their native place; and their worship is conformable to the world that God made. May they possess their own land, and may their influence come again from Italy to save from jar, and boasting, and ineptitude the foolish, valourless cities, and the garish crowds of shouting men.... And let us especially pray that the revival of the faith may do something for our poor old universities.

151

Already, when I heard all these directions, they seemed to argue a longer road than I had expected. It proved interminable.

It was now fully dark; the night was very cold from the height of the hills; a dense dew began to fall upon the ground, and the sky was full of stars. For hours I went on slowly down the lane that ran round the hollow of the wooded mountain, wondering why I did not reach the stream he spoke of. It was midnight when I came to the level, and yet I heard no water, and did not yet see the tower against the sky. Extreme fatigue made it impossible, as I thought, to proceed farther, when I saw a light in a window, and went to it quickly and stood beneath it. A woman from the window called me *Caro mio,* which was gracious, but she would not let me sleep even in the straw of the barn.

I hobbled on in despair of the night, for the necessity of sleep was weighing me down after four high hills climbed that day, and after the rough ways and the heat and the continual marching.

I found a bridge which crossed the deep ravine they had told me of. This high bridge was new, and had been built of fine stone, yet it was broken and ruined, and a gap suddenly showed in the dark. I stepped back from it in fear. The clambering down to the stream and up again through the briars to regain the road broke me yet more, and when, on the hill beyond, I saw the tower faintly darker against the dark sky, I went up doggedly to it, fearing faintness, and reaching it where it stood (it was on the highest ground overlooking the Secchia valley), I sat down on a stone beside it and waited for the morning.

The long slope of the hills fell away for miles to where, by daylight, would have lain the misty plain of Emilia. The darkness confused the landscape. The silence of the mountains and the awful solemnity of the place lent that vast panorama a sense of the terrible, under the dizzy roof of the stars. Every now and again some animal of the night gave a cry in the undergrowth of the valley, and the great rock of Castel-Nuovo, now close and enormous--bare, rugged, a desert place--added something of doom.

The hours were creeping on with the less certain stars; a very faint and unliving grey touched the edges of the clouds. The cold possessed me, and I rose to walk, if I could walk, a little farther.

What is that in the mind which, after (it may be) a slight disappointment or a petty accident, causes it to suffer on the scale of grave things?

I have waited for the dawn a hundred times, attended by that mournful, colourless spirit which haunts the last hours of darkness; and influenced especially by the great timeless apathy that hangs round the first uncertain promise of increasing light. For there is an hour before daylight when men die, and when there is nothing above the soul or around it, when even the stars fail.

And this long and dreadful expectation I had thought to be worst when one was alone at sea in a small boat without wind; drifting beyond one's harbour in the ebb of the outer channel tide, and sogging back at the first flow on the broad, confused movement of a sea without any waves. In such lonely mornings I have watched the Owers light turning, and I have counted up my gulf of time, and wondered that moments could be so stretched out in the clueless mind. I have prayed for the morning or for a little draught of wind, and this I have thought, I say, the extreme of absorption into emptiness and longing.

But now, on this ridge, dragging myself on to the main road, I found a deeper abyss of isolation and despairing fatigue than I had ever known, and I came near to turning eastward and imploring the hastening of light, as men pray continually without reason for things that can but come in a due order. I still went forward a little, because when I sat down my loneliness oppressed me like a misfortune; and because my feet, going painfully and slowly, yet gave a little balance and rhythm to the movement of my mind.

I heard no sound of animals or birds. I passed several fields, deserted in the half-darkness; and in some I felt the hay, but always found it wringing wet with dew, nor could I discover a good shelter from the wind that blew off the upper snow of the summits. For a little space of time there fell upon me, as I crept along the road, that shadow of sleep which numbs the mind, but it could not compel me to lie down, and I accepted it only as a partial and beneficent oblivion which covered my desolation and suffering as a thin, transparent cloud may cover an evil moon.

Then suddenly the sky grew lighter upon every side. That cheating gloom (which I think the clouds in purgatory must reflect) lifted from the valley as though to a slow order given by some calm and good influence that was marshalling in the day. Their colours came back to things; the trees recovered their shape, life, and trembling; here and there, on the face of the mountain opposite, the mists by their movement took part in the new life, and I thought I heard for the first time the tumbling water far below me in the ravine. That subtle barrier was drawn which marks to-day from yesterday; all the night and its despondency became the past and entered memory. The road before me, the pass on my left (my last ridge, and the entry into Tuscany), the mass of the great hills, had become mixed into the increasing light, that is, into the familiar and invigorating Present which I have always found capable of opening the doors of the future with a gesture of victory.

My pain either left me, or I ceased to notice it, and seeing a little way before me a bank above the road, and a fine grove of sparse and

153

dominant chestnuts, I climbed up thither and turned, standing to the east.

There, without any warning of colours, or of the heraldry that we have in the north, the sky was a great field of pure light, and without doubt it was all woven through, as was my mind watching it, with security and gladness. Into this field, as I watched it, rose the sun.

The air became warmer almost suddenly. The splendour and health of the new day left me all in repose, and persuaded or compelled me to immediate sleep.

I found therefore in the short grass, and on the scented earth beneath one of my trees, a place for lying down; I stretched myself out upon it, and lapsed into a profound slumber, which nothing but a vague and tenuous delight separated from complete forgetfulness. If the last confusion of thought, before sleep possessed me, was a kind of prayer-- and certainly I was in the mood of gratitude and of adoration--this prayer was of course to God, from whom every good proceeds, but partly (idolatrously) to the Sun, which, of all the things He has made, seems, of what we at least can discover, the most complete and glorious.

Therefore the first hours of the sunlight, after I had wakened, made the place like a new country; for my mind which received it was new. I reached Collagna before the great heat, following the fine highroad that went dipping and rising again along the mountain side, and then (leaving the road and crossing the little Secchia by a bridge), a path, soon lost in a grassy slope, gave me an indication of my way. For when I had gone an hour or so upwards along the shoulder of the hill, there opened gradually before me a silent and profound vale, hung with enormous woods, and sloping upwards to where it was closed by a high bank beneath and between two peaks. This bank I knew could be nothing else than the central ridge of the Apennines, the watershed, the boundary of Tuscany, and the end of all the main part of my journey. Beyond, the valleys would open on to the Tuscan Plain, and at the southern limit of that, Siena was my mark; from Siena to Rome an eager man, if he is sound, may march in three long days. Nor was that calculation all. The satisfaction of the last lap, of the home run, went with the word Tuscany in my mind; these cities were the approaches and introduction of the end.

When I had slept out the heat, I followed the woods upward through the afternoon. They stood tangled and huge, and the mosses under them were thick and silent, because in this last belt of the mountains height and coolness reproduced the north. A charcoal burner was making his furnace; after that for the last miles there was no sound. Even the floor of the vale was a depth of grass, and no torrent ran in it but only a little hidden stream, leafy like our streams at home.

154

At last the steep bank, a wall at the end of the valley, rose immediately above me. It was very steep and bare, desolate with the many stumps of trees that had been cut down; but all its edge and fringe against the sky was the line of a deep forest.

After its laborious hundreds of feet, when the forest that crowned it evenly was reached, the Apennines were conquered, the last great range was passed, and there stood no barrier between this high crest and Rome.

The hither side of that bank, I say, had been denuded of its trees; the roots of secular chestnuts stood like graves above the dry steep, and had marked my last arduous climb. Now, at the summit, the highest part was a line of cool forest, and the late afternoon mingled with the sanctity of trees. A genial dampness pervaded the earth beneath; grasses grew, and there were living creatures in the shade.

Nor was this tenanted wood all the welcome I received on my entry into Tuscany. Already I heard the noise of falling waters upon every side, where the Serchio sprang from twenty sources on the southern slope, and leapt down between mosses, and quarrelled, and overcame great smooth dark rocks in busy falls. Indeed, it was like my own country in the north, and a man might say to himself--'After so much journeying, perhaps I am in the Enchanted Wood, and may find at last the fairy Melisaunde.'

A glade opened, and, the trees no longer hiding it, I looked down the vale, which was the gate of Tuscany. There--high, jagged, rapt into the sky--stood such a group of mountains as men dream of in good dreams, or see in the works of painters when old age permits them revelations. Their height was evident from the faint mist and grey of their hues; their outline was tumultuous, yet balanced; full of accident and poise. It was as though these high walls of Carrara, the western boundary of the valley, had been shaped expressly for man, in order to exalt him with unexpected and fantastic shapes, and to expand his dull life with a permanent surprise. For a long time I gazed at these great hills.

Then, more silent in the mind through their influence, I went down past the speech and companionship of the springs of the Serchio, and the chestnut trees were redolent of evening all round. Down the bank to where the streams met in one, down the river, across its gaping, ruinous bridge (which some one, generations ago, had built for the rare travellers--there were then no main roads across the Apennine, and perhaps this rude pass was in favour); down still more gently through the narrow upper valley I went between the chestnut trees, and calm went with me for a companion: and the love of men and the expectation of good seemed natural to all that had been made in this blessed place. Of Borda, where the peasants directed me, there is no need to speak, till crossing the Serchio once more, this time on a trestle bridge of wood, I passed by a wider path through the groves, and entered the

155

dear village of Sillano, which looks right into the pure west. And the peaks are guardians all about it: the elder brothers of this remote and secluded valley.

An inn received me: a great kitchen full of men and women talking, a supper preparing, a great fire, meat smoking and drying in the ingle-nook, a vast timbered roof going up into darkness: there I was courteously received, but no one understood my language. Seeing there a young priest, I said to him--

'Pater, habeo linguam latinam, sed non habeo linguam Italicam. Visne mi dare traductionem in istam linguam Toscanam non nullorum verborum?'

To this he replied, 'Libenter,' and the people revered us both. Thus he told me the name for a knife was cultello; for a room, camera par domire; for 'what is it called?' 'come si chiama?'; for 'what is the road to?' 'quella e la via a ...?' and other phrases wherein, no doubt, I am wrong; but I only learnt by ear.

Then he said to me something I did not understand, and I answered, 'Pol-Hercle!' at which he seemed pleased enough.

Then, to make conversation, I said, 'Diaconus es?'

And he answered me, mildly and gravely, 'Presbyter sum.'

And a little while after he left for his house, but I went out on to the balcony, where men and women were talking in subdued tones. There, alone, I sat and watched the night coming up into these Tuscan hills. The first moon since that waning in Lorraine--(how many nights ago, how many marches!)--hung in the sky, a full crescent, growing into brightness and glory as she assumed her reign. The one star of the west called out his silent companions in their order; the mountains merged into a fainter confusion; heaven and the infinite air became the natural seat of any spirit that watched this spell. The fire-flies darted in the depths of vineyards and of trees below; then the noise of the grasshoppers brought back suddenly the gardens of home, and whatever benediction surrounds our childhood. Some promise of eternal pleasures and of rest deserved haunted the village of Sillano.

In very early youth the soul can still remember its immortal habitation, and clouds and the edges of hills are of another kind from ours, and every scent and colour has a savour of Paradise. What that quality may be no language can tell, nor have men made any words, no, nor any music, to recall it--only in a transient way and elusive the recollection of what youth was, and purity, flashes on us in phrases of the poets, and is gone before we can fix it in our minds--oh! my friends, if we could but recall it! Whatever those sounds may be that are beyond our sounds, and whatever are those keen lives which remain alive there under memory--whatever is Youth--Youth came up that valley at evening, borne upon a southern air. If we deserve or attain beatitude, such things shall at last be our settled state; and their now sudden influence upon the soul in short ecstasies is the proof that they stand outside time, and are not subject to decay.

This, then, was the blessing of Sillano, and here was perhaps the highest moment of those seven hundred miles--or more. Do not therefore be astonished, reader, if I now press on much more hurriedly to Rome, for the goal is almost between my hands, and the chief moment has been enjoyed, until I shall see the City.

Now I cry out and deplore me that this next sixty miles of way, but especially the heat of the days and the dank mists of the night, should have to be told as of a real journey in this very repetitive and sui-similar world. How much rather I wish that being free from mundane and wide-awake (that is to say from perilously dusty) considerations and droughty boredoms, I might wander forth at leisure through the air and visit the regions where everything is as the soul chooses: to be dropped at last in the ancient and famous town of Siena, whence comes that kind of common brown paint wherewith men, however wicked, can produce (if they have but the art) very surprising effects of depth in painting: for so I read of it in a book by a fool, at six shillings, and even that was part of a series: but if you wish to know anything further of the matter, go you and read it, for I will do nothing of the kind.

Oh to be free for strange voyages even for a little while! I am tired of the road; and so are you, and small blame to you. Your fathers also tired of the treadmill, and mine of the conquering marches of the Republic. Heaven bless you all!

But I say that if it were not for the incredulity and doubt and agnostico-schismatical hesitation, and very cumbersome air of questioning-and-peering-about, which is the bane of our moderns, very certainly I should now go on to tell of giants as big as cedars, living in mountains of precious stones, and drawn to battle by dragons in cars of gold; or of towns where the customs of men were remote and unexpected; of countries not yet visited, and of the gods returning. For though it is permissible, and a pleasant thing (as Bacon says), to mix a little falsehood with one's truth (so St Louis mixed water with his wine, and so does Sir John Growl mix vinegar with his, unless I am greatly mistaken, for if not, how does he give it that taste at his dinners? eh? There, I think, is a question that would puzzle him!) yet is it much more delectable, and far worthier of the immortal spirit of man to soar into the empyrean of pure lying--that is, to lay the bridle on the neck of Pegasus and let him go forward, while in the saddle meanwhile one sits well back, grips with the knee, takes the race, and on the energy of that steed visits the wheeling stars.

This much, then, is worth telling of the valley of the Serchio, that it is narrow, garrulous with water brawling, wooded densely, and contained by fantastic mountains. That it has a splendid name, like the clashing of cymbals--Garfagnana; that it leads to the Tuscan plain, and that it is over a day's march long. Also, it is an oven.

Never since the early liars first cooked eggs in the sand was there such heat, and it was made hotter by the consciousness of folly, than which there is no more heating thing; for I think that not old Championnet himself, with his Division of Iron, that fought one to three and crushed the aged enormities of the oppressors as we would crush an empty egg, and that found the summer a good time for fighting in Naples, I say that he himself would not have marched men up the Garfagnana in such a sun. Folly planned it, Pride held to it, and the devils lent their climate. Garfagnana! Garfagnana! to have such a pleasant name, and to be what you are!

Not that there were not old towers on the steep woods of the Apennine, nor glimpses of the higher peaks; towns also: one castle surrounded by a fringe of humble roofs--there were all these things. But it was an oven. So imagine me, after having passed chapels built into rocks, and things most curious, but the whole under the strain of an intolerable sun, coming, something after midday, to a place called Castel-Nuovo, the first town, for Campogiamo is hardly a town.

At Castel-Nuovo I sat upon a bridge and thought, not what good men think (there came into my memory no historical stuff; for all I know, Liberty never went by that valley in arms); no appreciation of beauty filled me; I was indifferent to all save the intolerable heat, when I suddenly recognized the enormous number of bridges that bespattered the town.

'This is an odd thing,' I mused. 'Here is a little worriment of a town up in the hills, and what a powerful lot of bridges!'

I cared not a fig for the thousand things I had been told to expect in Tuscany; everything is in a mind, and as they were not in my mind they did not exist. But the bridges, they indeed were worthy of admiration!

Here was a horrible little place on a torrent bank. One bridge was reasonable for by it went the road leading south to Lucca and to Rome; it was common honour to let men escape. But as I sat on that main bridge I counted seven others; indeed there must have been a worship of a bridge-god some time or other to account for such a necklace of bridges in such a neglected borough.

You may say (I am off hard on the road to Borgo, drooping with the heat, but still going strongly), you may say that is explicable enough. First a thing is useful, you say, then it has to become routine; then the habit, being a habit, gets a sacred idea attached to it. So with bridges:

e.g. Pontifex; Dervorguilla, our Ballici saint that built a bridge; the devil that will hinder the building of bridges; *cf.* the Porphyry Bridge in the Malay cosmogony; Amershickel, Brueckengebildung im kult-Historischer. Passenmayer; Durat, *Le pont antique, etude sur les origines Toscanes;* Mr Dacre's *The Command of Bridges in Warfare; Bridges and Empire,* by Captain Hole, U.S.A. You may say all this; I shall not reply. If the heat has hindered me from saying a word of the fine open valley on the left, of the little railway and of the last of the hills, do you suppose it will permit me to discuss the sanctity of bridges? If it did, I think there is a little question on 'why should habit turn sacred?' which would somewhat confound and pose you, and pose also, for that matter, every pedant that ever went blind and crook-backed over books, or took ivory for horn. And there is an end of it. Argue it with whom you will. It is evening, and I am at Borgo (for if many towns are called Castel-Nuovo so are many called Borgo in Italy), and I desire to be free of interruption while I eat and sleep and reflect upon the error of that march in that heat, spoiling nearly thirty miles of road, losing so many great and pleasurable emotions, all for haste and from a neglect of the Italian night.

And as I ate, and before I slept, I thought of that annotated Guide Book which is cried out for by all Europe, and which shall tell blunt truths. Look you out *'Garfagnana, district of, Valley of Serchio'* in the index. You will be referred to p. 267. Turn to p. 267. You will find there the phrase--

'One can walk from the pretty little village of Sillano, nestling in its chestnut groves, to the flourishing town of Borgo on the new Bagni railway in a day.'

You will find a mark[1] after that phrase. It refers to a footnote. Glance (or look) at the bottom of the page and you will find:

So I slept late and uneasily the insufficient sleep of men who have suffered, and in that uneasy sleep I discovered this great truth: that if in a southern summer you do not rest in the day the night will seem intolerably warm, but that, if you rest in the day, you will find coolness and energy at evening.

The next morning with daylight I continued the road to Lucca, and of that also I will say nothing.

LECTOR. Why on earth did you write this book?

AUCTOR. For my amusement.

LECTOR. And why do you suppose I got it?

---

[1] But if one does one is a fool.

AUCTOR. I cannot conceive ... however, I will give up this much, to tell you that at Decimo the mystery of cypress trees first came into my adventure and pilgrimage: of cypress trees which henceforward were to mark my Tuscan road. And I will tell you that there also I came across a thing peculiar (I suppose) to the region of Lucca, for I saw it there as at Decimo, and also some miles beyond. I mean fine mournful towers built thus: In the first storey one arch, in the second two, in the third three, and so on: a very noble way of building.

And I will tell you something more. I will tell you something no one has yet heard. To wit, why this place is called Decimo, and why just below it is another little spot called Sexta.

LECTOR.. ..

AUCTOR. I know what you are going to say! Do not say it. You are going to say: 'It is because they were at the sixth and tenth milestones from Lucca on the Roman road.' Heaven help these scientists! Did you suppose that I thought it was called Decimo because the people had ten toes? Tell me, why is not every place ten miles out of a Roman town called by such a name? Eh? You are dumb. You cannot answer. Like most moderns you have entirely missed the point. We all know that there was a Roman town at Lucca, because it was called Luca, and if there had been no Roman town the modern town would not be spelt with two *c's*. All Roman towns had milestones beyond them. But why did *this* tenth milestone from *this* Roman town keep its name?

LECTOR. I am indifferent.

AUCTOR. I will tell you. Up in the tangle of the Carrara mountains, overhanging the Garfagnana, was a wild tribe, whose name I forget (unless it were the Bruttii), but which troubled the Romans not a little, defeating them horribly, and keeping the legionaries in some anxiety for years. So when the soldiers marched out north from Luca about six miles, they could halt and smile at each other, and say 'At *Sextant*... that's all right. All safe so far!' and therefore only a little village grew up at this little rest and emotion. But as they got nearer the gates of the hills they began to be visibly perturbed, and they would say: 'The eighth mile! cheer up!' Then 'The ninth mile! Sanctissima Madonna! Have you seen anything moving on the heights?' But when they got to the *tenth* milestone, which stands before the very jaws of the defile, then indeed they said with terrible emphasis, *'Ad Decimam!'* And there was no restraining them: they would camp and entrench, or die in the venture: for they were Romans and stern fellows, and loved a good square camp and a ditch, and sentries and a clear moon, and plenty of sharp stakes, and all the panoply of war. That is the origin of Decimo.

For all my early start, the intolerable heat had again taken the ascendant before I had fairly entered the plain. Then, it being yet but morning, I entered from the north the town of Lucca, which is the neatest, the regularest, the exactest, the most fly-in-amber little town in the world, with its uncrowded streets, its absurd fortifications, and its contented silent houses--all like a family at ease and at rest under its high sun. It is as sharp and trim as its own map, and that map is as clear as a geometrical problem. Everything in Lucca is good.

I went with a short shadow, creeping when I could on the eastern side of the street to save the sunlight; then I came to the main square, and immediately on my left was the Albergo di Something-or-other, a fine great hotel, but most unfortunately right facing the blazing sky. I had to stop outside it to count my money. I counted it wrong and entered. There I saw the master, who talked French.

'Can you in an hour,' said I, 'give me a meal to my order, then a bed, though it is early day?' This absurd question I made less absurd by explaining to him my purpose. How I was walking to Rome and how, being northern, I was unaccustomed to such heat; how, therefore, I had missed sleep, and would find it necessary in future to walk mainly by night. For I had now determined to fill the last few marches up in darkness, and to sleep out the strong hours of the sun.

All this he understood; I ordered such a meal as men give to beloved friends returned from wars. I ordered a wine I had known long ago in the valley of the Saone in the old time of peace before ever the Greek came to the land. While they cooked it I went to their cool and splendid cathedral to follow a late Mass. Then I came home and ate their admirable food and drank the wine which the Burgundians had trodden upon the hills of gold so many years before. They showed me a regal kind of a room where a bed with great hangings invited repose.

All my days of marching, the dirty inns, the forests, the nights abroad, the cold, the mists, the sleeplessness, the faintness, the dust, the dazzling sun, the Apennines--all my days came over me, and there fell on me a peaceful weight, as his two hundred years fell upon Charlemagne in the tower of Saragossa when the battle was done; after he had curbed the valley of Ebro and christened Bramimonde.

So I slept deeply all day long; and, outside, the glare made a silence upon the closed shutters, save that little insects darted in the outer air.

When I woke it was evening. So well had they used me that I paid what they asked, and, not knowing what money remained over, I left their town by the southern gate, crossed the railway and took the road.

My way lay under the flank of that mountain whereby the Luccans cannot see Pisa, or the Pisans cannot see Lucca--it is all one to me, I shall not live in either town, God willing; and if they are so eager to squint at one another, in Heaven's name, cannot they be at the pains to walk round the end of the hill? It is this laziness which is the ruin of

161

many; but not of pilgrims, for here was I off to cross the plain of Arno in one night, and reach by morning the mouth and gate of that valley of the Elsa, which same is a very manifest proof of how Rome was intended to be the end and centre of all roads, the chief city of the world, and the Popes' residence--as, indeed, it plainly is to this day, for all the world to deny at their peril, spiritual, geographical, historical, sociological, economic, and philosophical.

For if some such primeval and predestinarian quality were not inherent in the City, how, think you, would the valley of the Serchio--the hot, droughty, and baking Garfagnana--lead down pointing straight to Rome; and how would that same line, prolonged across the plain, find fitting it exactly beyond that plain this vale of the Elsa, itself leading up directly towards Rome? I say, nowhere in the world is such a coincidence observable, and they that will not take it for a portent may go back to their rationalism and consort with microbes and make their meals off logarithms, washed down with an exact distillation of the root of minus one; and the peace of fools, that is the deepest and most balmy of all, be theirs for ever and ever.

Here again you fall into errors as you read, ever expecting something new; for of that night's march there is nothing to tell, save that it was cool, full of mist, and an easy matter after the royal entertainment and sleep of the princely Albergo that dignifies Lucca. The villages were silent, the moon soon left the sky, and the stars could not show through the fog, which deepened in the hours after midnight.

A map I had bought in Lucca made the difficulties of the first part of the road (though there were many cross-ways) easy enough; and the second part, in midnight and the early hours, was very plain sailing, till--having crossed the main line and having, at last, very weary, come up to the branch railway at a slant from the west and north, I crossed that also under the full light--I stood fairly in the Elsa valley and on the highroad which follows the railway straight to Siena. That long march, I say, had been easy enough in the coolness and in the dark; but I saw nothing; my interior thoughts alone would have afforded matter for this part; but of these if you have not had enough in near six hundred miles of travel, you are a stouter fellow than I took you for.

Though it was midsummer, the light had come quickly. Long after sunrise the mist dispersed, and the nature of the valley appeared.

It was in no way mountainous, but easy, pleasant, and comfortable, bounded by low, rounded hills, having upon them here and there a row of cypresses against the sky; and it was populous with pleasant farms. Though the soil was baked and dry, as indeed it is everywhere in this south, yet little regular streams (or canals) irrigated it and nourished many trees--- but the deep grass of the north was wanting.

162

For an hour or more after sunrise I continued my way very briskly; then what had been the warmth of the early sun turned into the violent heat of day, and remembering Merlin where he says that those who will walk by night must sleep by day, and having in my mind the severe verses of James Bayle, sometime Fellow of St Anne's, that 'in Tuscan summers as a general rule, the days are sultry but the nights are cool' (he was no flamboyant poet; he loved the quiet diction of the right wing of English poetry), and imagining an owlish habit of sleeping by day could be acquired at once, I lay down under a tree of a kind I had never seen; and lulled under the pleasant fancy that this was a picture-tree drawn before the Renaissance, and that I was reclining in some background landscape of the fifteenth century (for the scene was of that kind), I fell asleep.

When I woke it was as though I had slept long; but I doubted the feeling. The young sun still low in the sky, and the shadows not yet shortened, puzzled me. I looked at my watch, but the dislocation of habit which night marches produce had left it unwound. It marked a quarter to three, which was absurd. I took the road somewhat stiffly and wondering. I passed several small white cottages; there was no clock in them, and their people were away. At last in a Trattoria, as they served me with food, a woman told me it was just after seven; I had slept but an hour.

Outside, the day was intense; already flies had begun to annoy the darkened room within. Through the half-curtained door the road was white in the sun, and the railway ran just beyond.

I paid my reckoning, and then, partly for an amusement, I ranged my remaining pence upon the table, first in the shape of a Maltese cross, then in a circle (interesting details!). The road lay white in the sunlight outside, and the railway ran just beyond.

I counted the pence and the silver--there was three francs and a little over; I remembered the imperial largesse at Lucca, the lordly spending of great sums, where, now in the pocket of an obsequious man, the pounds were taking care of themselves. I remembered how at Como I had been compelled by poverty to enter the train for Milan. How little was three francs for the remaining twenty-five miles to Siena! The road lay white in the sunlight, and the railway ran just beyond.

I remembered the pleasing cheque in the post-office of Siena; the banks of Siena, and the money changers at their counters changing money at the rate of change.

'If one man,' thought I, 'may take five per cent discount on a sum of money in the exchange, may not another man take discount off a walk of over seven hundred miles? May he not cut off it, as his due, twenty-five miserable little miles in the train?' Sleep coming over me after my meal increased the temptation. Alas! how true is the great phrase of

Averroes (or it may be Boa-ed-din: anyhow, the Arabic escapes me, but the meaning is plain enough), that when one has once fallen, it is easy to fall again (saving always heavy falls from cliffs and high towers, for after these there is no more falling).... Examine the horse's knees before you buy him; take no ticket-of-leave man into your house for charity; touch no prospectus that has founders' shares, and do not play with firearms or knives and never go near the water till you know how to swim. Oh! blessed wisdom of the ages! sole patrimony of the poor! The road lay white in the sun, and the railway ran just beyond.

If the people of Milo did well to put up a statue in gold to the man that invented wheels, so should we also put one up in Portland stone or plaster to the man that invented rails, whose property it is not only to increase the speed and ease of travel, but also to bring on slumber as can no drug: not even poppies gathered under a waning moon. The rails have a rhythm of slight falls and rises ... they make a loud roar like a perpetual torrent; they cover up the mind with a veil.

Once only, when a number of men were shouting 'POGGI-BON-SI,' like a war-cry to the clank of bronze, did I open my eyes sleepily to see a hill, a castle wall, many cypresses, and a strange tower bulging out at the top (such towers I learned were the feature of Tuscany). Then in a moment, as it seemed, I awoke in the station of Siena, where the railway ends and goes no farther.

It was still only morning; but the glare was beyond bearing as I passed through the enormous gate of the town, a gate pierced in high and stupendous walls that are here guarded by lions. In the narrow main street there was full shade, and it was made cooler by the contrast of the blaze on the higher storeys of the northern side. The wonders of Siena kept sleep a moment from my mind. I saw their great square where a tower of vast height marks the guildhall. I heard Mass in a chapel of their cathedral: a chapel all frescoed, and built, as it were, out of doors, and right below the altar-end or choir. I noted how the city stood like a queen of hills dominating all Tuscany: above the Elsa northward, southward above the province round Mount Amiato. And this great mountain I saw also hazily far off on the horizon. I suffered the vulgarities of the main street all in English and American, like a show. I took my money and changed it; then, having so passed not a full hour, and oppressed by weariness, I said to myself:

'After all, my business is not with cities, and already I have seen far off the great hill whence one can see far off the hills that overhang Rome.'

With this in my mind I wandered out for a quiet place, and found it in a desolate green to the north of the city, near a huge, old red-brick church like a barn. A deep shadow beneath it invited me in spite of the scant and dusty grass, and in this country no one disturbs the wanderer. There, lying down, I slept without dreams till evening.

164

AUCTOR. Turn to page 94.

LECTOR. I have it. It is not easy to watch the book in two places at once; but pray continue.

AUCTOR. Note the words from the eighth to the tenth lines.

LECTOR. Why?

AUCTOR. They will make what follows seem less abrupt.

Once there was a man dining by himself at the Cafe Anglais, in the days when people went there. It was a full night, and he sat alone at a small table, when there entered a very big man in a large fur coat. The big man looked round annoyed, because there was no room, and the first man very courteously offered him a seat at his little table. They sat down and ate and talked of several things; among others, of Bureaucracy. The first maintained that Bureaucracy was the curse of France.

'Men are governed by it like sheep. The administrator, however humble, is a despot; most people will even run forward to meet him halfway, like the servile dogs they are,' said he.

'No,' answered the Man in the Big Fur Coat, 'I should say men were governed just by the ordinary human sense of authority. I have no theories. I say they recognize authority and obey it. Whether it is bureaucratic or not is merely a question of form.'

At this moment there came in a tall, rather stiff Englishman. He also was put out at finding no room. The two men saw the manager approach him; a few words were passed, and a card; then the manager suddenly smiled, bowed, smirked, and finally went up to the table and begged that the Duke of Sussex might be allowed to share it. The Duke hoped he did not incommode these gentlemen. They assured him that, on the contrary, they esteemed his presence a favour.

'It is our prerogative,' said the Man in the Big Fur Coat, 'to be the host Paris entertaining her Guest.'

They would take no denial; they insisted on the Duke's dining with them, and they told him what they had just been discussing. The Duke listened to their theories with some *morgue*, much *spleen*, and no little *phlegm*, but with *perfect courtesy,* and then, towards the coffee, told them in fluent French with a strong accent, his own opinion. (He had had eight excellent courses; Yquem with his fish, the best Chambertin during the dinner, and a glass of wonderful champagne with his dessert.) He spoke as follows, with a slight and rather hard smile:

'My opinion may seem to you impertinent, but I believe nothing more subtly and powerfully affects men than the aristocratic feeling. Do not misunderstand me,' he added, seeing that they would protest; 'it is not my own experience alone that guides me. All history bears witness to the same truth.'

The simple-minded Frenchmen put down this infatuation to the Duke's early training, little knowing that our English men of rank are the simplest fellows in the world, and are quite indifferent to their titles save in business matters.

The Frenchmen paid the bill, and they all three went on to the Boulevard.

'Now,' said the first man to his two companions, 'I will give you a practical example of what I meant when I said that Bureaucracy governed mankind.'

He went up to the wall of the Credit Lyonnais, put the forefinger of either hand against it, about twenty-five centimetres apart, and at a level of about a foot above his eyes. Holding his fingers thus he gazed at them, shifting them slightly from time to time and moving his glance from one to the other rapidly. A crowd gathered. In a few moments a pleasant elderly, short, and rather fat gentleman in the crowd came forward, and, taking off his hat, asked if he could do anything for him.

'Why,' said our friend, 'the fact is I am an engineer (section D of the Public Works Department) and I have to make an important measurement in connexion with the Apothegm of the Bilateral which runs to-night precisely through this spot. My fingers now mark exactly the concentric of the secondary focus whence the Radius Vector should be drawn, but I find that (like a fool) I have left my Double Refractor in the cafe hard by. I dare not go for fear of losing the place I have marked; yet I can get no further without my Double Refractor.'

'Do not let that trouble you,' said the short, stout stranger; 'I will be delighted to keep the place exactly marked while you run for your instrument.'

The crowd was now swelled to a considerable size; it blocked up the pavement, and was swelled every moment by the arrival of the curious. The little fat elderly man put his fingers exactly where the other's had been, effecting the exchange with a sharp gesture; and each watched intently to see that it was right to within a millimetre. The attitude was constrained. The elderly man smiled, and begged the engineer not to be alarmed. So they left him with his two forefingers well above his head, precisely twenty-five centimetres apart, and pressing their tips against the wall of the Credit Lyonnais. Then the three friends slipped out of the crowd and pursued their way.

'Let us go to the theatre,' said the experimenter, 'and when we come back I warrant you will agree with my remarks on Bureaucracy.'

They went to hear the admirable marble lines of Corneille. For three hours they were absorbed by the classics, and, when they returned, a crowd, now enormous, was surging all over the Boulevard, stopping the traffic and filled with a noise like the sea. Policemen were attacking it with the utmost energy, but still it grew and eddied; and in the centre-- a little respectful space kept empty around him--still stretched the poor little fat elderly man, a pitiable sight. His knees were bent, his head wagged and drooped with extreme fatigue, he was the colour of old blotting-paper; but still he kept the tips of his two forefingers exactly twenty-five centimetres apart, well above his head, and pressed against the wall of the Credit Lyonnais.

'You will not match that with your aristocratic sentiment!' said the author of the scene in pardonable triumph.

'I am not so sure,' answered the Duke of Sussex. He pulled out his watch. 'It is midnight,' he said, 'and I must be off; but let me tell you before we part that you have paid for a most expensive dinner, and have behaved all night with an extravagant deference under the impression that I was the Duke of Sussex. As a fact my name is Jerks, and I am a commercial traveller in the linseed oil line; and I wish you the best of good evenings.'

'Wait a moment,' said the Man in the Big Fur Coat; 'my theory of the Simple Human Sense of Authority still holds. I am a detective officer, and you will both be good enough to follow me to the police station.'

And so they did, and the Engineer was fined fifty francs in correctional, and the Duke of Sussex was imprisoned for ten days, with interdiction of domicile for six months; the first indeed under the Prefectorial Decree of the 18th of November 1843, but the second under the law of the 12th germinal of the year VIII.

In this way I have got over between twenty and thirty miles of road which were tramped in the dark, and the description of which would have plagued you worse than a swarm of hornets.

Oh, blessed interlude! no struggling moon, no mist, no long-winded passages upon the genial earth, no the sense of the night, no marvels of the dawn, no rhodomontade, no religion, no rhetoric, no sleeping villages, no silent towns (there was one), no rustle of trees--just a short story, and there you have a whole march covered as though a brigade had swung down it. A new day has come, and the sun has risen over the detestable parched hillocks of this downward way.

No, no, Lector! Do not blame me that Tuscany should have passed beneath me unnoticed, as the monotonous sea passes beneath a boat in full sail. Blame all those days of marching; hundreds upon hundreds of miles that exhausted the powers of the mind. Blame the fiery and angry sky of Etruria, that compelled most of my way to be taken at night. Blame St Augustine, who misled me in his Confessions by talking like an African of 'the icy shores of Italy'; or blame Rome, that now more and more drew me to Herself as She approached from six to five, from five to four, from four to three--now She was but *three* days off. The third sun after that I now saw rising would shine upon the City.

I did indeed go forward a little in the heat, but it was useless. After an hour I abandoned it. It was not so much the sun, though that was intemperate and deadly; it was rather the inhuman aspect of the earth which made me despair. It was as though the soil had been left imperfect and rough after some cataclysm; it reminded me of those bad lands in the west of America, where the desert has no form, and where the crumbling and ashy look of things is more abhorrent than their mere desolation. As soon march through evil dreams!

The north is the place for men. Eden was there; and the four rivers of Paradise are the Seine, the Oise, the Thames, and the Arun; there are grasses there, and the trees are generous, and the air is an unnoticed pleasure. The waters brim up to the edges of the fields. But for this bare Tuscany I was never made.

How far I had gone I could not tell, nor precisely how much farther San Quirico, the neighbouring town, might be. The imperfect map I had bought at Siena was too minute to give me clear indications. I was content to wait for evening, and then to go on till I found it. An hour or so in the shade of a row of parched and dusty bushes I lay and ate and drank my wine, and smoked, and then all day I slept, and woke a while, and slept again more deeply. But how people sleep and wake, if you do not yet know it after so much of this book you never will.

It was perhaps five o'clock, or rather more, when I rose unhappily and took up the ceaseless road.

Even the goodness of the Italian nature seemed parched up in those dry hollows. At an inn where I ate they shouted at me, thinking in that way to make me understand; and their voices were as harsh as the grating of metal against stone. A mile farther I crossed a lonely line of railway; then my map told me where I was, and I went wearily up an indefinite slope under the declining sun, and thought it outrageous that only when the light had gone was there any tolerable air in this country.

Soon the walls of San Quirico, partly ruinous, stood above the fields (for the smallest places here have walls); as I entered its gate the sun set, and as though the cool, coming suddenly, had a magic in it, everything turned kinder. A church that could wake interest stood at the entry of the town; it had stone lions on its steps, and the pillars were so carved as to resemble knotted ropes. There for the first time I saw in procession one of those confraternities which in Italy bury the dead; they had long and dreadful hoods over their heads, with slits for the eyes. I spoke to the people of San Quirico, and they to me. They were upstanding, and very fine and noble in the lines of the face. On their walls is set a marble tablet, on which it is registered that the people of Tuscany, being asked whether they would have their hereditary Duke or the House of Savoy, voted for the latter by such and such a great majority; and this kind of tablet I afterwards found was common to all these small towns. Then passing down their long street I came, at the farther gate, to a great sight, which the twilight still permitted me to receive in its entirety.

For San Quirico is built on the edge of a kind of swell in the land, and here where I stood one looked over the next great wave; for the shape of the view was, on a vast scale, just what one sees from a lonely boat looking forward over a following sea.

The trough of the wave was a shallow purple valley, its arid quality hidden by the kindly glimmer of evening; few trees stood in it to break its sweep, and its irregularities and mouldings were just those of a sweep of water after a gale. The crest of the wave beyond was seventeen miles away. It had, as have also such crests at sea, one highest, toppling peak in its long line, and this, against the clear sky, one could see to be marked by buildings. These buildings were the ruined castle and walls of Radicofani, and it lay straight on my way to Rome.

It is a strange thing, arresting northern eyes, to see towns thus built on summits up into the sky, and this height seemed the more fantastic because it was framed. A row of cypress trees stood on either side of the road where it fell from San Quirico, and, exactly between these, this high crest, a long way off, was set as though by design.

With more heart in me, and tempted by such an outline as one might be by the prospect of adventure, I set out to cross the great bare run of the valley. As I went, the mountain of Amiato came more and more nearly abreast of me in the west; in its foothills near me were ravines and unexpected rocks; upon one of them hung a village. I watched its church and one tall cypress next it, as they stood black against the last of daylight. Then for miles I went on the dusty way, and crossed by old bridges watercourses in which stood nothing but green pools; and the night deepened.

It was when I had crossed the greater part of the obscure plain, at its lowest dip and not far from the climb up to Radicofani, that I saw lights shining in a large farmhouse, and though it was my business to walk by night, yet I needed companionship, so I went in.

There in a very large room, floored with brick and lit by one candle, were two fine old peasants, with faces like apostles, playing a game of cards. There also was a woman playing with a strong boy child, that could not yet talk: and the child ran up to me. Nothing could persuade the master of the house but that I was a very poor man who needed sleep, and so good and generous was this old man that my protests seemed to him nothing but the excuses and shame of poverty. He asked me where I was going. I said, 'To Rome.' He came out with a lantern to the stable, and showed me there a manger full of hay, indicating that I might sleep in it... His candle flashed upon the great silent oxen standing in rows; their enormous horns, three times the length of what we know in England, filled me with wonder ... Well! (may it count to me as gain!), rather than seem to offend him I lay down in that manger, though I had no more desire to sleep than has the flittermouse in our Sussex gloamings; also I was careful to offer no money, for that is brutality. When he had left me I took the opportunity for a little rest, and lay on my back in the hay wide-awake and staring at darkness.

The great oxen champed and champed their food with a regular sound; I remembered the steerage in a liner, the noise of the sea and the regular screw, for this it exactly resembled. I considered in the darkness the noble aspect of these beasts as I had seen them in the lantern light, and I determined when I got to Rome to buy two such horns, and to bring them to England and have them mounted for drinking horns--great drinking horns, a yard deep--and to get an engraver to engrave a motto for each. On the first I would have--

   King Alfred was in Wantage born
He drank out of a ram's horn.
Here is a better man than he,
Who drinks deeper, as you see.

Thus my friends drinking out of it should lift up their hearts and no longer be oppressed with humility. But on the second I determined for a rousing Latin thing, such as men shouted round camp fires in the year 888 or thereabouts; so, the imagination fairly set going and taking wood-cock's flight, snipe-fashion, zigzag and devil-may-care- for-the-rules, this seemed to suit me--

Salve, cornu cornuum!
Cornutorum vis Boum.
Munus excellent Deum!
Gregis o praesidium!
Sitis desiderium!
Dignum cornuum cornu
Romae memor salve tu!
Tibi cornuum cornuto--

LECTOR. That means nothing.

AUCTOR. Shut up!

Tibi cornuum cornuto
Tibi clamo, te saluto
Salve cornu cornuum!
Fortunatam da Domunt!

And after this cogitation and musing I got up quietly, so as not to offend the peasant: and I crept out, and so upwards on to the crest of the hill.

But when, after several miles of climbing, I neared the summit, it was already beginning to be light. The bareness and desert grey of the distance I had crossed stood revealed in a colourless dawn, only the Mont' Amiata, now somewhat to the northward, was more gentle, and softened the scene with distant woods. Between it and this height ran a vague river-bed as dry as the stones of a salt beach.

The sun rose as I passed under the ruined walls of the castle. In the little town itself, early as was the hour, many people were stirring. One gave me good-morning--a man of singular character, for here, in the very peep of day, he was sitting on a doorstep, idle, lazy and contented, as though it was full noon. Another was yoking oxen; a third going out singing to work in the fields.

I did not linger in this crow's nest, but going out by the low and aged southern gate, another deeper valley, even drier and more dead than the last, appeared under the rising sun. It was enough to make one despair! And when I thought of the day's sleep in that wilderness, of the next night's toil through it--

LECTOR. What about the Brigand of Radicofani of whom you spoke in Lorraine, and of whom I am waiting to hear?

AUCTOR. What about him? Why, he was captured long ago, and has since died of old age. I am surprised at your interrupting me with such questions. Pray ask for no more tales till we get to the really absorbing story of the Hungry Student.

Well, as I was saying, I was in some despair at the sight of that valley, which had to be crossed before I could reach the town of Acquapendente, or Hanging-water, which I knew to lie somewhere on the hills beyond. The sun was conquering me, and I was looking hopelessly for a place to sleep, when a cart drawn by two oxen at about one mile an hour came creaking by. The driver was asleep, his head on the shady side. The devil tempted me, and without one struggle against temptation, nay with cynical and congratulatory feelings, I jumped up behind, and putting my head also on the shady side (there were soft sacks for a bed) I very soon was pleasantly asleep.

We lay side by side for hour after hour, and the day rose on to noon; the sun beat upon our feet, but our heads were in the shade and we slept heavily a good and honest sleep: he thinking that he was alone, but I knowing that I was in company (a far preferable thing), and I was right and he was wrong. And the heat grew, and sleep came out of that hot sun more surely than it does out of the night air in the north. But no dreams wander under the noon.

From time to time one or the other of us would open our eyes drowsily and wonder, but sleep was heavy on us both, and our minds were sunk in calm like old hulls in the dark depths of the sea where there are no storms.

We neither of us really woke until, at the bottom of the hill which rises into Acquapendente, the oxen stopped. This halt woke us up; first me and then my companion. He looked at me a moment and laughed. He seemed to have thought all this while that I was some country friend of his who had taken a lift; and I, for my part, had made more or less certain that he was a good fellow who would do me no harm. I was right, and he was wrong. I knew not what offering to make him to compensate him for this trouble which his heavy oxen had taken. After some thought I brought a cigar out of my pocket, which he smoked with extreme pleasure. The oxen meanwhile had been urged up the slow hill, and it was in this way that we reached the famous town of Acquapendente. But why it should be called famous is more than I can understand. It may be that in one of those narrow streets there is a picture or a church, or one of those things which so attract unbelieving men. To the pilgrim it is simply a group of houses. Into one of these I went, and, upon my soul, I have nothing to say of it except that they furnished me with food.

I do not pretend to have counted the flies, though they were numerous; and, even had I done so, what interest would the number have, save to the statisticians? Now as these are patient men and foolish, I heartily recommend them to go and count the flies for themselves.

Leaving this meal then, this town and this people (which were all of a humdrum sort), and going out by the gate, the left side of which is made up of a church, I went a little way on the short road to San Lorenzo, but I had no intention of going far, for (as you know by this time) the night had become my day and the day my night.

I found a stream running very sluggish between tall trees, and this sight sufficiently reminded me of my own country to permit repose. Lying down there I slept till the end of the day, or rather to that same time of evening which had now become my usual waking hour ... And now tell me, Lector, shall I leave out altogether, or shall I give you some description of, the next few miles to San Lorenzo?

LECTOR. Why, if I were you I would put the matter shortly and simply, for it is the business of one describing a pilgrimage or any other matter not to puff himself up with vain conceit, nor to be always picking about for picturesque situations, but to set down plainly and shortly what he has seen and heard, describing the whole matter.

AUCTOR. But remember, Lector, that the artist is known not only by what he puts in but by what he leaves out.

LECTOR. That is all very well for the artist, but you have no business to meddle with such people.

AUCTOR. How then would you write such a book if you had the writing of it?

LECTOR. I would not introduce myself at all; I would not tell stories at random, nor go in for long descriptions of emotions, which I am sure other men have felt as well as I. I would be careful to visit those things my readers had already heard of (AUCTOR. The pictures! the remarkable pictures! All that is meant by culture! The brown photographs! Oh! Lector, indeed I have done you a wrong!), and I would certainly not have the bad taste to say anything upon religion. Above all, I would be terse.

AUCTOR. I see. You would not pile words one on the other, qualifying, exaggerating, conditioning, superlativing, diminishing, connecting, amplifying, condensing, mouthing, and glorifying the mere sound: you would be terse. You should be known for your self-restraint. There should be no verbosity in your style (God forbid!), still less pomposity, animosity, curiosity, or ferocity; you would have it neat, exact, and scholarly, and, above all, chiselled to the nail. A fig (say you), the pip of a fig, for the rambling style. You would be led into no hilarity, charity, vulgarity, or barbarity. Eh! my jolly Lector? You would simply say what you had to say?

LECTOR. Precisely; I would say a plain thing in a plain way.

AUCTOR. So you think one can say a plain thing in a plain way? You think that words mean nothing more than themselves, and that you can talk without ellipsis, and that customary phrases have not their connotations? You think that, do you? Listen then to the tale of Mr Benjamin Franklin Hard, a kindly merchant of Cincinnati, O., who had no particular religion, but who had accumulated a fortune of six hundred thousand dollars, and who had a horror of breaking the Sabbath. He was not 'a kind husband and a good father,' for he was unmarried; nor had he any children. But he was all that those words connote.

This man Hard at the age of fifty-four retired from business, and determined to treat himself to a visit to Europe. He had not been in Europe five weeks before he ran bang up against the Catholic Church. He was never more surprised in his life. I do not mean that I have exactly weighed all his surprises all his life through. I mean that he was very much surprised indeed--and that is all that these words connote.

He studied the Catholic Church with extreme interest. He watched High Mass at several places (hoping it might be different). He thought it was what it was not, and then, contrariwise, he thought it was not what it was. He talked to poor Catholics, rich Catholics, middle-class Catholics, and elusive, wellborn, penniless, neatly dressed, successful Catholics; also to pompous, vain Catholics; humble, uncertain Catholics; sneaking, pad-footed Catholics; healthy, howling, combative Catholics; doubtful, shoulder-shrugging, but devout Catholics; fixed, crabbed, and dangerous Catholics; easy, jovial, and shone-upon-by-the-heavenly-light Catholics; subtle Catholics; strange Catholics, and *(quod tibi manifeste absurdum videtur)* intellectual, *pince-nez,* jejune, twisted, analytical, yellow, cranky, and introspective Catholics: in fine, he talked to all Catholics. And when I say 'all Catholics' I do not mean that he talked to every individual Catholic, but that he got a good, integrative grip of the Church militant, which is all that the words connote.

Well, this man Hard got to know, among others, a certain good priest that loved a good bottle of wine, a fine deep dish of poulet a la casserole, and a kind of egg done with cream in a little platter; and eating such things, this priest said to him one day: 'Mr Hard, what you want is to read some books on Catholicism.' And Hard, who was on the point of being received into the Church as the final solution of human difficulties, thought it would be a very good thing to instruct his mind before baptism. So he gave the priest a note to a bookseller whom an American friend had told him of; and this American friend had said:

'You will find Mr Fingle (for such was the bookseller's name) a hard-headed, honest, business man. He can say a *plain thing in a plain way.'*

'Here,' said Mr Hard to the priest, 'is ten pounds. Send it to this bookseller Fingle and he shall choose books on Catholicism to that amount, and you shall receive them, and I will come and read them here with you.'

So the priest sent the money, and in four days the books came, and Mr Hard and the priest opened the package, and these were the books inside:

Auricular Confession: a History. By a Brand Saved from the Burning.

Isabella; or, The Little Female Jesuit. By 'Hephzibah'.

Elisha MacNab: a Tale of the French Huguenots.

England and Rome. By the Rev. Ebenezer Catchpole of Emmanuel, Birmingham.

174

Nuns and Nunneries. By 'Ruth', with a Preface by Miss Carran, lately rescued from a Canadian Convent.

History of the Inquisition. By Llorente.

The Beast with Seven Heads; or, the Apocalyptical Warning.

No Truce with the Vatican.

The True Cause of Irish Disaffection.

Decline of the Latin Nations.

Anglo-Saxons the Chosen Race, and their connexion with the Ten Lost Tribes: with a map.

Finally, a very large book at the bottom of the case called *Giant Pope*.

And it was no use asking for the money back or protesting. Mr Fingle was an honest, straightforward man, who said a plain thing in a plain way. They had left him to choose a suitable collection of books on Catholicism, and he had chosen the best he knew. And thus did Mr Hard (who has recently given a hideous font to the new Catholic church at Bismarckville) learn the importance of estimating what words connote.

LECTOR. But all that does not excuse an intolerable prolixity?

AUCTOR. Neither did I say it did, dear Lector. My object was merely to get you to San Lorenzo where I bought that wine, and where, going out of the gate on the south, I saw suddenly the wide lake of Bolsena all below.

It is a great sheet like a sea; but as one knows one is on a high plateau, and as there is but a short dip down to it; as it is round and has all about it a rim of low even hills, therefore one knows it for an old and gigantic crater now full of pure water; and there are islands in it and palaces on the islands. Indeed it was an impression of silence and recollection, for the water lay all upturned to heaven, and, in the sky above me, the moon at her quarter hung still pale in the daylight, waiting for glory.

I sat on the coping of a wall, drank a little of my wine, ate a little bread and sausage; but still song demanded some outlet in the cool evening, and companionship was more of an appetite in me than landscape. Please God, I had become southern and took beauty for granted.

Anyhow, seeing a little two-wheeled cart come through the gate, harnessed to a ramshackle little pony, bony and hard, and driven by a little, brown, smiling, and contented old fellow with black hair, I made a sign to him and he stopped.

This time there was no temptation of the devil; if anything the advance was from my side. I was determined to ride, and I sprang up beside the driver. We raced down the hill, clattering and banging and rattling like a piece of ordnance, and he, my brother, unasked began to sing. I sang in turn. He sang of Italy, I of four countries: America, France, England, and Ireland. I could not understand his songs nor he mine, but there was wine in common between us, and *salami* and a merry heart, bread which is the bond of all mankind, and that prime solution of ill-ease--I mean the forgetfulness of money.

That was a good drive, an honest drive, a human aspiring drive, a drive of Christians, a glorifying and uplifted drive, a drive worthy of remembrance for ever. The moon has shone on but few like it though she is old; the lake of Bolsena has glittered beneath none like it since the Etruscans here unbended after the solemnities of a triumph. It broke my vow to pieces; there was not a shadow of excuse for this use of wheels: it was done openly and wantonly in the face of the wide sky for pleasure. And what is there else but pleasure, and to what else does beauty move on? Not I hope to contemplation! A hideous oriental trick! No, but to loud notes and comradeship and the riot of galloping, and laughter ringing through old trees. Who would change (says Aristippus of Pslinthon) the moon and all the stars for so much wine as can be held in the cup of a bottle upturned? The honest man! And in his time (note you) they did not make the devilish deep and fraudulent bottoms they do now that cheat you of half your liquor.

Moreover if I broke my vows (which is a serious matter), and if I neglected to contemplate the heavens (for which neglect I will confess to no one, not even to a postulate sub-deacon; it is no sin; it is a healthy omission), if (I say) I did this, I did what peasants do. And what is more, by drinking wine and eating pig we proved ourselves no Mohammedans; and on such as he is sure of, St Peter looks with a kindly eye.

Now, just at the very entry to Bolsena, when we had followed the lovely lake some time, my driver halted and began to turn up a lane to a farm or villa; so I, bidding him good-night, crossed a field and stood silent by the lake and watched for a long time the water breaking on a tiny shore, and the pretty miniatures of waves. I stood there till the stars came out and the moon shone fully; then I went towards Bolsena under its high gate which showed in the darkness, and under its castle on the rock. There, in a large room which was not quite an inn, a woman of great age and dignity served me with fried fish from the lake, and the men gathered round me and attempted to tell me of the road to Rome, while I in exchange made out to them as much by gestures as by broken words the crossing of the Alps and the Apennines.

176

Then, after my meal, one of the men told me I needed sleep; that there were no rooms in that house (as I said, it was not an inn), but that across the way he would show me one he had for hire. I tried to say that my plan was to walk by night. They all assured me he would charge me a reasonable sum. I insisted that the day was too hot for walking. They told me, did these Etruscans, that I need fear no extortion from so honest a man.

Certainly it is not easy to make everybody understand everything, and I had had experience already up in the mountains, days before, of how important it is not to be misunderstood when one is wandering in a foreign country, poor and ill-clad. I therefore accepted the offer, and, what was really very much to my regret, I paid the money he demanded. I even so far fell in with the spirit of the thing as to sleep a certain number of hours (for after all, my sleep that day in the cart had been very broken, and instead of resting throughout the whole of the heat I had taken a meal at Acquapendente). But I woke up not long after midnight--perhaps between one and two o'clock--and went out along the borders of the lake.

The moon had set; I wish I could have seen her hanging at the quarter in the clear sky of that high crater, dipping into the rim of its inland sea. It was perceptibly cold. I went on the road quite slowly, till it began to climb, and when the day broke I found myself in a sunken lane leading up to the town of Montefiascone.

The town lay on its hill in the pale but growing light. A great dome gave it dignity, and a castle overlooked the lake. It was built upon the very edge and lip of the volcano-cup commanding either side.

I climbed up this sunken lane towards it, not knowing what might be beyond, when, at the crest, there shone before me in the sunrise one of those unexpected and united landscapes which are among the glories of Italy. They have changed the very mind in a hundred northern painters, when men travelled hither to Rome to learn their art, and coming in by her mountain roads saw, time and again, the set views of plains like gardens, surrounded by sharp mountain-land and framed.

The road did not pass through the town; the grand though crumbling gate of entry lay up a short straight way to the right, and below, where the road continued down the slope, was a level of some eight miles full of trees diminishing in distance. At its further side an ample mountain, wooded, of gentle flattened outline, but high and majestic, barred the way to Rome. It was yet another of those volcanoes, fruitful after death, which are the mark of Latium: and it held hidden, as did that larger and more confused one on the rim of which I stood, a lake in its silent crater. But that lake, as I was to find, was far smaller than the glittering sea of Bolsena, whose shores now lay behind me.

177

The distance and the hill that bounded it should in that climate have stood clear in the pure air, but it was yet so early that a thin haze hung over the earth, and the sun had not yet controlled it: it was even chilly. I could not catch the towers of Viterbo, though I knew them to stand at the foot of the far mountain. I went down the road, and in half-an-hour or so was engaged upon the straight line crossing the plain.

I wondered a little how the road would lie with regard to the town, and looked at my map for guidance, but it told me little. It was too general, taking in all central Italy, and even large places were marked only by small circles.

When I approached Viterbo I first saw an astonishing wall, perpendicular to my road, untouched, the bones of the Middle Ages. It stood up straight before one like a range of cliffs, seeming much higher than it should; its hundred feet or so were exaggerated by the severity of its stones and by their sheer fall. For they had no ornament whatever, and few marks of decay, though many of age. Tall towers, exactly square and equally bare of carving or machicolation, stood at intervals along this forbidding defence and flanked its curtain. Then nearer by, one saw that it was not a huge castle, but the wall of a city, for at a corner it went sharp round to contain the town, and through one uneven place I saw houses. Many men were walking in the roads alongside these walls, and there were gates pierced in them whereby the citizens went in and out of the city as bees go in and out of the little opening in a hive.

But my main road to Rome did not go through Viterbo, it ran alongside of the eastern wall, and I debated a little with myself whether I would go in or no. It was out of my way, and I had not entered Montefiascone for that reason. On the other hand, Viterbo was a famous place. It is all very well to neglect Florence and Pisa because they are some miles off the straight way, but Viterbo right under one's hand it is a pity to miss. Then I needed wine and food for the later day in the mountain. Yet, again, it was getting hot. It was past eight, the mist had long ago receded, and I feared delay. So I mused on the white road under the tall towers and dead walls of Viterbo, and ruminated on an unimportant thing. Then curiosity did what reason could not do, and I entered by a gate.

The streets were narrow, tortuous, and alive, all shaded by the great houses, and still full of the cold of the night. The noise of fountains echoed in them, and the high voices of women and the cries of sellers. Every house had in it something fantastic and peculiar; humanity had twined into this place like a natural growth, and the separate thoughts of men, both those that were alive there and those dead before them, had decorated it all. There were courtyards with blinding whites of sunlit walls above, themselves in shadow; and there were many carvings and paintings over doors. I had come into a great living place after the loneliness of the road.

There, in the first wide street I could find, I bought sausage and bread and a great bottle of wine, and then quitting Viterbo, I left it by the same gate and took the road.

For a long while yet I continued under the walls, noting in one place a thing peculiar to the Middle Ages, I mean the apse of a church built right into the wall as the old Cathedral of St Stephen's was in Paris. These, I suppose, enemies respected if they could; for I have noticed also that in castles the chapel is not hidden, but stands out from the wall. So be it. Your fathers and mine were there in the fighting, but we do not know their names, and I trust and hope yours spared the altars as carefully as mine did.

The road began to climb the hill, and though the heat increased--for in Italy long before nine it is glaring noon to us northerners (and that reminds me: your fathers and mine, to whom allusion has been made above {as they say in the dull history books--[LECTOR. How many more interior brackets are we to have? Is this algebra? AUCTOR. You yourself, Lector, are responsible for the worst.]} your fathers and mine coming down into this country to fight, as was their annual custom, must have had a plaguy time of it, when you think that they could not get across the Alps till summer-time, and then had to hack and hew, and thrust and dig, and slash and climb, and charge and puff, and blow and swear, and parry and receive, and aim and dodge, and butt and run for their lives at the end, under an unaccustomed sun. No wonder they saw visions, the dear people! They are dead now, and we do not even know their names.)--Where was I?

LECTOR. You were at the uninteresting remark that the heat was increasing.

AUCTOR. Precisely. I remember. Well, the heat was increasing, but it seemed far more bearable than it had been in the earlier places; in the oven of the Garfagnana or in the deserts of Siena. For with the first slopes of the mountain a forest of great chestnut trees appeared, and it was so cool under these that there was even moss, as though I were back again in my own country where there are full rivers in summer-time, deep meadows, and all the completion of home.

Also the height may have begun to tell on the air, but not much, for when the forest was behind me, and when I had come to a bare heath sloping more gently upwards--a glacis in front of the topmost bulwark of the round mountain--- I was oppressed with thirst, and though it was not too hot to sing (for I sang, and two lonely carabinieri passed me singing, and we recognized as we saluted each other that the mountain was full of songs), yet I longed for a bench, a flagon, and shade.

And as I longed, a little house appeared, and a woman in the shade sewing, and an old man. Also a bench and a table, and a tree over it.

179

There I sat down and drank white wine and water many times. The woman charged me a halfpenny, and the old man would not talk. He did not take his old age garrulously. It was his business, not mine; but I should dearly have liked to have talked to him in Lingua Franca, and to have heard him on the story of his mountain: where it was haunted, by what, and on which nights it was dangerous to be abroad. Such as it was, there it was. I left them, and shall perhaps never see them again.

The road was interminable, and the crest, from which I promised myself the view of the crater-lake, was always just before me, and was never reached. A little spring, caught in a hollow log, refreshed a meadow on the right. Drinking there again, I wondered if I should go on or rest; but I was full of antiquity, and a memory in the blood, or what not, impelled me to see the lake in the crater before I went to sleep: after a few hundred yards this obsession was satisfied.

I passed between two banks, where the road had been worn down at the crest of the volcano's rim; then at once, far below, in a circle of silent trees with here and there a vague shore of marshy land, I saw the Pond of Venus: some miles of brooding water, darkened by the dark slopes around it. Its darkness recalled the dark time before the dawn of our saved and happy world.

At its hither end a hill, that had once been a cone in the crater, stood out all covered with a dense wood. It was the Hill of Venus.

There was no temple, nor no sacrifice, nor no ritual for the Divinity, save this solemn attitude of perennial silence; but under the influence which still remained and gave the place its savour, it was impossible to believe that the gods were dead. There were no men in that hollow; nor was there any memory of men, save of men dead these thousands of years. There was no life of visible things. The mind released itself and was in touch with whatever survives of conquered but immortal Spirits.

Thus ready for worship, and in a mood of adoration; filled also with the genius which inhabits its native place and is too subtle or too pure to suffer the effect of time, I passed down the ridge-way of the mountain rim, and came to the edge overlooking that arena whereon was first fought out and decided the chief destiny of the world.

For all below was the Campagna. Names that are at the origin of things attached to every cleft and distant rock beyond the spreading level, or sanctified the gleams of rivers. There below me was Veii; beyond, in the Wall of the Apennines, only just escaped from clouds, was Tibur that dignified the ravine at the edge of their rising; that crest to the right was Tusculum, and far to the south, but clear, on a mountain answering my own, was the mother of the City, Alba Longa. The Tiber, a dense, brown fog rolling over and concealing it, was the god of the wide plain.

There and at that moment I should have seen the City. I stood up on the bank and shaded my eyes, straining to catch the dome at least in the sunlight; but I could not, for Rome was hidden by the low Sabinian hills.

Soracte I saw there--Soracte, of which I had read as a boy. It stood up like an acropolis, but it was a citadel for no city. It stood alone, like that soul which once haunted its recesses and prophesied the conquering advent of the northern kings. I saw the fields where the tribes had lived that were the first enemies of the imperfect state, before it gave its name to the fortunes of the Latin race.

Dark Etruria lay behind me, forgotten in the backward of my march: a furnace and a riddle out of which religion came to the Romans--a place that has left no language. But below me, sunlit and easy (as it seemed in the cooler air of that summit), was the arena upon which were first fought out the chief destinies of the world.

And I still looked down upon it, wondering.

Was it in so small a space that all the legends of one's childhood were acted? Was the defence of the bridge against so neighbouring and petty an alliance? Were they peasants of a group of huts that handed down the great inheritance of discipline, and made an iron channel whereby, even to us, the antique virtues could descend as a living memory? It must be so; for the villages and ruins in one landscape comprised all the first generations of the history of Rome. The stones we admire, the large spirit of the last expression came from that rough village and sprang from the broils of that one plain; Rome was most vigorous before it could speak. So a man's verse, and all he has, are but the last outward appearance, late and already rigid, of an earlier, more plastic, and diviner fire.

'Upon this arena,' I still said to myself, 'were first fought out the chief destinies of the world'; and so, played upon by an unending theme, I ate and drank in a reverie, still wondering, and then lay down beneath the shade of a little tree that stood alone upon that edge of a new world. And wondering, I fell asleep under the morning sun.

But this sleep was not like the earlier oblivions that had refreshed my ceaseless journey, for I still dreamt as I slept of what I was to see, and visions of action without thought--pageants and mysteries--surrounded my spirit; and across the darkness of a mind remote from the senses there passed whatever is wrapped up in the great name of Rome.

When I woke the evening had come. A haze had gathered upon the plain. The road fell into Ronciglione, and dreams surrounded it upon every side. For the energy of the body those hours of rest had made a fresh and enduring vigour; for the soul no rest was needed. It had attained, at least for the next hour, a vigour that demanded only the physical capacity of endurance; an eagerness worthy of such great occasions found a marching vigour for its servant.

In Ronciglione I saw the things that Turner drew; I mean the rocks from which a river springs, and houses all massed together, giving the steep a kind of crown. This also accompanied that picture, the soft light which mourns the sun and lends half-colours to the world. It was cool, and the opportunity beckoned. I ate and drank, asking every one questions of Rome, and I passed under their great gate and pursued the road to the plain. In the mist, as it rose, there rose also a passion to achieve.

All the night long, mile after mile, I hurried along the Cassian Way. For five days I had slept through the heat, and the southern night had become my daytime; and though the mist was dense, and though the moon, now past her quarter, only made a vague place in heaven, yet expectation and fancy took more than the place of sight. In this fog I felt with every step of the night march the approach to the goal.

Long past the place I had marked as a halt, long past Sette Vene, a light blurred upon the white wreaths of vapour; distant songs and the noise of men feasting ended what had been for many, many hours--for more than twenty miles of pressing forward--an exaltation worthy of the influence that bred it. Then came on me again, after the full march, a necessity for food and for repose. But these things, which have been the matter of so much in this book, now seemed subservient only to the reaching of an end; they were left aside in the mind.

It was an inn with trellis outside making an arbour. In the yard before it many peasants sat at table; their beasts and waggons stood in the roadway, though, at this late hour, men were feeding some and housing others. Within, fifty men or more were making a meal or a carousal.

What feast or what necessity of travel made them keep the night alive I neither knew nor asked; but passing almost unobserved amongst them between the long tables, I took my place at the end, and the master served me with good food and wine. As I ate the clamour of the peasants sounded about me, and I mixed with the energy of numbers.

With a little difficulty I made the master understand that I wished to sleep till dawn. He led me out to a small granary (for the house was full), and showed me where I should sleep in the scented hay. He would take no money for such a lodging, and left me after showing me how the door latched and unfastened; and out of so many men, he was the last man whom I thanked for a service until I passed the gates of Rome.

Above the soft bed which the hay made, a square window, unglazed, gave upon the southern night; the mist hardly drifted in or past it, so still was the air. I watched it for a while drowsily; then sleep again fell on me.

But as I slept, Rome, Rome still beckoned me, and I woke in a struggling light as though at a voice calling, and slipping out I could not but go on to the end.

The small square paving of the Via Cassia, all even like a palace floor, rang under my steps. The parched banks and strips of dry fields showed through the fog (for its dampness did not cure the arid soil of the Campagna). The sun rose and the vapour lifted. Then, indeed, I peered through the thick air--but still I could see nothing of my goal, only confused folds of brown earth and burnt-up grasses, and farther off rare and un-northern trees.

I passed an old tower of the Middle Ages that was eaten away at its base by time or the quarrying of men; I passed a divergent way on the right where a wooden sign said 'The Triumphal Way', and I wondered whether it could be the road where ritual had once ordained that triumphs should go. It seemed lonely and lost, and divorced from any approach to sacred hills.

The road fell into a hollow where soldiers were manoeuvring. Even these could not arrest an attention that was fixed upon the approaching revelation. The road climbed a little slope where a branch went off to the left, and where there was a house and an arbour under vines. It was now warm day; trees of great height stood shading the sun; the place had taken on an appearance of wealth and care. The mist had gone before I reached the summit of the rise.

There, from the summit, between the high villa walls on either side-- at my very feet I saw the City.

And now all you people whatsoever that are presently reading, may have read, or shall in the future read, this my many-sided but now-ending book; all you also that in the mysterious designs of Providence may not be fated to read it for some very long time to come; you then I say, entire, englobed, and universal race of men both in gross and regardant, not only living and seeing the sunlight, but dead also under the earth; shades, or to come in procession afterwards out of the dark places into the day for a little, swarms of you, an army without end; all you black and white, red, yellow and brown, men, women, children and poets--all of you, wherever you are now, or have been, or shall be in your myriads and deka myriads and hendeka myriads, the time has come when I must bid you farewell--

Ludisti satis, edisti satis, atque bibisti;
Tempus abire tibi est....

Only Lector I keep by me for a very little while longer with a special purpose, but even he must soon leave me; for all good things come to

183

an end, and this book is coming to an end--has come to an end. The leaves fall, and they are renewed; the sun sets on the Vexin hills, but he rises again over the woods of Marly. Human companionship once broken can never be restored, and you and I shall not meet or understand each other again. It is so of all the poor links whereby we try to bridge the impassable gulf between soul and soul. Oh! we spin something, I know, but it is very gossamer, thin and strained, and even if it does not snap time will at last dissolve it.

Indeed, there is a song on it which you should know, and which runs--

[Bar of music]

So my little human race, both you that have read this book and you that have not, good-bye in charity. I loved you all as I wrote. Did you all love me as much as I have loved you, by the black stone of Rennes I should be rich by now. Indeed, indeed, I have loved you all! You, the workers, all puffed up and dyspeptic and ready for the asylums; and you, the good-for-nothing lazy drones; you, the strong silent men, who have heads quite empty, like gourds; and you also, the frivolous, useless men that chatter and gabble to no purpose all day long. Even you, that, having begun to read this book, could get no further than page 47, and especially you who have read it manfully in spite of the flesh, I love you all, and give you here and now my final, complete, full, absolving, and comfortable benediction.

To tell the truth, I have noticed one little fault about you. I will not call it fatuous, inane, and exasperating vanity or self- absorption; I will put it in the form of a parable. Sit you round attentively and listen, dispersing yourselves all in order, and do not crowd or jostle.

Once, before we humans became the good and self-respecting people we are, the Padre Eterno was sitting in heaven with St Michael beside him, and He watched the abyss from His great throne, and saw shining in the void one far point of light amid some seventeen million others, and He said:

'What is that?'

And St Michael answered:

'That is the Earth,' for he felt some pride in it.

'The Earth?' said the Padre Eterno, a little puzzled . . . 'The Earth? ...?... I do not remember very exactly . . .'

'Why,' answered St Michael, with as much reverence as his annoyance could command, 'surely you must recollect the Earth and all the pother there was in heaven when it was first suggested to create it, and all about Lucifer--'

184

'Ah!' said the Padre Eterno, thinking twice, 'yes. It is attached to Sirius, and--'

'No, no,' said St Michael, quite visibly put out. 'It is the Earth. The Earth which has that changing moon and the thing called the sea.'

'Of course, of course,' answered the Padre Eterno quickly, 'I said Sirius by a slip of the tongue. Dear me! So that is the Earth! Well, well! It is years ago now ... Michael, what are those little things swarming up and down all over it?'

'Those,' said St Michael, 'are Men.'

'Men?' said the Padre Eterno, 'Men ... I know the word as well as any one, but somehow the connexion escapes me. Men ...' and He mused.

St Michael, with perfect self-restraint, said a few things a trifle staccato, defining Man, his dual destiny, his hope of heaven, and all the great business in which he himself had fought hard. But from a fine military tradition, he said nothing of his actions, nor even of his shrine in Normandy, of which he is naturally extremely proud: and well he may be. What a hill!

'I really beg your pardon,' said the Padre Eterno, when he saw the importance attached to these little creatures. 'I am sure they are worthy of the very fullest attention, and' (he added, for he was sorry to have offended) 'how sensible they seem, Michael! There they go, buying and selling, and sailing, driving, and wiving, and riding, and dancing, and singing, and the rest of it; indeed, they are most practical, business-like, and satisfactory little beings. But I notice one odd thing. Here and there are some not doing as the rest, or attending to their business, but throwing themselves into all manner of attitudes, making the most extraordinary sounds, and clothing themselves in the quaintest of garments. What is the meaning of that?'

'Sire!' cried St Michael, in a voice that shook the architraves of heaven, 'they are worshipping You!'

'Oh! they are worshipping *me*! Well, that is the most sensible thing I have heard of them yet, and I altogether commend them. *Continuez*,' said the Padre Eterno, '*continuez!*'

And since then all has been well with the world; at least where *Us continuent*.

And so, carissimi, multitudes, all of you good-bye; the day has long dawned on the Via Cassia, this dense mist has risen, the city is before

185

me, and I am on the threshold of a great experience; I would rather be alone. Good-bye my readers; good-bye the world.

At the foot of the hill I prepared to enter the city, and I lifted up my heart.

There was an open space; a tramway: a tram upon it about to be drawn by two lean and tired horses whom in the heat many flies disturbed. There was dust on everything around.

A bridge was immediately in front. It was adorned with statues in soft stone, half-eaten away, but still gesticulating in corruption, after the manner of the seventeenth century. Beneath the bridge there tumbled and swelled and ran fast a great confusion of yellow water: it was the Tiber. Far on the right were white barracks of huge and of hideous appearance; over these the Dome of St Peter's rose and looked like something newly built. It was of a delicate blue, but made a metallic contrast against the sky.

Then (along a road perfectly straight and bounded by factories, mean houses and distempered walls: a road littered with many scraps of paper, bones, dirt, and refuse) I went on for several hundred yards, having the old wall of Rome before me all this time, till I came right under it at last; and with the hesitation that befits all great actions I entered, putting the right foot first lest I should bring further misfortune upon that capital of all our fortunes.

And so the journey ended.

It was the Gate of the Poplar--not of the People. (Ho, Pedant! Did you think I missed you, hiding and lurking there?) Many churches were to hand; I took the most immediate, which stood just within the wall and was called Our Lady of the People--(not 'of the Poplar'. Another fall for the learned! Professor, things go ill with you to-day!). Inside were many fine pictures, not in the niminy-piminy manner, but strong, full-coloured, and just.

To my chagrin, Mass was ending. I approached a priest and said to him:

'Pater, quando vel a quella hora e la prossimma Missa?'

'Ad nonas,' said he.

'Pol! Hercle!' (thought I), 'I have yet twenty minutes to wait! Well, as a pilgrimage cannot be said to be over till the first Mass is heard in Rome, I have twenty minutes to add to my book.'

So, passing an Egyptian obelisk which the great Augustus had nobly dedicated to the Sun, I entered....

186

LECTOR. But do you intend to tell us nothing of Rome?

AUCTOR. Nothing, dear Lector.

LECTOR. Tell me at least one thing; did you see the Coliseum?

AUCTOR. ... I entered a cafe at the right hand of a very long, straight street, called for bread, coffee, and brandy, and contemplating my books and worshipping my staff that had been friends of mine so long, and friends like all true friends inanimate, I spent the few minutes remaining to my happy, common, unshriven, exterior, and natural life, in writing down this

DITHYRAMBIC

EPITHALAMIUM OR THRENODY

In these boots, and with this staff   Two hundred leaguers and a half--

(That means, two and a half hundred leagues. You follow? Not two hundred and one half league.... Well--)

Two hundred leaguers and a half
Walked I, went I, paced I, tripped I,
Marched I, held I, skelped I, slipped I,
Pushed I, panted, swung and dashed I;
Picked I, forded, swam and splashed I,
Strolled I, climbed I, crawled and scrambled,
Dropped and dipped I, ranged and rambled;
Plodded I, hobbled I, trudged and tramped I,
And in lonely spinnies camped I,
And in haunted pinewoods slept I,
Lingered, loitered, limped and crept I,
Clambered, halted, stepped and leapt I;
Slowly sauntered, roundly strode I,

And... (Oh! Patron saints and Angels
That protect the four evangels!
And you Prophets vel majores
Vel incerti, vel minores,
Virgines ac confessores
Chief of whose peculiar glories
Est in Aula Regis stare
Atque orare et exorare
Et clamare et conclamare
Clamantes cum clamoribus
Pro nobis peccatoribus.)

Let me not conceal it... Rode I.
(For who but critics could complain Of 'riding' in a railway train?)
Across the valleys and the high-land,
With all the world on either hand.
Drinking when I had a mind to,
Singing when I felt inclined to;
Nor ever turned my face to home
Till I had slaked my heart at Rome.

THE END AGAIN

LECTOR. But this is dogg--

AUCTOR. Not a word!

FINIS

Lightning Source UK Ltd.
Milton Keynes UK
18 August 2009

142789UK00001B/166/A